An illustrated history of
BRITISH RAILWAY HOTELS
1838-1983
Oliver Carter

Sir William Towle, 1849-1929

Controller, Midland Railway Hotels, 1885-1914

"....The nation owes a debt of gratitude to the railway companies for the provision of many good hotels which would certainly never have been built by other capital...."

Silver Link Publishing
The Coach House, Garstang Road, St Michael's, Lancashire, PR3 OTG.

Below: (and rear cover): *Liverpool Exchange Station Hotel*, as depicted in a much-retouched publicity photograph, produced during LMS days. The hotel's name, the people standing on the footpaths and the motor cars are all the work of a skilled artist! *Authors collection.*

Inset: The logo used by the LMS Hotel Services department during the 1930s. *Author's collection.*

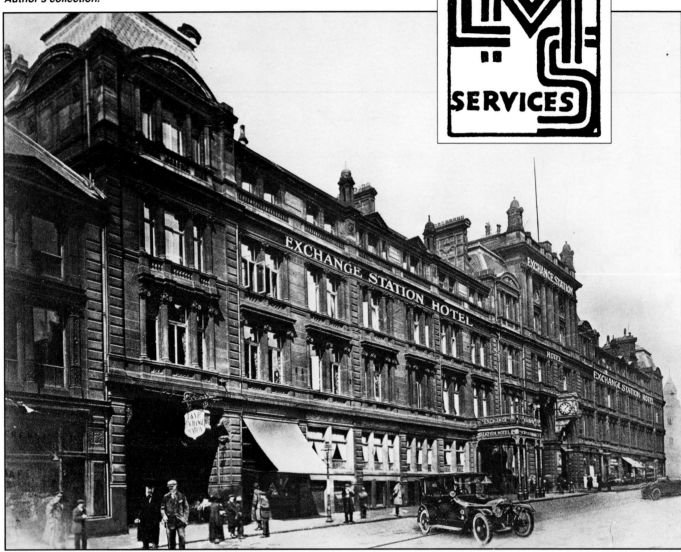

FRONT COVER:
Probably the best-known railway hotel of them all – the one-time *Midland Grand*, at St Pancras, closed in 1935 and subsequently used by BR as offices. The original plans for this splendid building featured five floors - but the thrifty Midland Railway company reduced this to four to trim expenditure. *Brian Morrison.*

TITLE PAGE:
Sir William Towle, Controller of the Midland Railway's Hotels, 1885 to 1914. He was head of a family which for a combined 150 years exerted the most profound effect on railway hotels and catering: Sir William's sons, Lt. Col. Sir Francis William Towle (1876-1951) and Arthur Edward Towle (1878-1949) both followed their father into the MR's hotel business and enjoyed successful careers in this important aspect of railway development. William Towle and his elder son were amongst the first members of the hotel profession to be honoured with knighthoods. *National Railway Museum.*

REAR COVER (UPPER LEFT):
The immaculate head porter at the *Euston Hotel*, around 1905. Not a gentleman to tolerate any nonsense! *Author's collection.*

Copyright © Oliver Carter & Silver Link Publishing Ltd, May 1990.

First published in the United kingdom, May 1990

Imagesetting by Ps&Qs, Liverpool, and printed in the UK by The Amadeus Press, Huddersfield, Yorkshire.

Designed by Barbara Allen, Leading Edge Press & Publishing Ltd, Hawes, North Yorkshire.

Jacket design by Nigel Harris.

British Library Cataloguing in Publication Data
Carter, Oliver
    An illustrated history of railway hotels, 1840-1989
    1. Great Britain. Hotels, history
    I. Title
    647'.944101'09

ISBN 0-947971-36-X

AN ILLUSTRATED HISTORY OF RAILWAY HOTELS

CONTENTS

Authors Preface 4

Introduction..5

CHAPTER 1: LOCATION
   London 8
   Towns and Cities...15
   Seaports and Harbours...28
   Seaside and Inland Resorts..35
      England and Wales 35
      Scotland...42
   Ireland 49

CHAPTER 2: PLANNING AND AMENITIES
   Style 55
   Construction and Amenities 61

CHAPTER 3: MANAGEMENT AND STAFF
   Management...80
      Powers to Build or Purchase 80
      Leaseholds...81
      Joint Participation 83
      Hotel Committees 83
      Hotel Controllers...86
      Constructions Committees..89
      The 'Big Four' Period: 1923-1947..90
      Nationalisation of the Railways: 1948..91
      Profitability 92
   Staff...94

CHAPTER 4: PUBLICITY
   Naming 102
   Advertising...104
   Guide Books 105
   Timetables 107
   Brochures 108
   Postcards..112
   Tariffs 113
   Recent Trends in Classification 115
   Openings..115
   Royal Visits and State Occasions..115
   Closures...118

APPENDICES
   Appendix 1:
      List of principal railway hotels built or purchased by the railways
      in Great Britain and Ireland, arranged under the 'Big Four' companies 120
   Appendix 2:
      List of the 19 British Transport Hotels Sold in 1983, and their buyers 124
      Leading Hotel Operators in Britain at the end of 1970 125
      Leading Hotel Operators in Britain at the end of 1976 125
      Receipts and Expenditure incurred by the 23 Hotel-owning Railway Companies in the United Kingdom
       & Ireland for 1913 (Compiled to Conform with the requirements of the Railway Accounts Act, 1911)............126
      Receipts and Expenditure on Hotel, Refreshment Room and Dining Car
      Services, incurred by UK and Irish Railways, 1933 126
      Operating Profits of the Hotels Executive, 1948-1972 and British Transport Hotels Ltd, 1973-1982....................126
      Operating costs incurred by British Transport Hotels Ltd, 1971-1972 127
      Great Southern Hotels, Operated by Ostlanna Iompair Eireann (OCIE)
      The wholly owned subsidiary of Coras Iompair Eireann (CIE) 20-year statement....................127
      Local Acts of Parliament relating to railway hotels..127
      Detailed Examination of the local Acts of Parliament relating to railway hotels (These Railway Acts
      reveal a number of projects which were subsequently abandoned at the planning stage) 128
      Non-residential hotels, inns and other properties owned by the railways 128
   Appendix 3:
      References 129
   Appendix 4:
      Index 130

AUTHOR'S PREFACE

THE idea for this book has its roots in my childhood, when home was in South Manchester. The most convenient way into the city centre was by train to the erstwhile Central station (which lives on as the G-Mex exhibition centre) where passengers could not fail to be aware of the neighbouring *Midland Hotel*. Porters and page boys from the hotel wore distinctive plum-coloured uniforms, giving the hotel a prominent visual profile, whilst the aroma of cooking from the basement kitchens were usually tempting. The comings and goings of wicker laundry baskets, deliveries by the Manchester Ice Company or by meat, fruit, vegetable and fish merchants all combined to ensure that the 'Midland' made you aware of its presence! These were all indications of a very busy hotel.

Several years later, as an architecture student, I saw the interior of the *Midland Hotel* for the first time, when attending trade shows and seminars, and I was very impressed by the workmanship of its Edwardian builders. During my studies, I wrote a biography of Francis Thompson (1808-1895) an architect whose work included one of the first purpose-built railway hotels, as part of the magnificent Derby station project of 1839-1840. My review of Thompson's work was subsequently published in *The Architectural Review*, and read by the late Sir John Betjeman. He was enthusiastic about the new light I had shed on Thompson's work and suggested that it was time more was written about the railway hotels generally. It was an interesting suggestion....but without a great deal of background information the task was formidable.

The late George Dow help set me on course, partly by an introduction to Paul Long, formerly Secretary to British Transport Hotels. Paul Long in turn introduced me to Frank Hole, recently (at the time of writing) retired as Controller of the BTH organisation. I continued collecting information and, slowly, a picture began to emerge.

This book tells the story of the railways 145 years in the hotel business. Sadly, the year 1983 marked the end of active railway ownership, with the sale of the last BTH hotels, but the new owners have embarked on many improvements, and names like *The Midland Hotel*, in Manchester, live on in tribute to the famous companies which built them.

Oliver Carter,
Caldbeck,
Cumbria,
January 1990.

Above: In their heyday, there were more than 140 railway hotels, in all parts of the kingdom, serving a variety of business and leisure needs. In Scotland, the Glasgow & South Western Railway promoted its hotels through postcards, for example, as shown here, featuring the *St Enoch Hotel*, Glasgow, the *Station Hotel*, Ayr, the *Station Hotel* Dumfries and the *Station Hotel*, Turnberry. *Author's Collection.*

AN ILLUSTRATED HISTORY OF RAILWAY HOTELS

INTRODUCTION

Above: *The Felix Hotel*, at Felixstowe, opened in 1903 and purchased by the Great Eastern Railway in 1920. *John Alsop Collection.*

The railways pioneered the hotel industry in Britain and spent 145 years as hoteliers. It is a story which began at Euston in 1838 and ended in 1983 following the sale of British Transport Hotels' remaining assets, prompted by the Transport Act of 1981. This marked the end of a rather sad period for the railway hotels, for the rumours of impending privatisation during the mid-1970s had led to a growing loss of confidence in the once-profitable undertaking, and financial deficits for the years 1980-82. In the Republic of Ireland, the former railway hotels have been placed under the control of the state-sponsored Council for Education,(Recruitment and Training with the Hotel Catering and allied industries).

The railways' hotel empire, once the largest in the world, numbered more than 140 properties, and also extended to the ownership of smaller inns and licensed premises. The railway companies had built or purchased their hotels to satisfy a range of needs: in towns, cities and seaports, for the traveller and visitor, at seaside and inland resorts for the holiday maker and golfer, and they provided accommodation for public meetings and other functions. The high standards and extensive accommodation provided sometimes attracted criticism, but in most cases the passing of years proved that hotels were often too small, and complete rebuilding or the building of extensions was needed to keep pace with demand.

In the words of Sir William Towle (1849-1929), Controller of the Midland Railway's hotels, from 1885 to 1914: "The nation owes a debt of gratitude to the railway companies for the provision of many good hotels which would certainly never have been built by other capital." *(1)*

As leaders of a new industry, the railways had to learn the art of hotel management largely unaided. In London, several railway hotels were soon in competition with each other, whilst Birmingham, Liverpool, Leeds, Bradford, Edinburgh and Glasgow were also able to boast more than one railway-owned hotel. By the end of the 19th century, other hotel and catering companies were emerging. Gordon Hotels, Frederick Hotels, Spiers & Pond, and, later, Trust Houses were all anxious to tender for hotels and catering contracts from those railways which chose not to operate their own hotels.

Many of the staff who worked in the hotels devoted the whole of their working lives to the industry. For example, Sir William Towle spent 50 years with the Midland Railway and developed his company's reputation in the hotel business to one of unquestioned pre-eminence. Life was tough for staff. They were usually housed in the hotel's basements or attics, and worked long hours. For the less-indus-

Above: Railway hotel interiors were often very grand and most elegant. This view shows the Palm Court, at *The Felix Hotel*, Felixstowe – a very pleasant and relaxing room in which to pass an hour or two in reading or conversation, perhaps over afternoon tea. The Hotel was one of the most popular on the East Coast during the 1920s and 1930s. *John Alsop Collection.*

Above, left: The railway hotels were enthusiastic about promoting their names, and everything from cutlery to drinking glasses, table cloths and cruet carried the hotel and company's monogram. These table settings feature LNWR and GSWR items. *Author's collection.*

Above, right: In the days before private bathrooms, the hotels were also obliged to provide a range of altogether more personal facilites for their patrons, as illustrated by this Great Central Railway chamber pot. *George Dow Collection.*

trious, reprimands and fines were commonplace, and union representation among railway hotel staff was never very high. During the 1970s, for example, only 30% of staff were members of a trade union, compared with a 100% membership among train catering staff.

Railway-owned hotels were an institution not confined to the British Isles, for French and several other European railways once owned them too. However, it was in

Canada that the work started in Britain has continued in more recent times, and is now aimed towards the international hotel market. Sir William C. Van Horne (1843-1915) builder and late president of the Canadian Pacific Railway, saw his railway as a means of opening up unsettled territory. He masterminded the building of the CPR's first hotel in Vancouver in 1887. The opening of *Le Chateau Frontenac* in Quebec (1893) and the *Royal York Hotel* in Toronto

AN ILLUSTRATED HISTORY OF RAILWAY HOTELS

(1929) – the largest hotel in the Commonwealth – were important steps forward. Ambitious plans to build in London during the 1930s failed, but CP.Hotels did move overseas in March and June 1973 when they took over the management of two hotels in Mexico. Canada's other equally famous railway, Canadian National, entered the hotel business in 1910 when the *Prince Arthur Hotel* opened.

Meanwhile, in Britain now that privatisation is matter of history, one cannot help but speculate on the bright future which undoubtedly lies ahead for the hotel industry, and in particular the famous former railway hotels. In Edinburgh, the *Caledonian Hotel* has (at the time of writing) recently celebrated its 80th birthday and a £2 million facelift. Its stately elegance and timeless standards of quality and service continue to underpin a formula which is already reaping rich rewards for its new owners. Nearby, the *North British Hotel* is undergoing a similar facelift and the replanning of its lower floors. In

Manchester, the famous *Midland Hotel* has begun a new career as the *Holiday Inn Midland Hotel,* and is a vital partner in the redevelopment of the neighbouring *G-Mex* centre (the former Central Station) into one of the finest exhibition, sporting and conference complexes in Europe.

In later years, faster travel and changing holiday patterns (especially the cheap, overseas package) has prompted the decline of most of the seaport and seaside resorts hotels. However, the town centre and popular inland resorts and golf hotels were meanwhile frequently modernised and upgraded, as far as funds permitted.

The names of the railway hotels will live on as a reminder of the companies which owned them for so long, and of those far-off years before the amalgamation of the railways, nationalisation and privatisation were ever dreamed of. For the collector, more tangible reminders exist in the form of many highly prized items: uniform buttons, cutlery, crockery, coloured postcards and guide books.

Above: The splendid Gothic frontage of the former *Midland Grand Hotel,* at St Pancras, is a very familiar sight – but its interior magnificence is much less well-known, for the hotel closed in 1935 and has since been used as offices by BR. This interesting view shows the staircase and first floor landing at St Pancras, about 1920. and features the redecoration carried out in 1901, when T. Wallace Hay painted the frescoes of the *Garden of Deduit and Romance of the Rose. Author's Collection.*

Chapter 1

LOCATIONS
London

"EUSTON" & "VICTORIA" HOTELS,

LONDON & NORTH-WESTERN RAILWAY COMPANY.

These hotels are situated one on each side of the entrance to Euston station.

The Porters attend the Arrival of the Trains.

EUSTON STATION, LONDON.

The opening of Euston station by the London & Birmingham Railway on July 20 1837 was a bold and, as later events proved, a permanent move for the company. Ten months later the Board of Directors, revealing vision and an instinct for business, issued a prospectus containing illustrations by Philip Hardwick inviting shareholders to purchase £25 shares in a company to be entitled the London & Birmingham Hotels & Dormitories. At a Special General Meeting of the railway company on July 11 1838, it was resolved to let the site in front of their station in Euston Grove to the hotel syndicate, "Believing the advantages to be derived by the company from this appropriation of the land in question will more than counterbalance any pecuniary advantage that might otherwise by obtained from it". It was stipulated that the railway directors should "have a permanent control over an undertaking, the main object of which is to promote the success of the railway by providing for the comfort of families and individuals who travel on it" (1)

The design adopted was largely that shown on the prospectus, with a pair of identical buildings flanking the approach to the Doric Arch. It was at first proposed to name the superior accommodation to the east side after Adelaide, the Dowager Queen of William IV, but before the opening in December 1839, the name has been changed to the *Euston Hotel*. The dormitory accommodation on the west side, named after the young Queen Victoria, had

Above: The world's first railway hotels: The *Victoria Hotel* opened in September 1839 and the *Euston Hotel* in December 1839. They are featured here in a London & North Western Railway's Tourist Guide of 1876. *Authors collection.*

Below: Euston in the 1920s, showing the newly-built LNWR war memorial, and the vista of the hotel link block (completed in 1881) which hides the famous Doric Arch from view. *SLP collection.*

meanwhile opened during the last week of September 1839, and could rightly claim to be the first railway-owned hotel in Britain. Its site is occupied by today's station.

A ruling by the Directors stated that no person would

meet the need for accommodation in this rapidly developing area of London, a private developer opened the *Prince of Wales Hotel*, a "Commercial Inn for families and Gentlemen" on the south side of the line next to the temporary terminus. *(3)*

These arrangements were to last some 12 years until February 1851, when the GWR's Directors decided to build a more conveniently placed and prestigious terminus on a new site fronting Conduit Street East. Observing that the *Prince of Wales Hotel* was a profitable enterprise, it was resolved to build an hotel on the road frontage immediately in front of the proposed terminus. The new Paddington station opened on January 16 1854, and was followed by the opening of the hotel on June 9. With 103 bedrooms and 15 sitting rooms, the hotel was the finest in London and its need was proved over many years. Subsequent additions and alterations increased the hotel's capacity to approximately 250 bedrooms.

Top: The *Euston Hotel*. A detail view of the ornate classical facade of the 'link block,' designed by J. B. Stansby. The piers of the Doric Arch can be seen through the right hand portals. *Authors collection.*

Above: The *Great Western Royal Hotel*, London, featured in the *Illustrated London News* for December 18 1852. Philip Hardwick Jnr. provided the finest hotel London had seen at that time.

Right: The *Great Northern Hotel*, at King's Cross, is shown here in a deceptively rural setting! Visitors needed to be aware of the 'extras' which could be more the double the price of a bedroom. *Facsimile published by the Great Northern Hotel, 1974*

be allowed to occupy a room for more than three consecutive nights if the accommodation was required for the use of railway passengers. The attractive but limited amount of accommodation and the 'together but apart' arrangements became an increasing nuisance until 1881, when the buildings were linked by a new block, bridging the avenue and hiding the view of the Doric Arch from Euston Road. The total accommodation available was increased to 300 rooms.

Two miles away to the west, the Great Western Railway first established itself in London at a terminus which opened on June 4 1838, adjacent to Bishops Road bridge, Paddington. While construction was taking place, the GWR's Directors decided to purchase the nearby Mint public house because: "conversion of the public house into a Coffee Tavern would be useful for the servants". *(2)* To

JUNE 1854

Great Northern Railway Hotel,
KING'S CROSS, LONDON
PRICES OF APARTMENTS.

Ground Floor ...	...	Sitting Room...	4s.	0d.
		Small ditto	3	0
First Floor ...	...	Sitting Room	4	0
		Small ditto	3	0
		Bed Room, large bed, two persons...	3	0
Second Floor ...	...	Ditto Ditto Ditto	3	0
		Ditto, single person	2	6
		Ditto, with two beds	4	0
Third and Fourth Floor ...		Ditto, large bed, two persons ...	2	6
		Ditto, single person	2	0
		Ditto, with two beds	3	0
Dressing Room ...	...	... ...	1	6
Servant's Bed ...		... ...	1	6
Sitting Room Fire (per day) ...		... ...	1	6
Ditto ditto (half day) ...	...	... ...	1	0
Bed Room ditto		... ...	1	0
Wax Lights ...	...	... ...	1	6
Dinner, as per Bill of Fare.				
Breakfast, plain ...		... ...	1	6
Ditto, with Cold Meat or Eggs ...		... ...	2	0
Ditto, with Broiled Ham or Chop ...		... ...	2	6
Hot Bath ...	...	... ...	2	0

It is particularly requested that NO FEES be offered to any of the Servants. In lieu thereof, One Shilling and Sixpence will be charged to each Visitor for attendance for the first day, and One Shilling per day afterwards; and to a family of more than three persons half the first charge after the first day. This charge includes the removal of Luggage, and for services rendered throughout the Hotel.

Visitors are earnestly requested to communicate to the Proprietor any cause of complaint arising from incivility or inattention, that it may be immediately investigated and rectified.

The Porters of the Hotel await the arrival of each Train at the Station for the removal of Luggage, &c. to the Hotel.

BROUGHAMS, CLARENCES, FAMILY CARRIAGES AND POST HORSES
BY THE DAY   OR HOUR
Lock-up Coach Houses and Excellent Stables.

The year 1854 also marked the opening of the Great Northern Railway's terminus and hotel at King's Cross. One of the least-altered of London's stations, Lewis Cubitt's design has a simple elegance and the curved boundary to which the hotel was built provided an attractive departure from the normally flat-fronted facades.

The Midland Railway meanwhile had reached London, via Rugby, to Euston after concluding a running powers agreement. Following the opening of King's Cross, similar arrangements were made with the Great Northern Railway, and Midland Railway trains began through-running in 1858, by way of Bedford and Hitchin. The MR was determined that its own London terminus would not only cater for its trains but would also provide hotel and headquarters accommodation for the Company. Unfortunately rising costs forced the Midland Directors to reduce Sir George Gilbert Scott's prizewinning design from five principal floor levels to four floors and abandon the office move from Derby to London. Under the regime of William Towle, St. Pancras did, however, become the headquarters of the Company's Hotels, Refreshments Room & Restaurant Car Department and, following the closure of the *Midland Grand Hotel* in 1935, provided a permanent home for the

MIDLAND GRAND,
LONDON.
WILLIAM TOWLE, Manager.

The MIDLAND GRAND is designed and arranged to meet the requirements of those who desire either the most sumptuous Apartments or a modest Bachelor's Bed-room ; and the Cuisine and Wine List will be found to embrace the elegance of the French Cuisine and the choicest Vintages, and the simplest meals with the wine of the Gironde or the Rhone at one shilling the half-bottle.

The MIDLAND GRAND forms the Terminus of the Midland Railway, whence Express Trains depart for Scotland, Manchester, Liverpool and all principal Manu-facturing Towns.

The MIDLAND GRAND *charges for Attendance and Gas have been abolished.* One Hundred Rooms at 3s. 6d. and 4s. per day, inclusive. Board, Apartments, &c., 10s. 6d. per day for the Winter.

The MIDLAND GRAND has Passenger Elevators, Electric Light, Telegraph, Telephone to Theatres and business centres. Special service of comfortable Broughams, at very low fares. Table d'Hôte open to non-residents.

For the increased comfort of ladies and families visiting London, the Ladies' Coffee Room is now open. It is on the first floor and en suite with the Music, Reading, Drawing and Billiard Rooms. The corridors are well-warmed and ventilated ; the service is the best in London, and the tariff, which is exceptionally low, is the same as in the General Coffee Room.

The Midland Omnibuses will meet Families coming to the Midland Grand Hotel.

Within Shilling Cab-fare of important business and West End centres and nearly all theatres. Close to Euston and King's Cross.

The QUEEN'S HOTEL, LEEDS, MIDLAND HOTEL, DERBY, and MIDLAND HOTEL, MORECAMBE, *are under the same Management.*

88

16

Above: Sir George Gilbert Scott's original plans for the *Midland Grand Hotel* provided five floor levels – but only four were built, to reduce costs. Nevertheless, the Midland Railway used the original drawings for publicity purposes, as shown in this advertisement from Whitackers Almanac for 1888.

Left: The former *Midland Grand Hotel* from the south-west. Guests could sit out on the balcony above the entrance porch. Count the floors, compared with the illustration above. *SLP.*

Facing page: A sitting room at the *Midland Grand*, St Pancras, containing some of the furniture supplied by Gillow's. Note the piano and the electric wall lights added at the turn of the century. *Authors collection.*

LMS Hotels Department and subsequently the Hotels Executive and finally British Transport Hotels Ltd.

A considerable gap of four and a half years separated the opening of St. Pancras Station on October 1 1868, and the opening of the *Midland Grand Hotel* on May 5 1873. This was the result of financial uncertainty, but with this accomplished, the four railway companies entering London from the North and West were able to accommodate some 600 visitors in their own hotels.

Developments on the south bank of the River Thames focussed on London's first railway terminal, which had opened on December 14 1836, at London Bridge. The first railway service was to Deptford and, a little later, to Greenwich. Parliament's first insistence that London should have only one railway route from the south caused a great deal of congestion. Within seven years the London & Greenwich Railway was sharing facilities with the London & Brighton Railway (opened in 1841) and the South Eastern Railway, which commenced its services to Folkestone and Dover in 1843 and 1844 respectively. The South Eastern Railway eased the congestion to some extent by opening its own terminus at Bricklayer's Arms in 1842, but the only permanent solution lay in the crossing of the Thames, and the building of stations nearer to the centre of the capital.

The initiative was taken by London Brighton & South Coast Railway with the opening of Victoria station in October 1860. Two weeks later, the South Eastern Railway's competitor, the London Chatham & Dover Railway, also established itself at Victoria using temporary platforms on the eastern side of the station, and completed permanent facilities two years later. Meanwhile, on the western side of the station, fronting Buckingham Palace Road, the LBSCR's

Grosvenor Hotel was taking shape. Massively-built and occupying a frontage of 262ft by 150ft, the hotel proved a success and received a 150-room extension in 1907.

The South Eastern Railway, determined to follow suit, embarked on an exercise from which it never made a complete financial recovery. Commencing with new high-level station at London Bridge it constructed two river crossings, one to a new station, named the City Terminus (opened in 1866) whilst the other, to the West End, at Charing Cross, opened in 1865. The cost of the work was reported to be £1,000 per lineal yard - a huge sum.

With the congestion at London Bridge eased, the London Bridge Terminus Hotel Company, composed largely of railway shareholders, nevertheless thought it opportune to build an hotel on the south-west side of the station. The opening was announced in Bradshaw's guide for September/October,1862, but the venture proved unprofitable and in 1893 the building was acquired by the LBSCR, which converted the building into offices.

Alone among the railways of the Southern Counties, the London & South Western Railway, whose terminus at Nine Elms had opened in 1839, remained on the South Bank and did not provided hotel accommodation at its new Waterloo

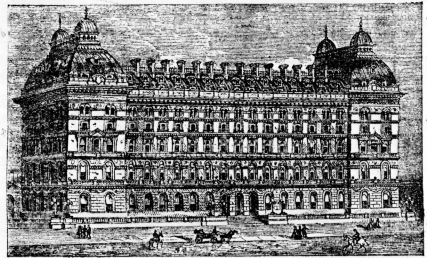

Has a direct approach from the Station, is situated in the most fashionable quarter of the Metropolis, near the Queen's Palace, and in the vicinity of the Parks and Clubs.

It contains every convenience for the comfort of Visitors at a moderate scale of charges.

FREDERIC SMITH,
Manager.

RESIDENTS HAVE THE OPTION OF BOARDING AS PER TARIFF, OR AT A FIXED PRICE OF 10s. 6d. PER DAY.

Above: The *Grosvenor Hotel*, opened in 1861, was one of the first to include a lift – or 'rising room' as they were known at the time. Medallions placed between the first floor windows featured notable personalities of their day! *GER Timetable, 1872.*

terminus, when it opened in July 1848.

The London Chatham & Dover Railway, aware of the success of the South Eastern Railway's *City Terminus Hotel,* decided to incorporate an hotel in its own City terminus, at Holborn Viaduct, *(4)* in 1877. Of the newcomers from the south, the *Charing Cross Hotel* was undoubtedly the most successful. Well-placed in the West End, the hotel had a 90-bedroom annexe in Villiers Street, linked by way of a footbridge in 1878, and within 12 years, the *Craven Hotel* in the neighbouring street of the same name was acquired.

An interesting observation about the development of hotel provision in London was made in a locally-published guide in 1879: "One of the greatest changes in London during the last score or so years is in the matter of hotels. In proportion to its size London is still far worse provided in this respect than most of the great Continental or American towns. Almost every great railway, however, with the exception of the Great Eastern and the South Western, now has a handsome hotel in connection with its terminus. The most especially noticeable being the *Great Western Hotel:* the *Grosvenor* at the Victoria Station of the London, Brighton and South Coast Railway; the *Charing Cross Hotel* belonging to the South-Eastern Railway; the *Great Northern Hotel* at the gates of the Great Northern; and the gorgeous Gothic pile which forms the front of the St. Pancras (Midland) terminus." One other railway hotel, the *Great Eastern Hotel* at Liverpool Street, opened in 1884.

The year 1879 was an interesting point in the development of the hotel industry in London. It marked virtually the end of the railways' involvement in hotel building – and it also marked the beginning of Frederick Gordon's plans for a large hotel empire. Frederick Gordon (1835-1904) the son of a house painter, was the creator of the world's first great hotel empire. Before his arrival, the railways' chief competitors were the *Westminster Palace* (1859); the *Palace,* Buckingham Gate (1861); and the

Langham, Portland Place (1865). However, within the space of 12 years, Gordon created a hotel mecca in the West End of London. The *Grand Hotel,* on the site of Northumberland House was built in 1881; followed by the *First Avenue Hotel*, Holborn, in 1883; the *Metropole Hotel* in 1885; and the purchase of the *Northumberland Avenue Hotel* in 1893, following the disgrace and imprisonment (for fraud) of its promoter Jabez Balfour. Two more hotels, this time not of Gordon's funding, were added as the century came to a close. The *Hotel Cecil,* advertised as: "the largest and most magnificent hotel in Europe, and three minutes from Charing Cross," opened in 1896, *(5)* and the more luxurious *Carlton,* built on the site of the former *Her Majesty's Theatre*, opened in 1899.

One final act came to fruition in July 1899, the floating of Frederick Hotels, named after the Henry Frederick Syndicate. With a subscription of £200,000 from Sir John Blundell Maple and the name of Frederick Gordon as Chairman, the company quickly acquired two brand-new hotels, the *Hotel Great Central* at Marylebone Station, and the *Hotel Russell.*

New generations of hotels joined the London scene during the Edwardian Era, the 1920s and 1930s, and also in the so-called 'high rise' era of more recent years. However, the railways took no part in these developments. Nevertheless it is interesting to reflect on the demise of the Gordon hotels, and the resilience displayed by London's railway hotels, which were well-managed and which enjoyed consistently good reputations. Of Gordon's empire, the *Grand Hotel* closed in 1927, the *First Avenue* followed in 1935, the *Metropole* disappeared in 1936, and the *Northumberland Avenue* closed in 1940, although by then it had been renamed the *Victoria Hotel.* The huge *Hotel Cecil* had a career that lasted barely 34 years. The *Langham* became one of the homes of the BBC in 1946, whilst the *Hotel Great Central* was bought by the LNER in 1947 and used thereafter as offices. Of the railway hotels that did close, the *London Bridge Terminus Hotel* was subsequently used railway offices and was gutted by fire bombs on December 29 1940. The *Holborn Viaduct Hotel* became the main office of Henley's Wireless Telegraph Works Ltd, and likewise became a war casualty in 1941. A third war casualty, again in 1941, was the *City Terminus Hotel*, which had earlier changed its name to the *Cannon Street Station*

Hotel. (6) The most sumptuous of all railway hotels, the *Midland Grand Hotel,* at St. Pancras, closed in 1935 following a decision not to embark on internal modernisation, whilst the *Euston Hotel* was demolished in 1963 in the wake of the Euston station rebuilding scheme and the destruction of London's monument to the Railway Age, the Doric Arch.

Right and below: The *Charing Cross Hotel*, **opened in 1863, sustained war damage during bombing in 1941. The lower illustration shows the two attic floors as subseqeuntly re-designed and rebuilt. Note also the Queen Eleanor cross in the forecourt.** *Authors Collection*

Towns and Cities

Above: The *Crewe Arms Hotel*. This hotel was built by Lord Crewe in 1836 and purchased by the LNWR in 1877. *Author's collection.*

ELSEWHERE in the British Isles, railway hotels appeared in many localities. Sometimes they were built in existing towns, simply to fulfil the demand for more accommodation. Existing towns sometimes became important railway junctions and an hotel was built adjacent to the station to cater for passengers wishing to make an overnight break of journey, for example at Birmingham or York.

In the larger towns of the Industrial Revolution, the demand for accommodation (principally by businessmen and commercial travellers) was greater and sometimes two or more new hotels were built in rapid succession. Towns often looked to their railways to provide accommodation, but it was not always the railways which took the initiative of providing hotel accommodation at stations. Crewe, which stood in open fields when the Grand Junction Railway arrived in 1837, was a mere hamlet of about 55 dwellings. Lord Crewe, aware of the likely influx of travellers, built the *Crewe Arms Hotel* in 1836 and subsequently leased the premises to the LNWR in 1864, at £225 per annum. *(7)* Birmingham's growth as a vital rail

junction dated from July 1837, with the opening of the route to Liverpool. London was reached in September,1838, Derby in August 1839, Gloucester in December 1840, and Manchester in August 1842. A second route to London, by way of the GWR's broad gauge, opened in October 1852. A rapid influx of visitors and the British Association for the Advancement of Science's choice of Birmingham for its Annual Conference in 1839, taxed the meagre accommodation available at the *Hen and Chickens*, then the borough's only up-to-date hotel!

Meanwhile the Boards of the London & Birmingham and the Grand Junction Railways, aware of the need for hotel accommodation, met in March 1839, and asked Philip Hardwick, architect of the stations at Euston and Curzon street, Birmingham, to consider the problem and write a report. Soon afterwards he advised that the Boardroom at Curzon Street could be converted for hotel use, at a cost of about £1,000. The work was completed by the end of 1839 and named the *Victoria Hotel. (7)* To meet further demand, R.B. Dockray added a wing to the building in 1840-41, during which time the accommodation was renamed the *Queens Hotel*.

Robert Benson Dockray (1811-1871) was Resident Engineer of the Southern Division of the London & North Western Railway from 1846 to 1852. He kept a diary, and

Facing page: The *Holborn Viaduct Hotel* opened in 1877. Its magnificent dining room featured roundels containing the Coats-of-Arms of towns through which the owning railway (the LCDR) passed. *Authors collection.*

ENTRANCE TO
BIRMINGHAM (CURZON STREET) STATION, 1838.

QUEEN'S HOTEL BIRMINGHAM.

AN ILLUSTRATED HISTORY OF RAILWAY HOTELS

Above: The Second World War intervened before work could start on a modern hotel at the GWR's Snow Hill Station. This author's sketch is based on an illustration published in the Birmingham *Evening Despatch* of January 28 1939. *Author.*

fortunately three annual volumes, covering the years 1850 (from which the pages for June 24-September 5 have been removed), 1853 and 1860, have survived. The entry for December 16 1850, reads: "I went to Great George Street (offices of Robert Stephenson) to enquire after the drawings of the Birmingham New Station. Mr Berkeley found them, but they were so splendid in design we both thought it would not do to show them to our Board. They were made by Thompson and are most handsome and elegant but quite out of the question for a railway station in these times". *(8)*

It is clear that, after a little over ten years, the Curzon Street Station and hotel were overcrowded, but with the chill wind of increased economies beginning to blow through Boardrooms, funds were no longer available. The 'Thompson' referred to was more likely Francis Thompson (1808-1895) one of the most accomplished architects of the early Victorian period, best known for the *Midland Hotel* and station at Derby, and the stations at Chester and Cambridge.

Two and a half years later, plans for a new *Queens Hotel* for Birmingham, to the design of William Livock, at an estimated cost of £9,957 were approved, and subsequently opened on May 1 1854. The building formed a 504ft long frontage to the new station, and remained unaltered until 1911, when more bedrooms were added. By this time, the hotel was 'bulging at the seams,' with 4,140 travellers being turned away in 1910; on one day alone, 168

Facing page, upper: The Curzon Street Arch, at Birmingham, designed by Philip Hardwick in 1838. From 1838 to 1854, hotel accommodation was provided on the upper floors and in the extension on the right. *Author's collection.*

Facing page, lower: The famous *Queens Hotel*, Birmingham. Designed by William Livock in 1853 and extended in 1911, 1917 and 1925. It was closed amidst much protest on December 31 1965. In this official view, the hotel carries the name *Queens North Western Hotel*. *Authors collection.*

would-be guests were unable to obtain accommodation. *(7)* A new west wing and a 40-room extension followed in 1917 and 1925 respectively. More land was purchased in 1935, but further plans were dashed by uncertainties about the future.

Meanwhile, the GWR, earlier frustrated at not being able to participate in a joint venture with the London & North Western Railway for a new central station in Birmingham, opened its own small hotel at Snow Hill Station in 1869. In words of *The Graphic*, the hotel was: "One of the most elegant, comfortable and economical in the three Kingdoms". *(9)* Grand words for the comparatively limited accommodation.

Peaceful rivalry between Birmingham's two railway hotels lasted barely three years when, in 1872, Isaac Horton (a private developer) announced plans to build a 200-room hotel in New Street, opposite the *Queens Hotel*. It was rumoured that the hotel was to be named the *North Western*. Alarmed, the LNWR renamed its own hotel the *North Western Queens Hotel* in June of that year. In reply, Isaac Horton named his hotel the *Midland Hotel*, giving the false impression that the well-known railway company were its owners. Horton's second venture, the opening of the *Grand Hotel*, followed in 1875. The LNWR, taken aback by the rapid increase in competition, mentioned only the *Hen and Chickens Hotel*, and the *North Western Queens Hotel*, in its Official Tourist and Picturesque Guide for 1876.

In 1905, the GWR decided to reconstruct Snow Hill station and convert the hotel, which would have been difficult to enlarge due to site limitations, into office accommodation, but retain the ground floor for remodelling into up-to date restaurant.

By 1939 the *Queens Hotel*, the *Midland Hotel* and the *Grand Hotel* had become age-worn in spite of some modernisation, and the GWR stepped in with an announcement that a brand new hotel was to be built on

DERBY STATION — NORTH MIDLAND RAILWAY.
FRANCIS THOMPSON, ARCHT
Under the directions of R. Stephenson, Esq.

Above: Francis Thompson's attractive station square at Derby, of 1838/40, included a well-appointed hotel shown at the right of this illustration. The Midland Railway bought the hotel in 1862. *Author's collection.*

Right: The *Great Northern Hotel* at Peterborough, built to the design of a local architect. Henry Goddard & Son. This hotel opened in 1851. *Author's collection.*

The *Royal Station Hotel,*
Hull, opened in 1851. One of
several railway hotels designed
by G. T. Andrews. An ever-popular
venue, the building was extended in 1909
and 1935. Queen Victoria visited the hotel in 1854.
Illustrated London News, October 21 1854.

the Colmore Row frontage at Snow Hill. But World War II was about to begin and the ambitious plans were abandoned. *(10)*

The caution exercised by the London & Birmingham and Grand Junction Railways in the modest provision of about 10 bedrooms at Birmingham back in 1839, was a typical attitude of the time, and was a result of two principal factors. Railways were still in their infancy and it was largely a matter of conjecture as to how many passengers were likely to need accommodation, and where it should be provided. Secondly, the financial burden of railway construction often drained funds to the limit and companies were reluctant to dig deeper into their pockets, especially for facilities which did not guarantee a return. In these circumstances, the contractor who had been paid for building the railway and its stations was often prepared to finance the construction of an hotel. Thomas Jackson of Pimlico, who carried out several of the civil engineering contracts and the building of the Derby station for the North Midland Railway (1837-40) gained the company's approval for his offer (of December 17 1839) to build an hotel adjoining the station. Fortunately, Jackson obtained a design for the hotel from Francis Thompson, who had been responsible for the North Midland stations and a happy unity of style was maintained for what can rightly be claimed as the earliest planned station square in the provinces. *(11)* David Nicholson, of Wandsworth, who was responsible for the construction of most of the stations on the London & Southampton Railway, was another

contractor who stepped forward as an hotelier. He built the *Junction Hotel,* at Bishopstoke, late in 1841. Like Thomas Jackson, he obtained the services of the architect of the line, in this instance, none other than Sir William Tite (1798-1873), architect of the Royal Exchange and a leading architect of his generation.

The somewhat unusual circumstances relating to the provisions of hotel and refreshment room facilities at Swindon in 1842 were also brought about by the participation of a willing contractor, J. & C. Rigby, who had built several of the GWR stations. The GWR was anxious to avoid further heavy expenditure in the provision of the hotel and housing accommodation and entered into an agreement with Rigby's, whereby the contractors, at their own expense, were to build Swindon station and 300 workmen's cottages in return for a 99-years lease of the proposed hotel and refreshment rooms at the station, at a rental of one penny a year. *(12)*

Custom was assured because it was further agreed that all regular trains would stop for about ten minutes, to allow passengers to alight for refreshment. The accommodation occupied the twin buildings, one of which still stands; one on the Up platform and one on the Down platform. The basements contained the kitchens, the platform levels were occupied by large refreshment rooms and the first floors of both buildings were linked by a covered bridge which formed the hotel. The coffee room and sitting rooms occupied the south block whilst the bedrooms occupied the north block. The hotel had several changes of name; it

Above: The *Queens Hotel*, Leeds, as completely rebuilt in 1937 to the design of W. Curtis Green in association with W. Hamlyn. *Author's collection.* Below: The *Great Northern Hotel*, Leeds, opened in 1869. This building suffered fire damage in 1906. *Illustration courtesy of Hadfield, Cawkwell & Davidson, successors to M. E. Hadfield, who designed the Hotel.*

Above: The *Midland Hotel*, Bradford, opened in 1890 to the design of Charles Trubshaw. The famous actor Sir Henry Irving died at the hotel in 1905. *Author's collection.*

Above: The *Midland Hotel*, Manchester, was one of the most ambitious of the Midland Railway's Hotel building projects, completed to the design of Charles Trubshaw. The hotel had its own post-mark, until 1949. *Author's collection.*

was first referred to as the *Queen Arms Inn*, later the *Queens Hotel* and finally the *Queens Royal Hotel*. But to confuse matters, a second hotel had appeared by 1848, and occupied the site opposite the station entrance. Known as the *Queen Arms Hotel* this building and its companions on the platform were owned and managed by the Swindon Junction Hotel Company which the lessees had formed to look after their hotel and catering activities. The situation, which had for long proved both inconvenient and annoying to the now prosperous GWR, came to an end in 1895 when the lease was bought out for £100,000, by the GWR. Swindon station changed radically; express trains no longer stopped, the platform hotel was closed within three years and the adjoining *Queens Arms Hotel*, opposite the station entrance, was leased to the Weymouth Brewery Company

As the railway companies grew and began to pay their way, they also took a greater interest in hotel building and assumed the role which had earlier been taken by private developers. Thus, in 1848, the Great Northern Railway took its first step into the hotel business, by purchasing the residence of Richard Moon at Lincoln, and extensively

AN ILLUSTRATED HISTORY OF RAILWAY HOTELS

remodelling it as a new hotel to the design of H. Goddard. *(13)* The ancient Cathedral City became the meeting point of lines from Gainsborough, Market Razen, Peterborough and later Grantham. Lincoln's *Great Northern Hotel* soon became a popular place of call.

Small railway companies too, were responsible for some of the earliest and most attractively-sited hotels. The Northern Staffordshire Railway station and hotel at Stoke-on Trent, both designed by R.A. Hunt, remain as one of the most interesting station squares. The hotel, opened in June 1849 cost a little over £1,900 and became so well patronised that it was enlarged in 1878. *(7)* It was later referred to as the *Five Towns Hotel* in an Arnold Bennett novel.

Facing page: The *Station Hotel*, Inverness. This hotel was opened in 1856 and purchased by the Highland Railway 1878. *Author's collection.*

Right: The *Central Station Hotel*, Glasgow opened 1885 and is seen here as sketched in an LMS brochure of 1937. *Author's collection.*

Below: The *Central Station Hotel*, Glasgow. The dining room with its curved walls was located at the corner of the building shown in the illustration. *Author's collection.*

Yorkshire and the North East of England were also the scene of determined development in the later 1840s and early 1850s, with railway hotels being built at Tweedmouth and Tynemouth, both opened in 1847, and three attractive hotels constructed to the designs of G.T. Andrews of York. These were the attractive terminus buildings taken over by the NER at this time at Gateshead, opened in 1844, followed by the *Station Hotel* at Hull in 1851 and the *Station Hotel* at York, opened in 1852, for the North Eastern Railway. Andrews gave his stations an air of importance and treated the hotels as an integral of the overall design. John Dobson (1787-1865), architect of the magnificent station at Newcastle-upon-Tyne, also designed the modest 50-bedroomed hotel to the left of the station frontage. Steady demand led to the accommodation being enlarged to 133 bedrooms in 1892.

The industrial West Riding of Yorkshire. and in particular the thriving towns of Leeds and Bradford, featured prominently in hotel building schemes of the 1860s. Leeds became the first town outside London to have two large railway-owned hotels, one of which also happened to be the first hotel to be built by the Midland Railway. The MR, like its competitors was by then sufficiently powerful to dictate building policy and a scheme which had been started by the Leeds Hotel

Company in 1859 actually came to fruition under the sole control of the Midland Railway. The Leeds Hotel Company, which had been in search of a suitable site and half the capital required to float the scheme, obtained the MR's agreement to sell a piece of land near the station. However, the MR Board of Directors insisted on its own shareholders first agreeing to acquire a one-third interest in the nominal capital of the hotel company. The value of the site and buildings was to form part of the proposed subscription, and it further required that the railway should be represented by one-third of the members of the Hotels Management Committee. The Leeds Hotel Company rejected these terms, but the Midland Board, aware of the need for an hotel in the locality, declared that the hotel should be under the control of the MR. This proposal was duly confirmed in principal and endorsed by the railway shareholders on August 16 1859.

The Chairman of the MR, referring to the vote of £15,000 for the new hotel, remarked that: "he had given the subject a long and careful consideration and seeing that in another year the Lancaster and Carlisle Company would have opened its line from Low Gill to Ingleton, which

Below: The *Station Hotel*, Perth. A distinctly Scottish Baronial design by Andrew Heiton, in 1890. *Author's collection.*

AN ILLUSTRATED HISTORY OF RAILWAY HOTELS

egrams - BRITISH, EDINBURGH.
phones - 8966-8972 Central
EDINBURGH 24051.

NORTH BRITISH STATION HOTEL Edinburgh

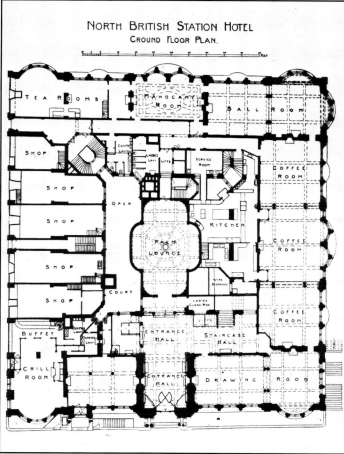

NORTH BRITISH STATION HOTEL
GROUND FLOOR PLAN

Above: The *North British Hotel*, Edinburgh. This postcard features its earlier name and a change of telephone number - ever thrifty, the railway company simply had the old cards overprinted! *John Alsop Collection.*

Left: A ground floor plan from the *North British Hotel*. From the coffee room, guests enjoyed a magnificent view of the city's castle and gardens. *Author's collection.*

would give them a through route both to the North of Ireland, and to Scotland, and seeing also that it was now admitted that the Midland Company was entitled to consideration in respect of that traffic, the directors found that some resting place was absolutely necessary for families, midway between these points. They believe that this hotel would influence the traffic to a very large extent and they were assured that the rent would be amply repay the interest upon the cost of the outlay; it would yield a fair return directly to the company and indirectly it would add largely to the revenue." (7)

The necessary powers to build the hotel were obtained in the Midland Railway Act of 1861 and the *Queens Hotel* opened on January 10 1863. The hotel was an immediate success and its accommodation was extended in 1867, and again in 1898, and was completely rebuilt in 1936/7. Leeds became such an important rail junction that the Great Northern Railway also built an hotel of its own; it was named it after the company and opened for business on July 1 1869. The pair of railway hotels were later joined by the privately owned *Metropole Hotel*, which opened in 1899. In neighbouring Bradford, a similar pattern occurred with three principal hotels, two of which were railway-owned. The *Victoria Hotel* (1867) was later bought by the Great Northern Railway, and was followed by the *Alexandra Hotel* (1877) and the *Midland Hotel* (1890) which was built by the MR as part of the Foster Square scheme completed that year. The *Victoria Hotel* (Bradford) renamed the *Great Northern Victoria Hotel*, was a popular haunt of merchants. The 1871 census returns revealed that they had come from countries as far afield as America, Russia, Turkey, Italy, Germany and France. The neighbouring Midland Hotel was the scene of the death, on October 13 1905, of the renowned actor Sir Henry Irving (born 1838) whilst he was 'on tour.'

Across the Pennines into industrial Lancashire, the cotton metropolis of Manchester was poorly provided with hotel accommodation. In fact, the *Queens Hotel,* in Piccadilly (opened in 1845) was the only sizeable hotel in the city centre. The *Victoria Hotel*, built by Manchester Corporation and opened in 1866, proved to be a financial disaster. The *Grosvenor Hotel* (opened in 1879) and the *Grand Hotel* (opened in 1883) met with greater success. The LNWR's Additional Powers Act of 1881 authorised the building of hotels at Manchester's London Road Station, also at Rugby and Dublin, but after due consideration only the hotel at Dublin was built.

The MR first reached Manchester in 1867, by way of its own route from Derby, through the Peak District to New Mills, and then via Manchester, Sheffield & Lincolnshire Railway metals to London Road. The opportunity for serious thought about building a modern railway hotel, which would outshine all the existing competition, came to the MR in June 1877. That year, work commenced on the building of the Manchester South District Railway, which gave the Midland a direct access to Manchester at a new terminus at Central Station. The Cheshire Lines Committee, a partnership formed by the Great Northern Railway, the Manchester, Sheffield & Lincolnshire Railway and Midland Railway, failed to reach a firm decision about the building of an hotel at the new Central Station, and the MR decided to proceed with its own plans. In 1896, £365,000 was spent on the purchase of a two-acre island site in front of the station, for an hotel. It was to cost £1,250,000 and would rival the best which Europe or America could offer. Among the buildings which had to be demolished to make way for the new hotel were two places of entertainment; the most important of these was the Gentleman's Concert Hall, erected by private subscription in 1831. Charles Halle made his first appearance in the hall and later founded his orchestra there. The other was a music hall called the Casino, or familiarly, the 'Old Cass.'

Charles Heywood, the owner of the Concert Hall, agreed to sell the building to the MR, providing that a Theatre/Concert Hall of equal size was included in the accommodation to be provided in the new hotel. The 800-seat theatre subsequently provided was so popular that within a year of its opening in September 1903, other theatre managers in the City opposed the renewal of its licence. This attempt failed and in 1907 theatrical history was made when Miss Horniman introduced her company to the hotel theatre audience before taking over The Gaiety as the home of England's first repertory company.

With 400 bedrooms, the **Midland Hotel** was the ultimate in provincial hotels. In the words of Sir James Hoy, a former Lord Mayor of Manchester, at the opening dinner on Saturday September 5 1903: "There was, in the hotel, everything of the very best that had been done on the face

of the globe." *(14)* Nine months later the Hon Stewart Rolls and Henry Royce met at the *Midland Hotel* to discuss the merger of their business interests.....the outcome, as they say, is history!

Not the most attractive of buildings externally, Professor Reilly, of Liverpool University, likened it to "An ant-heap". *(15)* But no one could deny the magnificence of the interior. The completion of the *Midland Hotel,* Manchester, also filled an important gap in the coverage paid by the LNWR and MR to the western side of England, and to their routes from London to Carlisle.But the opening of the *Midland Hotel* did not meet with universal approval. When Spiers & Pond shareholders met in July 1904, their Chairman referred to: "unfair competition, as in the case of the Midland Railways one-and-a-quarter million pound hotel. That had had the effect that every other hotel in Manchester was practically doing no business, for the new hotel was more than sufficient to supply all the wants of Manchester." This was reported in *The Globe* of July 11 1904.

The provision of railway hotels in Scotland followed the 'discovery' of the highlands, made possible by the opening of new trunk routes from England. The *Station Hotel,* Inverness (opened in 1856) was purchased by the Highland Railway in 1878, just a year before Scotland's first purpose-built railway hotel opened at St. Enoch Station, Glasgow, in July 1879. Glasgow's second railway hotel, the *Central Station Hotel,* was opened by the Caledonian Railway in June 1885. When the North British Railway rebuilt its Queen Street station in Glasgow, in 1877, it also took over the adjacent hotel fronting George Square. This was later rebuilt with the addition of a third floor and reopened in May 1905. Perth should have had a railway hotel as early as 1865, when the necessary powers were obtained, but hesitation on the part of the owning companies delayed building operations until 1889.

Edinburgh was the scene of feverish construction in the opening years of the 20th century, first with large North British Hotel, opened in October 1902, and followed by the opening of the *Caledonian Hotel* in December 1903. The latter project had its origins in plans drawn-up in 1867, but subsequently shelved owing to lack of funds. Aberdeen, in the territory of the Great North of Scotland Railway, had two privately owned hotels, the *Station Hotel* opened in 1870 and the *Aberdeen Palace Hotel* opened in 1874. Both hotels were purchased by the railway company in 1890 and 1910 respectively.

Facing page: An official postcard, showing the Caledonian Railway's hotels at Glasgow and Edinburgh. Attractive postcards were a frequent part of promotion and publicity in these days. *John Alsop Collection.*

AN ILLUSTRATED HISTORY OF RAILWAY HOTELS

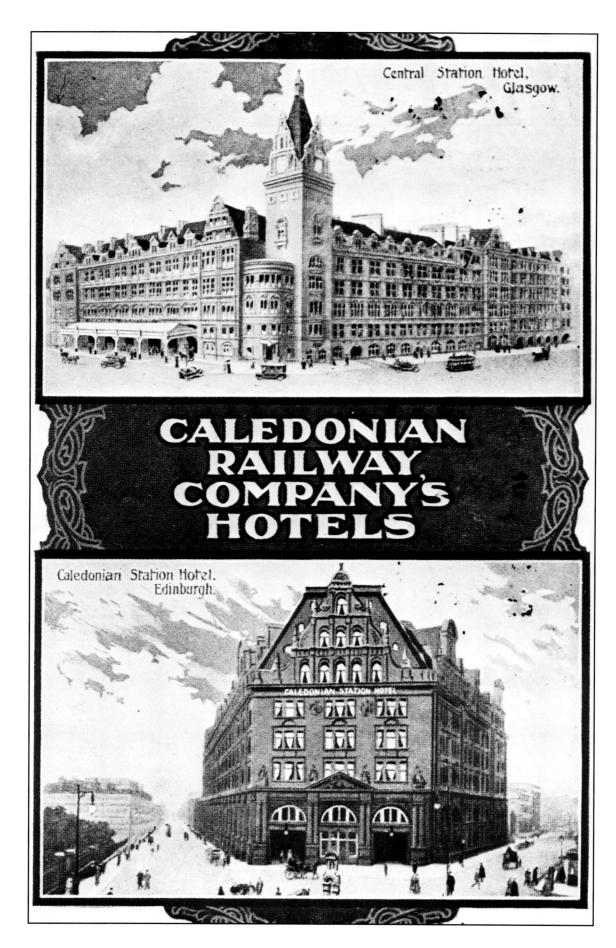

Central Station Hotel, Glasgow.

CALEDONIAN RAILWAY, COMPANY'S HOTELS

Caledonian Station Hotel, Edinburgh.

CALEDONIAN STATION HOTEL

Seaports and Harbours

The *Lord Warden Hotel*, Dover. This hotel was visited by Charles Dickens and described in not entirely complimentary terms! *Illustrated London News, September 10 1853.*

IN Victorian times, journeys by road and rail were tedious and travellers, often with a full day's journey behind them, were in need of a bed and refreshment before boarding ship, the following day.

For centuries the gateway to the continent had been by way of Dover. Then, with the coming of the railways, a new service operated by the South Eastern & Continental Steam Packet Company was inaugurated in 1845 to ply between Dover and Folkestone to Calais, Boulogne and Ostend. The SER later obtained powers in 1853 to own and run its own service from the Admiralty Pier at Dover. Samuel Beazley (1786-1851) more at home designing churches, did not live to see the opening of the *Lord Warden Hotel*, Dover, which he had designed for the SER. With about 40 bedrooms, the hotel enjoyed 85 years service before closure at the outbreak of the Second World War, in September 1939. Of Dover and the new hotel opened in 1853, Charles Dickens wrote. "I particularly detest Dover for the self-complacency with which it goes to bed. It always goes to bed (when I am going to Calais) with a more brilliant display of lamp and candle than any other town. Mr and Mrs. Birmingham host and hostess of the Lord Warden Hotel, are my much esteemed friends, but they are too conceited about the comforts of that establishment when the Night Mail is starting. I know that it is a good house to stay at, and I don't want the fact insisted upon in all its warm bright windows at such an hour. I know the Warden is a stationary edifice

that never rolls or pitches and I object to its big outline seeming to insist upon that circumstance, and, as it were, to come over with it, when I am reeling on the deck of the boat." *(16)*

Not far to the west of Dover, the South Eastern Railway built the *Royal Pavilion Hotel* at Folkestone in 1843, for passengers using the New Commercial Steam Packet Company's service to Boulogne. Described under the guise of 'Pavilionstone' Dickens wrote: "The South Eastern Company have bought Pavilionstone into such vogue, with their tidal trains and splendid steam packets, that a new Pavilionstone is rising up .... The lion of Pavilionstone is its great hotel." *(17)* He went on to recall the dingy accommodation and cold beef that his earlier lodgings had provided, and then meted out praise for the railway for its efficient handling of the traffic for those who wished to proceed direct from train to ship. For those who chose to linger, the *Great Pavilionstone Hotel* provided a friendly welcome. In fact, the hotel was of modest size, with about 35 bedrooms. Dwindling demand prompted by faster journeys led to its sale in 1896.

In neighbouring Sussex, the London Brighton & South Coast Railway established an independent company in 1847, the Brighton & Continental Steam Packet Company and chose Newhaven for the port from which to run its London Victoria-Dieppe service. The old fishing town had little more than a creek to offer and frequent silting under the strong winds inevitably led to delays, necessitating overnight stays. To provide hospitality for passengers, the railway built the *London & Paris Hotel* in 1847. The harbour was subsequently improved by the addition of the new quays. The fares charged for the 64-miles journey to Dieppe were lower than those for Dover crossing and consequently the boats were often crowded, deck passengers often enduring miseries in bad weather. The more affluent passengers enjoyed the hospitality of the *London & Paris Hotel* and the building underwent an eventful career; it was bombed in March 1942 and finally closed, prior to demolition, in 1959.

Before opening of the railway hotels at Dover, Folkestone and Newhaven, these ports were not devoid of accommodation and boasted several long established coaching inns. Southampton, the chief mail packet station on the south coast, also had several well-respected establishments including the *Royal, Dolphin, Radleys, Star* and *Crown Hotels.* The railways reached Southampton in June 1839, by way of the LSWR, and this company later became established in the steamer service by powers obtained in 1848. In France, the Western Railways reached Havre in 1847 and frequent sailings to Southampton and from Southampton to the Channel Islands, St. Malo and Honfleur brought a steadily growing number of passengers into the docks. Other companies developed services to North and South America, the West Indies and Africa. *(18)* To meet the demand for more hotel accommodation the LSWR bought the *Imperial Hotel* in 1882 and leased it to tenants. *(19)*

The great visionary, Isambard Kingdom Brunel laid more ambitious plans. He looked to the west and saw the GWR's empire extending to America by way of the Great Western Steamship Company's service to New York. So ambitious were the plans that Brunel's wooden auxiliary paddle steamer the *Great Western*, made her voyage to New York on April 8 1838, a little over three years before the railway from Paddington to Bristol was opened. Bristol, for long an important port, was well-provided with inns, but two enterprising hoteliers, Messrs. Leigh and Rogers, with an eye on attracting patronage from travellers en route to and from America, opened the *Royal Western Hotel,* at

Above: Known as the *Imperial Hotel* when it opened at Southampton in 1866, the London & South Western Railway purchased and renamed this hotel, as shown here, in 1882. The hotel belonged to the era of the transatlantic liners and closed in 1939. *John Alsop Collection.*

Bristol, on April 18 1839. (20) The future seemed bright and Brunel's second ship, the *Great Britain* was launched in 1843. However, in February 1842, high port dues had forced the steamship company to operate alternate voyages from Bristol and Liverpool, and shortly afterwards the service was moved to Liverpool, only to be wound up in 1850 and both ships sold.

Undaunted by the misfortunes of the Great Western Steamship Company, Brunel had another port in mind, the natural deep water inlet of Milford Haven. The site chosen was Neyland and in 1856 the port was linked by rail to London, via Gloucester. With a journey time of more than eight hours to the capital, the provision of hotel accommodation was essential. The owning company, the South Wales Railway, first asked Philip Hardwick Jnr to prepare plans in June 1856, but the plans were too ambitious and a more modest 12-bedroomed scheme by a Mr. Owen was prepared and authorised; the hotel opened in April 1858 *(21).* A thrice-weekly service to Waterford and a twice-weekly service to Cork, provided by Messrs. Ford & Jackson, brought many passengers into Neyland and the *South Wales Hotel* was extended later in 1858, to provide eight more rooms.

Above: The *London & Paris Hotel*, at Newhaven. The building sustained war damage in 1942 while serving as HMS Aggresive. *Newhaven Historical Society.*

Above: The *South Wales Hotel*, at Neyland (near Milford Haven) opened in April 1858. It was extended (on the right) later in 1858. This ill-fated hotel was built in anticipation of sea traffic which was later lost to Fishguard. *Author's sketch.*

Expectations of a trans-Atlantic service soared in 1860 when the Anglo-Luso-Brazilian Royal Mail Steam Navigation Company made Neyland a port of call, for their sailings from Portugal to Brazil. Brunel's third but unfortunate ship, the *Great Eastern,* arrived in August 1860, returning from her maiden voyage to New York, only to be laid-up for repairs. Hopes of a prosperous future faded and the *South Wales Hotel* relied on customers from passengers using the Irish services, until 1906, when the hotel lost its trade to the GWR's *Wyncliff Hotel* at Fishguard, following the transfer of traffic to the shorter sea route.

The phenomenal growth of Liverpool as a great passenger terminal and entrepot for the Lancashire cotton industry steadily outshone development at other ports. By 1875, the Liverpool docks had more than 18 miles of quay space, covering a water area of 267 acres. At the forefront of developments in steamship travel, Liverpool had welcomed the *Savannah*, the first steamship to cross the Atlantic, on June 20 1819, after her 28 day crossing. Nearly 20 years later, and hard on the heels of Brunel's *Great Western*, the Transatlantic Steamship Company, with its ships the *Royal William* and the *Liverpool,* completed successful Atlantic crossings on July 5 and October 20 1838 respectively. (22) By the early 1870s, the Cunard, White star, National, Inman, Allan and Guion companies were using Liverpool as their regular port of call. Passengers bound for New York paid between 15 and 20 guineas for a single journey and about 30 guineas for a return ticket. Liverpool was soon linked to the railway network too. Manchester was reached in September 1830, Birmingham in July 1837 and Preston in October 1838.

Travellers found Liverpool well provided, with about a dozen good hotels including the *Adelphi, Washington, Waterloo, Queens, Stork, Victoria, Angel* and *Compton Hotels*. In fact, the railways did not build an hotel of their own until the LNWR opened the 200-bedroom *Lime Street*

Station Hotel on March 1 1871. *(23)* However, the earlier absence of the railways from the hotel building scene was remedied by the attention which the Midland and the Lancashire & Yorkshire Railways paid to the city. Liverpool (and later Glasgow) were to be the only cities outside London to have three large railway hotels each.

The MR, anxious to build or purchase an hotel near its Liverpool terminus, bought the *Adelphi Hotel* in 1892. Built in 1826, this hotel was already famous and in Dickens' words: "undeniably perfect". Popularity however sometimes meant that larger premises were needed to cope with demand and the hotel was completely rebuilt in 1876. The MR later experienced a similar problem and its Chairman, G. Murray Smith, wrote: "For some years popularity of the Adelphi Hotel has been almost an embarrassment to the management in as much as the accommodation while considerable was not really enough. The Board determined therefore to build a new hotel that would meet all possible requirements in the future and would be at the same time building worthy of a great commercial city like Liverpool." The third *Adelphi Hotel* opened on March 14 1914 and was the ultimate in the MR's highly-regarded group of hotels. With nearly 600 rooms arranged on six floors, the magnificent classical interior contained in addition to the usual dining, coffee room and lounge facilities, a range of rooms for entertainment and sport. These included two ballrooms, a swimming pool, squash court, Turkish baths, gymnasium, rifle range and billiard room. *(24)* Liverpool's third railway hotel, the *Exchange Station Hotel*, with 80 bedrooms,was opened by the Lancashire & Yorkshire Railway in August 1888. *(25)* In the less prosperous 1930s, the LMS decided to close the *Lime Street Station Hotel* in March 1933 and transfer its business to the *Adelphi Hotel*. More recently, following the closure of the *Exchange Station Hotel*, (in July 1971) all trade was concentrated at the *Adelphi*.

Although Liverpool was concerned primarily with sailings to America and beyond, the LNWR competed with the City of Dublin Steam Packet Company for the lucrative Irish sea trade. The railway-owned boats reached Dublin at about 7am and as a place of recovery from the rigours of the crossing, the Company opened the *North Western Hotel*, on the North Wall in 1885. The hotel even had a garden, which was described as a 'green oasis' in the desert of docks and warehouses. When 'the troubles' came to Dublin, the hotel had its most unwelcome guests, a battallion of 'black and tans,' who remained until the truce of 1921, and then in 1924 the building was converted into office accommodation. The LNWR's route to Ireland, by way of Holyhead to Greenore, was ideal for the golfing traveller with a little time to spare. Both the *Station Hotel* at Holyhead (1880) and its namesake at Greenore (1873) included 18-hole courses among their amenities.

Continental traffic to Holland and North Germany came within the sphere of influence of the Great Eastern Railway, which inaugurated a once-weekly service between Harwich and Rotterdam in October 1863. The arrival of the *Blenheim* from Rotterdam on Saturday October 3 marked the end of a long struggle to obtain the consent of Parliament. The first setback came in 1843, when powers were refused to extend the London-Colchester main line from Ardleigh to Harwich. In August 1854, the branch from Manningtree to Harwich was opened, together with a small quay, but the railway was denied authority to establish a steamship service. Finally, amid strong opposition from other East Coast ports, the necessary Bill was passed in July 1863. *(26)*

To meet the demand for accommodation at Harwich, the railway opened the *Great Eastern Hotel* in January 1865. *(27)* In 1882/83 the company built a new £500,000 quay in a reclaimed site about

a mile from Harwich, and named the site Parkeston in honour of Mr. Parkes, Chairman of the Company. Again an hotel was included in the scheme: " for the accommodation of passengers who may desire to run down to Parkeston and stay until able to select a fine day for crossing the Channel, or for those who rest after leaving the steam packets before taking a railway journey." *(28)*

An influx of visitors and residents to the area also brought a new lease of life to the Harwich hotel and it was extensively renovated and refurbished in 1883. After

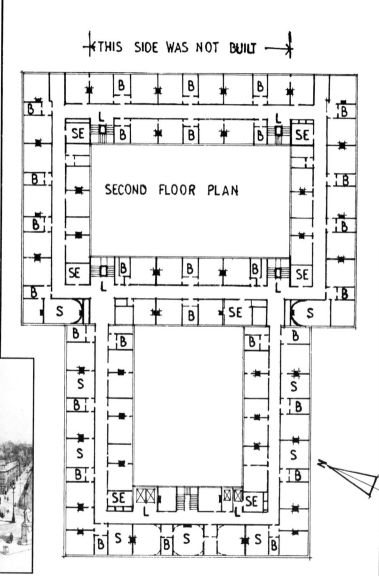

Above: A contemporary sketch of the *Adelphi Hotel*, at Liverpool. showing its commanding site. *Author's collection.*

Right: The *Adelphi Hotel* was the third hotel to occupy its site. It utilised moden steel-framed construction, but each room nevertheless had its own fireplace. *Author's sketch.*

THIS SIDE WAS NOT BUILT

SECOND FLOOR PLAN

ADELPHI HOTEL, LIVERPOOL. REBUILT 1912-14
STEEL FRAMED THROUGHOUT, PLANNED TO A 14'3" GRID.
KEY: B·BATH RM. S·SITTING RM. SE·SERVICE & STORES
L·LIFT. ALL OTHER LARGE ROOMS ARE BEDROOMS   FT.
ARCHT. R FRANK ATKINSON F.R.I.B.A.   10 20 30 40 50

AN ILLUSTRATED HISTORY OF RAILWAY HOTELS

requisitioning of both hotels in the World Wars, the Harwich hotel found a new use as the Town Hall in October 1951; the Parkeston hotel closed in 1963, and was later converted into office accommodation.

Another outlet to Germany and Holland was Grimsby. Among the property owned by the town's Royal Dock Company taken over in 1890 by the Manchester Sheffield & Lincolnshire Railway were two useful hotels, the *Royal* (1865), in the docks area, and the smaller *Yarborough Hotel,* which was considerably enlarged in 1891. By 1912,

the Great Central Railway (successor to the MSLR) was operating a daily service to Hamburg and thrice-weekly crossing to Antwerp and Rotterdam, which brought many transient visitors to both hotels.

The *Central Station Hotel,* Newcastle (1850 - described in more detail in *Towns & Cities,* see page 24), the *Royal Station Hotel,* Hull (1851) and the *Grand Hotel* at West Hartlepool (1899) have, over the years also catered for countless travellers en route for Scandinavian and Northern European ports.

Above: The *Station Hotel*, at Holyhead, was built in 1880 to replace a smaller hotel which had been purchased by the Chester & Holyhead Railway. *Author's collection.*

Facing page: Liverpool's *North Western Hotel* was designed by Alfred Waterhouse RA and opened in 1871. In 1933, business was transferred to the more modern *Adelphi* and the *Exchange Station* hotels. *Author's collection.*

Right: The *Royal Station Hotel*, at Newcastle Upon Tyne, opened in 1854 to the design of John Dobson. This view clearly shows the two additional floors added by William Bell in 1892. *Author's collection.*

GREEN EASTERN RAILWAY HOTEL, HARWICH, ESSEX.

This new and commodious first-class Hotel, belonging to the Great Eastern Railway Company, is now open for the reception of Families, Tourists, and other Visitors to this favorite and improving Marine resort.

The Hotel, which is extensive, elegantly furnished, and replete with every comfort, is pleasantly situated facing the Harbour, and commands delightful views of the scenery of the Rivers Orwell and Stour, and is adjacent to the Railway Station and Steam Boats.

Travellers to and from the Continent, *via* Harwich, to the Northern Ports of Germany and the Rhine, will find every accommodation at this Establishment.

The *cuisine* is of a varied and superior character, and the wines are selected from the choicest stocks.

Tariffs of charges can be obtained by application to the Manager, at the Hotel.

HOTEL PRICES.

COFFEE ROOM.

	s.	d.		s.	d.		s.	d.
Dinner off the Joint and Vegetables	2	6	Cold Meat	1	6	Cup of Coffee	0	6
Chops and Vegetables	2	0	Basin of Soup	1	0	Cup of Tea	0	6
Steaks and ditto	2	0	Plate of Sandwiches	0	6			

BREAKFASTS.

TEAS, &c.

	s.	d.		s.	d.		s.	d.
Plain	1	6	Broiled Ham and Eggs	2	6	Tea or Coffee and Bread and Butter	1	6
Cold Meat or Eggs	2	0	Chops, Steaks, or Plain Fish ...	3	0	Ditto with Cold Meat ...	2	0

PRIVATE DINNERS.

	s.	d.		s.	d.
Soup, Fish, off Joint, Entrée, Sweet, and Vegetables	5	0	Soup, off Joint, and Vegetables	3	0
Fish, off Joint, Entrée, Sweet, and Vegetables ...	4	0	Fish, off Joint, and Vegetables	3	0

Visitors' Servants' Bed per night. 1s. 6d.; Board and Lodging per day, 5s., or 30s. per week.

Sitting Rooms, from 4s. 0d. according to size and position.

FIRST AND SECOND FLOORS.			THIRD FLOOR.		
Bed Rooms, from	3s. 0d. to 4s. 0d.		Bed Rooms, from	2s. 6d. to 3s. 6d.	

BATHS.

Warm Sea Water	1s. 0d.	Cold Sea Water...	0s. 9d.

SERVICE.—Visitors will be charged 1s. 6d. per day each person. Casual Visitors, 3d. each meal.

PUBLIC & PRIVATE BILLIARD ROOMS.

A Tariff of Choice Wines and Liqueurs, selected with the greatest care, as per carte.

Liberal arrangements are made with Visitors staying any lengthened period.

The charge made for Attendance includes services rendered throughout the Establishment.

Visitors giving up Apartments are requested to give notice of their intention before noon,

Visitors are requested to communicate any cause of complaint to the Manager, that it may be immediately investigated and remedied.

All communications for Rooms, &c., to be addressed to the Manager, at the Hotel.

BY ORDER OF THE BOARD.

The *Great Eastern Hotel*, Harwich, opened in 1865, to the design of Thomas Allom. This detailed tariff was included in GER timetables of the period. *Stephenson Locomotive Society Library.*

Seaside and Inland Resorts

England and Wales

THE popularity of sea-bathing dates back to the mid-18th century and the publication of Dr. Richard Russel's treatise on Glandular Consumption, and the use of sea water for treating diseases of the glands. Published in Latin in 1750 and in English three years later, Russell's remedy acquired rapid favour and led to considerable changes in national taste. *(29)*

For example, fishing villages assumed new roles as fashionable watering places. Some resorts, on the other hand, had already acquired reputations as spas; Scarborough's medicinal springs had been discovered in the early 16th century. Other resorts-to-be, like Eastbourne, Hastings and Torquay had been known previously as coastal defence stations established during the Napoleonic wars. Although the railways played an important part in reaching out with new routes and branch lines to serve these resorts, they built few of their own seaside hotels. They saw their principal role as providing for the needs of passengers in towns and cities and at seaports. Leisure travel was hardly considered. There were also considerable financial risks to be taken in floating new ventures in hitherto insignificant fishing villages.

One of the railway's first seaside ventures, in 1848, on the shores of Morecambe Bay, in Lancashire, did meet with success. The Topographical Dictionary of England (published in 1831) observed: "Poulton has of late years become a favourite bathing place. It commands fine views of Morecambe Bay and the Westmoreland, Cumberland and Yorkshire mountains." The first railway to pass through the area was the Lancaster & Carlisle main line, opened in December 1846. The following year, the North Western Railway obtained powers to build an hotel at Poulton as part of its scheme to construct a railway from Skipton to Lancaster and Morecambe. The small hotel, named the

Above: An aerial view of the *Midland Hotel*, at Morecambe. Oliver Hill's exciting modern design of 1932 replaced a hotel of the same name, which had opened in 1848, but located elsewhere in the resort. *Author's collection.*

North Western, opened in September 1848, together with a branch line from Lancaster. Almost two years later, on June 1 1850, the completion of the railway to Skipton meant that visitors from Yorkshire could be added to those from Lancashire, who had already found the thriving little resort a pleasant place for family holidays.

By 1875, Poulton had become better known by its more familiar name of Morecambe, and the seafront hotel had been renamed the *Midland Hotel* in 1871. When the North Western Railway had been absorbed by the MR, *(30)* the company had set its sights on a new sea route to Belfast and the Isle of Man. Following the granting of powers to build a new harbour at nearby Heysham, in 1896, the MR purchased a private house, known as *Heysham Towers*, to supplement accommodation at the *Midland Hotel* and provide for visitors en route to Northern Ireland.

The *Heysham Towers Hotel* did not prosper and was sold in 1919. The *Midland Hotel* maintained its popularity, however, and in 1932 land was purchased by the LMS from Morecambe Corporation for the construction of a brand new modern hotel to replace the 84-years old veteran. Opened in July 1933, the 40-bedroomed *Midland Hotel* enjoyed nearly seven years of popularity before closing and spending nine years as a Royal Navy establishment. Changing patterns of demand and a decline in the attraction of Morecambe led to the sale of the hotel in 1952. It is still there today, opposite the station, as a monument to classic 1930s design.

The gamble taken by the North Western Railway at Morecambe had paid dividends, but a similar scheme doomed to failure was the proposal by a group of Hull and East Riding businessmen and landowners to choose Withernsea at the terminus for the projected 17-miles Hull and Holderness Railway. But for this scheme the small village might even have ceased to exist altogether!

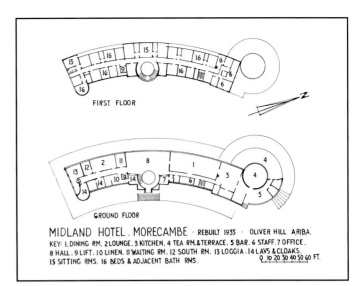

Above: A plan of the *Midland Hotel*, Morecambe. The principal rooms were arranged with a westerly view, out to sea. *Author's sketch.*

Neighbouring Owthorpe had already lost a considerable part of its land to the North sea, and extensive defence work had to be undertaken to reduce the risk of further erosion. Anthony Banister, who originated the scheme, was a prominent merchant and ship owner, and Mayor of Hull in 1851. He saw Withernsea as becoming an important seaside resort and fishing port. The plans included the building of the 40-bedroom *Station Hotel*, which, with the railway, was opened in June 1854. In the first four months, more than 60,000 passengers used the line and its future seemed bright. Eight years later the small independent company was absorbed by the North-Eastern Railway. *(31)*

Below : The *Queens Hotel*, Withernsea, opened in 1854. Hopes of a bright future for this resort were not fulfilled and the hotel was sold in 1892. *Author's sketch.*

AN ILLUSTRATED HISTORY OF RAILWAY HOTELS

Above: The *Zetland Hotel*, Saltburn by the Sea, opened in 1863. The hotel commanded magnificent sea views, and the turret included a telescope room at roof level. *Author's collection.*

However, the frequent risk of storm damage on the east coast and the introduction of fast steam trawlers prompted ship owners to use Hull, rather than tranship their catches to the railhead at Withernsea. Furthermore, the expectations of creating a 'second Scarborough' were not fulfilled and the railway hotel was becoming a 'white elephant.' In 1892, Francis and Sir James Reckitt stepped in and bought the hotel and its three acres of grounds, and handed them over to the Hull Royal Infirmary for use as a convalescent home for the poorer people of Hull and the East Riding. A few years later, the same benefactors opened a sanatorium close to the former hotel, and both buildings now form the General Hospital at Withernsea. The railway survived until October 19 1964 when the Beeching axe ended its useful service.

At the northern extremity of the Yorkshire coastline, a welcome escape from industrial Tees-side was created at Saltburn-by-sea. Of Saltburn, *The Newcastle Guardian's* correspondent wrote in 1863: "I found the place was just what I had hoped and longed for - a watering place, combining with the pleasures of the sea and beauties of country scenery." *The Yorkshire Post*, also impressed by the work which had been undertaken in 1861-63, made the journey by way of: "the Quakers line', as the Stockton &

Darlington Railway is familiarly termed, through the Black Country of Tees-side. Sight and sounds of industry were taken in by the eye and ear on all sides, ... as we hurried through miles of gigantic blast furnaces and extensive iron shipbuilding yards, long trains of ore and countless heaps of pigs (pig iron)." Pleasant countryside and a distant view of Captain Cook's monument were to be seen before the train arrived at: "this Brighton of the North-East coast .... which it is said originated from an idea of Mr Henry Pease, late MP for South Durham. However that may be, the project was taken up by the directors of the Stockton & Darlington Railway, and in the session of 1860-61 parliamentary powers were obtained to make a short branch line from Redcar to Saltburn, and build an hotel." *(32)*

A detailed description of the newly-built station and the *Zetland Hotel* followed and it was noticed that a few houses had been built for speculation and a permanent church was nearing completion, to replace a temporary structure. The completed private residences, terraced houses and several shops were seen to be: "more cheerful and clean looking than can scarcely be conceived." Saltburn-by-the-sea and its bastion, the *Zetland Hotel*, with 37 bedrooms, and the smaller privately-owned Alexandra

Above: Visitors to the *Zetland Hotel* arriving by train could alight at a glazed roof platform immediately behind the hotel, which enjoyed a commanding position above the seafront. *Author's collection.*

Hotel, became increasingly popular. An 1865 guide recommended the climate for "Unstrung men, languid women and weakly children," and the *Zetland Hotel* as: "a home for all classes, and the tariff so adjusted that the humble tradesman may be accommodated as comfortably and as economically as at an ordinary inn." The *Zetland's* fortunes changed with the coming of the Second World War. Requisitioning, followed by several precarious post-war years, were remedied to some extent by wise planning until, by 1960, the future appeared bright. But the increasing popularity of holidays abroad (the cheap package, again) was disastrous for Saltburn and a decision to sell the hotel came in 1975. Since then the new owners have converted the accommodation into self-contained apartments, and the railway is enjoying renewed popularity.

Although the NER's hotel at Saltburn proved viable over many years, the same company exercised caution at Scarborough. The huge *Grand Hotel* had opened in 1867, followed by the *Pavilion Hotel* in 1870 and the *Balmoral Hotel* 1889. Almost as a token gesture, the railway opened a

small residential hotel within the station buildings in 1883; it was not very successful and closed in 1898.

The development of Hunstanton on the north coast of Norfolk, as a seaside resort, originated with an idea put forward by Hamon le Strange, of Hunstanton Hall. When the Lynn & Hunstanton Railway arrived in 1862, land was set aside for an hotel. Opened in 1876 and named the *Sandringham Hotel*, its consistent popularity warranted the building of an extension on the seaward side, to provide a total of 55 bedrooms, in 1920. Meanwhile, Hunstanton had acquired a pier in 1870 and a theatre in 1896 and rivalled Cromer, Sheringham and Great Yarmouth as a favourite resort. Requisitioning during the Second World War, accompanied by subsequent changes in demand, brought about the demise of the *Sandringham Hotel* and it was sold in 1950. It was demolished in 1967.

Other successful small seaside hotels were built by the Taff Vale Railway at Penarth (the *Penarth Hotel*, opened in 1868 with about 30 bedrooms) and the SER (the *South Eastern Hotel*) at Deal, with about 60 bedrooms, in 1901. Many hotels relied on the sea front, adjacent beach, and sea

AN ILLUSTRATED HISTORY OF RAILWAY HOTELS

Left: The *Sandringham Hotel* at Hunstanton was opened in 1876 and extended in 1905. Popular with visitors from London and the Midlands, it was demolished in 1967. *Author's collection.*

Below: The *Penarth Hotel* was opened by the Taff Vale Railway in 1868 and had a comparatively brief career before becoming a childrens home in 1917. *Author's sketch.*

Lower: The *South Eastern Hotel*, at Deal, was opened in 1901 and was later renamed the *Queens Hotel. John Alsop Collection.*

bathing as the principal attractions for visitors. However, a new trend in seaside accommodation was to be found at the *Tregenna Castle Hotel*, St Ives, leased by the GWR in 1878, and at the *Seabrook Hotel* at Hythe, opened by the SER in 1880. These hotels stood in spacious grounds, and tennis courts, putting greens, and nine-hole golf courses were provided for guests as alternative pastimes to the beaches and sea bathing. The ultimate in seaside resort hotels, as far as the railway were concerned, was undoubtedly the *Felix Hotel* at Felixstowe. Purchased by the GER in 1920, the hotel stood in 16 acres of ground, had 21 tennis courts, croquet lawns and a nine-hole golf course, accompanied by boating, bathing and fishing facilities. Indoors, there were 106 single bedrooms (10 with baths) 93 double bedrooms (19 with baths) 20 bathrooms, three

Telephone:
St. Ives 38.

TREGENNA CASTLE HOTEL, St. Ives, Cornwall
(Under the management of the Great Western Railway Co.)

Telegrams:
"Tregotel," St. Ives
Cornwall.

Above: Dating from the 1770s and leased by the GWR in 1878, the *Tregenna Castle Hotel*, **at St Ives, Cornwall, became a very popular resort hotel.** *John Alsop Collection,.*

dining rooms, a ballroom, and three smoking rooms. The district was: "celebrated for its health-resorting climate and southerly aspect, which combined bracing air from the German ocean and an excess of brilliant sunshine, superior to that found in the South Coast resorts". *(33)* The *Felix Hotel* was yet another hotel which ended its career as a result of the changes brought about by the Second World War, and the building was sold to Fisons (the fertiliser company) for £122,500 in 1952, for use as offices.

The LNWR, which took an early interest in two inland resorts, by acquiring a part share in the ownership of the *Windermere Hotel* and the purchase of shares in the Buxton

Palace Hotel Company, embarked on a small venture entirely of its own funding. *(34)* When the new line from Llandudno to Betws-y-Coed and Blaenau Ffestiniog opened in July 1879, it was decided to encourage visitors to stay and explore the upper reaches of the Conway Valley and Snowdonia. The *North Western Hotel* was opened for this purpose in 1881, but quiet winters and the remoteness of Ffestiniog spelt an early demise for the hotel. In 1906, it was

Below: Built in 1907 as North Bovey Manor, at Moretonhampstead, the GWR purchased the building in 1929 to convert into the *Manor House Hotel*. **Detmar Blow designed the eight-window wide extension (on the left) in 1935.** *Richard Casserley collection.*

AN ILLUSTRATED HISTORY OF RAILWAY HOTELS

Above: The *Manor House Hotel's* elegant panelled and open-timbered minstrels gallery. *Sketched by Charles Mayo/Richard Casserley collection.*

Below: The *Welcombe Hotel*, at Stratford-upon-Avon. Built as a private residence in 1869, it was purchased by the LMS in 1930 and extended in 1933. The hotel is seen here on a postcard produced by the LMS. *John Alsop Collection.*

decided to sell the small hotel, which has since served as a public house.

In addition to the seaside and inland resort hotel, another type of hotel which found later but more permanent favour, was the country house hotel. When Viscount Hambleden's 5,450 acres North Bovey Manor Estate, on the edge of Dartmoor, came under the Auctioneer's hammer in November 1928, the lots included a Wesleyan chapel, a couple of inns, a fire station, post office, cattle market, several farms and orchards, and houses and cottages. But it was Lot 67 (193 acres) which aroused the interest of the GWR: "The Manor House, the family residence, completed in 1907, being a Jacobean replica in stone, with stone mullions and oak window frames.." However, Lot 67 was withdrawn without a bid reaching its modest reserve figure. Negotiations followed between the vendor and the GWR and in March 1929, a settlement was reached whereby the Manor House and 200 acres were purchased for £14,500. Following conversion as a hotel, the completion of an 18-hole golf course designed by Mr Abercromby, and tennis courts, The Manor House Hotel was launched on its very successful career in 1930. *(35)* It was extended in 1935 to increase its bedroom capacity to 66 rooms.

Not to be outdone, the LMS purchased Welcombe House, near Stratford-on-Avon, in December 1930, at a cost of £70,000, including the subsequent alterations and additions needed to provide 131 letting bedrooms and ancillary accommodation. Welcombe House had been built in 1869 by Mark Phillips, a Manchester cotton magnate, on the site of an earlier house. Tennis courts and nearby fishing and boating provided the hotel with ample amenities for its visitors. An earlier distinguished guest at the house had been President 'Teddy' Roosevelt, commemorated by a room bearing his name. *(36)*

The GWR intended to have an important say in the provision of resort hotels, when in 1936, the company announced that a grand seaside and resort hotel was to be built at Looe, in Cornwall. The distinguished architect Sir Edwin Lutyens was involved in the design of the proposed hotel, but the rumours and uncertainties about the coming war killed off the scheme, and it was not revived after 1945. *(36)*

Scotland

In 1890, the Great North of Scotland Railway, the last of the principal pre-Grouping railway companies to enter the hotel business, found immediate success with the purchase of the *Palace Hotel*, Aberdeen. In fact, the enlarged and modernised hotel was so busy between June and September that advance booking was essential. Two storeys (making five in all) were added in 1894, increasing the accommodation to 77 bedrooms. A second hotel, the *Station Hotel*, was purchased in 1910 and provided a further 51 letting bedrooms. Three years later, reassured by their success, the company decided to launch a venture which was new among the hotel-owning railways – an hotel to cater for the golfer. The site chosen was Cruden Bay, on the Buchan coast of Aberdeenshire. Its climate according to a later guide book was: "A dry bracing atmosphere, stimulating to the senses and strengthening to the system."

However, the nearest railway was some ten miles distant, at Ellon on the line from Aberdeen to Fraserburgh. Following the grant of the necessary powers, the locality became a scene of busy activity in the construction of a branch line, an imposing 96-bedroomed hotel built of local red granite, and a magnificent golf course. The branch line was opened in August 1896, and extended for a further five miles beyond Cruden Bay, to a terminus at Boddam. The attractive glass-roofed station at Cruden Bay was approximately one-third of a mile from the new hotel, and a 3ft 6in electric tramway was built to convey visitors on the final part of their journey. All was ready by Wednesday 1 March 1899, and the *Aberdeen Daily Free Press* set the scene: "The Directors of the GNSR will visit Cruden Bay today for the purpose of formally opening to public use the new hotel and the adjoining golf course. The Directors will make the journey to and from Aberdeen by special train. The hotel has been equipped in a handsome and thoroughly up-to-date style, and the golf course will, in the opinion of experts, take a leading place among the golfing greens of the country. The hotel has been erected to the designs of Mr John J. Smith, ARIBA, the Company's Architect. The golf course has been laid out under the supervision of Archie Simpson, the well-known golf professional." *(37)*

The hotel provided special quarters for golfers including bathrooms, heating and drying rooms and lockers. A bowling green, tennis courts, and croquet lawns were provided to cater for other interests. Sea bathing and

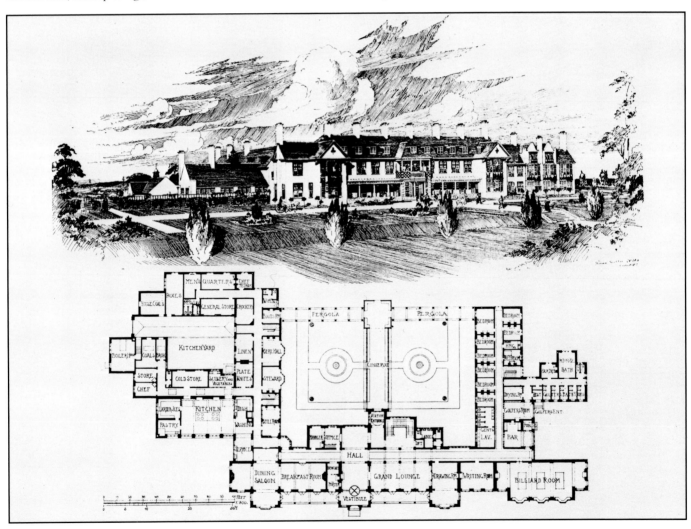

The *Turnberry Hotel* was one of the finest resort hotels built by the railways. It was designed by James Miller and opened in 1906. *Academy Architecture, 1904*

AN ILLUSTRATED HISTORY OF RAILWAY HOTELS

Turnberry Hotel

INCLUDING

First Class Return Railway Journey and Board and Residence in Turnberry Hotel

(Ceases after 31st May, 1927.)

	INCLUSIVE FARE	
	From GLASGOW (St. Enoch)	From EDINBURGH (Princes St.)
	s. d.	s. d.
Monday to Wednesday, ..		
Tuesday to Thursday, ..	47 6	—
Wednesday to Friday, ..		
Thursday to Saturday, ..		
Friday to Monday, ..	72 0	81 6
Saturday to Monday, ..	52 0	61 6

(Extension of Visit from Glasgow, 21/- per Day.)

The Coupons provide for Bedroom with attendance and meals Table d'Hôte, including Dinner on day of arrival and Breakfast on day of departure.

These Inclusive Bookings will be suspended during the Christmas, New Year, Easter and Whitsuntide Holidays.

Ayr Station Hotel

INCLUDING

First Class Return Railway Journey and Board and Residence in Ayr Station Hotel

(Ceases after 31st May, 1927.)

	INCLUSIVE FARE from GLASGOW (St. Enoch)
	s. d.
Monday to Wednesday, ...	
Tuesday to Thursday, ...	38 6
Wednesday to Friday, ...	
Thursday to Saturday, ...	
Friday to Monday, ...	58 6
Saturday to Monday, ...	43 6

(Extension of Visit, 15/- per Day.)

The Coupons provide for Bedroom with attendance and meals Table d'Hôte, including Dinner on day of arrival and Breakfast on day of departure.

These Inclusive Bookings will be suspended during the Christmas, New Year, Easter and Whitsuntide Holidays.

two miles of sandy beaches, and for the adventurous a sailing or fishing trip on the Emmanuel, Togo or Nile, combined to offer a very attractive holiday package.

Within a month of opening the hotel and golf course, the GNSR.was condemned for giving cheap trips on the line and enabling golfers "To desecrate the Sabbath day by playing golf." But a writer in Rural Notes in the local newspaper defended the railway's action for "beguiling a lot of idle fellows out to Cruden Bay, where I am sure they will be just as well employed in playing golf on Sundays as loafing about church doors and annoying worshippers, as they are complained of doing in Aberdeen". (37)

In contrast, there also came the rich, such as Sir Jeremiah Colman (who gave his name to the mustard); Sir William Burrell, of Glasgow (the ship-owner and collector); the Gilbeys (port wine importers); Thomas Wills (of the cigarette company); the McEwans (the brewers) and the Crawfords (the biscuit manufacturers) to mention but a few.

Sir Jeremiah Colman was remembered by one of his caddies, Mr Alexander Cruikshank: "There were about 100 boys waiting eagerly to be employed by the Caddymaster. On being chosen, the golfer paid one shilling for a caddy ticket and at the end of the round the caddy, on presenting this ticket to the caddymaster, received his payment. There were no caddy cars or tees in those days and the caddy had to lay down a little cone of sand for the golfer to play off. Sir Jeremiah played every day of his holiday and on the last day told the caddy to bring his clubs to the hotel and ask for Lady Colman. Her Ladyship would then appear, and with Sir Jeremiah hovering in the background, thank the caddy, present him with half a sovereign if this happened to

be his first year, and a whole sovereign for subsequent years, and then, what the boy dreaded, would kiss him on the cheek". *(38)*

All seemed set for a bright future, but the season was too short and the railway passed through comparatively poor country. As the years passed, the hotel simply, but gradually, faded out of existence. First the railway line closed to passenger traffic in October 1932, then the tramway in March 1941, and finally the hotel on November 7 1945, after serving as a wartime hospital. The golf course survived, however, and is still one of the most popular in Aberdeenshire and a lasting reminder of the hotel. The initial success of the GNSR at Cruden Bay, particularly in the provisions of the golf course, was a fact noted by the other Scottish railways, and it was thus important in paving the way for future developments elsewhere - which were much more successful.

In 1904-6 the Glasgow & South Western Railway, whose territory included the equable Ayrshire coast, built a magnificent 131-bedroomed holiday hotel and two golf courses at Turnberry. The *Ayr Advertiser* announced the opening arrangements on May 10 1906: "The Maidens and Dunure Railway will be opened on Thursday, 17th May, for passengers and merchandise traffic; simultaneously the Turnberry Station Hotel will be ready for the reception of visitors. Turnberry Golf Links are in excellent condition and

Gleneagles
Wondermazes

HOTEL
GOLF
TENNIS
"Nonesuch in Europe"

Gleneagles Hotel and Golf Courses

"The Eighth Wonder"

Above: The *Gleneagles Hotel*, at Auchterarder, was the ultimate amongst inland resort hotels. Its completion was delayed by the First World War until 1924. This is the jacket of an LMS publicity brochure of 1925. *Author's collection.*

will be open to hotel visitors." The following week, the correspondent of The Scotsman was impressed by the location of the hotel "on the breast of a hill overlooking the golf links and commanding uninterrupted views of the Firth of Clyde." Among the accommodation noted were "Salt water baths .... and the golfers corner, with its drying room and other accommodation, which cannot fail to be duly appreciated by the devotees of the Royal and Ancient game." (39) The location proved to be well-chosen and the *Turnberry Hotel*, as it was subsequently renamed, and its famous courses, the Ailsa and the Arran, have become household names in the world of international golf and a venue of the British Open Championship (in 1977) and the Walker Cup competition (in 1963).

Although Turnberry proved to be one of the best examples of a successful resort hotel, the Caledonian Railway took a step forward in 1913, which was to culminate 11 years later in the opening of the 114-bedroomed *Gleneagles Hotel*, Perthshire, one of the world's most famous golf hotels. Five days after the opening of the hotel on June 2 1924, *The Scotsman* observed: "Gleneagles Golf Course has attained unto world fame suddenly. It did not become great. It did not acquire a reputation gradually. Rather it was born great. Some imaginative mind discovered that Nature in one of her most pleasant and accommodating moods had fashioned those heather-clad hills and moors in a way which yielded easily to the treatment of the golf course architect. the result is two courses which are acclaimed among the best in Britain. In like manner there was conceived the idea of making Gleneagles a place to stay as well as a place to play. That aspiration has now

been realised and the Gleneagles Hotel this week accommodates its first visitors."

Promoted by a private company, the Caledonian Railway Order Confirmation Act of 1913, authorised the railway to participate in the venture, and by the Caledonian Railway Act of 1923, assume responsibility for the completion and ownership of the hotel and golf course. The Scotsman's report in June, 1924, noted that in addition to the golf courses, an indoor swimming pool was nearing completion, and that nine tennis courts had been carefully landscaped into the site as a protection against the wind. Bowling and croquet greens were also ready, and, for the angler, fishing rights had been acquired on neighbouring waters.

The Caledonian Railway had meanwhile become a constituent of the new London Midland & Scottish railway, and the new company was quick to recognise the importance of the Gleneagles project. A colour postcard sent from the hotel during the first month of business was entitled "Gleneagles Hotel in Perthshire, Britain's Premier Sports Hotel. The new Palace among the Scottish Mountains opened by the L.M.S.R. under the direction of Arthur Towle."

The golf courses, the King's Course and the Queen's Course designed by James Braid and the nine hole 'Wee Course,' did indeed become world-famous and have hosted the Penfold Tournament and many other competitions, including the popular Pro-celebrity Golf series shown on television.

Further north, the Highland Railway, whose territory extended from Perth to Inverness and the far North, and

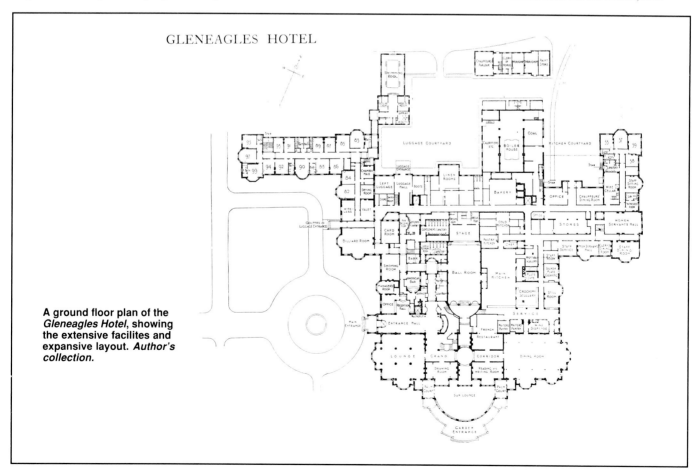

GLENEAGLES HOTEL

A ground floor plan of the *Gleneagles Hotel*, showing the extensive facilites and expansive layout. *Author's collection.*

The *Station Hotel*, at Dornoch Firth, opened in 1904 and was later renamed The Dornoch Hotel. It had a fine view over the adjacent Golf Course. *Author's sketch.*

Above: The *St Enoch Station Hotel*, Glasgow, which was opened in 1879. Thomas Wilson added some Scottish Baronial touches to his design, which owed much to St Pancras in overall concept. *The Mitchell Library.*

AN ILLUSTRATED HISTORY OF RAILWAY HOTELS

Above: The *Highland Hotel*, Strathpeffer (on the left) opened in 1911. Like the hotel at Dornoch Firth, it was designed by Cameron & Burnett. *Author's collection.*

Westwards to the Kyle of Lochalsh, played an increasing role as a tourist route. In 1870, a small private house at Achnasheen, adjacent to the new line to the Kyle of Lochalsh, was purchased and named the *Station Hotel*. In 1896, a larger private house at the Kyle was acquired and named the *Kyle of Lochalsh Hotel*. These hotels provided useful accommodation for visitors and passengers en route to Skye, but the HR was also attracted to the possibility of providing accommodation for the golfer. The opportunity came in 1902, when the company decided to build its first new hotel, at the Royal Burgh of Dornoch, Sutherland. Dornoch claimed to be the cradle of golf and it is on record that a match was played there in 1616. The new 83-bedroomed *Dornoch Hotel* opened in July 1904, and from its windows the Royal Dornoch Golf Courses and the sea beyond could be overlooked with ease.

To make the journey easier for visitors, Dornoch was linked by a branch line of slightly less than eight miles in length, to the Wick and Thurso-Inverness route, at the Mound. In spite of its attractive surroundings it was realised that the hotel would attract only summer visitors. Accordingly, the LMS, which inherited the hotel from the HR in the Grouping of 1923, decided to close down for the winter, normally from the last week in September until the

second or third week in May of the following year. War service from October 1940, until October 1944, followed by a steadily falling number of visitors, prompted the sale of the hotel in 1965.

The HR's second building venture, in 1911, was at the attractive spa of Strathpeffer. From Dingwall, the railway headed westwards to the Kyle and could have been carried through Strathpeffer to Garve and up the glen past the Falls of Rogie. Instead, Strathpeffer was avoided and it required the construction of a two-and-a-quarter mile branch to reach the line near Dingwall.

At the *Highland Hotel's* opening luncheon on June 13 1911, T.O. Fraser, Secretary to the Strathpeffer Spa Company observed the interest which the HR's hotel building scheme had aroused and felt "with much satisfaction the compliment paid by the Spa Company to the Highland Railway spending so much money in connection with the Spa (approximately £50,000). He considered that the new 90-bedroomed hotel would be a great benefit to the Spa and the whole neighbourhood. They had endeavoured to bring a new lot of people to the Spa, and it was to provide for those that the hotel had been erected, not to take away patrons from the other houses." To complete the celebrations for the large number of distinguished guests who had travelled from as far as field as London, a professional golf match on the Strathpeffer course took place with J.H. Taylor and A. Herd, the famous ex-champions, playing two local amateur players, J. Sutherland and C. Aylmer. *(40)*

Like the hotel at Dornoch, the problem of a short summer season again led the LMS to introduce winter closing between the end of September and the second or third week of May. Following war service, a decision to sell the hotel was made in 1946, but a further 12 years passed before a suitable purchaser was found in 1958.

The changing fortunes of the resort hotels built or purchased by the railways in Scotland was a problem not confined to the less-frequently visited parts of coastal Aberdeenshire and the north. The GSWR, which had opened the first large purpose-built railway hotel in Scotland in 1879 at St. Enoch Station, Glasgow, (97

bedrooms) built the *Station Hotel* at Ayr in 1886 and completely rebuilt its *Station Hotel* at Dumfries (purchased about 1880) in 1897 to provide 29 bedrooms. The *Station Hotel*, Ayr (45 bedrooms) thrived until the early 1920s and then dwindled so much in popularity that winter closing was considered in 1939. The hotel was sold in 1951.

The *Station Hotel*, Dumfries, provided a useful all-year service for the local community and received an annual summer boost from visitors to the south west. Even so, its fortunes steadily declined and the hotel was sold in 1972. On the other hand, the consistent popularity of golf in Britain, and Scotland in particular, assured the future of the conveniently situated hotels at Gleneagles and Turnberry, it also prompted British Transport Hotels to embark on its one and only new hotel building venture in 1968 at St. Andrews. The 80-bedroom hotel takes its name from the famous old course.

Above: The *Station Hotel*, at Dumfries, opened in 1897 to replace a smaller hotel. *Author's collection.*

AN ILLUSTRATED HISTORY OF RAILWAY HOTELS

Ireland

WITH the steady growth of railway routes to the Irish seaports, holiday-makers were tempted to make the crossing to the 'Emerald Isle' in growing numbers. In response, the principal Irish railways had by the 1890s built or purchased hotels in several widely-scattered localities. Earlier, the Midland Great Western Railway had built its main line from J.S. Mulvany's magnificent Broadstone Station, Dublin, directly westwards to Galway, a distance of 126 miles. To accommodate their passengers and holiday-makers the imposing *Railway Hotel* was built in 1848. Now known as the *Great Southern Hotel*, it continues to be one of the best known hotels in the West of Ireland – and with 115 bedrooms it is also one of the largest.

The same company later purchased two small hotels from the Royal Canal Company, the *Moy Valley Hotel* and the *Broadstone Harbour Hotel* in Dublin. Built between 1765 and 1788, these hotels had served as overnight staging posts for travellers using the canal. Another of the railway's acquisitions, the *Recess Hotel*, Connemara, was destroyed by fire during the Civil War, of 1922.

From junctions on its main line at Mullingar and Athlone the MGWR struck out north-westwards to the coast at Sligo and Mulrany respectively. At Mulrany the company acquired a 90-acres site for the construction of an hotel, a golf course, tennis courts and spacious wooded grounds. Opened in 1897 the hotel had 64 bedrooms and soon proved popular during the summer months, but the cold winters and remoteness necessitated winter closing usually between November and April.

The Great Northern Railway of Ireland headed northwards from Amiens Street, Dublin, to Belfast, and from a junction at Portadown, lines to Londonderry and Bundoran provided the company with useful outlets to the north and north west coasts. At Bundoran, overlooking Donegal Bay, the company purchased an hotel in 1895 and renamed it the *Great Northern Hotel*. Standing in a 130-acres site, a golf course, tennis courts, a swimming pool and nearby fishing and climbing combined to make a sportsman's paradise.

Below: *The Great Southern Hotel,* Killarney opened in 1854 and was subsequently extended. It is the second-oldest railway hotel in Ireland, after the *Great Southern Hotel* at Galway, which was opened in 1848. *Author's collection*

Above: A view of Killarney's *Great Southern Hotel*, as illustrated and published in the Jotter series of postcards. *John Alsop Collection.*

Below: The lounge at the *Great Southern Hotel*, Killarney, again from the Jotter series. *John Alsop Collection.*

AN ILLUSTRATED HISTORY OF RAILWAY HOTELS

Above: The *Slieve Donard Hotel*, at Newcastle, County Down, was opened by the Belfast & County Down Railway, in 1898. This is a postcard view. Below: Set in 180 acres, the *Great Southern Hotel* at Parknasilla (seen here illustrated on a postcard) opened in 1897 to the design of J.F. Fuller. *Author's collection.*

The Great Northern Railway of Ireland had another outlet, to a terminus at Warrenpoint on Carlingford Lough. Here, the *Beach Hotel* was purchased in 1899. And in nearby Rostrevor, two hotels were purchased that same year, the *Woodside Hotel* and the *Great Northern Hotel*. On the opposite side of Carlingford Lough, the London & North Western Railway of England owned a short mileage of railway which ran from the ports of Dundalk and Greenore to Newry. At Greenore, an imposing hotel was built in 1873, together with golf links and several holiday bungalows were added in 1903. The Belfast & County Down Railway, another of Ireland's small companies, erected a fine tourist hotel, with about 50 beds, at Newcastle in 1898, naming it the *Slieve Donard Hotel*.

The Belfast & Northern Countries Railway's principal outlets to the coast were at Larne, where the *Lahana Hotel* was purchased in 1909 to accommodate passengers using the sea crossing from Stranraer and Port rush on the Beautiful coast of Antrim, where an hotel was leased in 1891. The company also owned the *Midland Hotel* in Belfast, opened in 1898, and the *City Hotel* in Londonderry, both of modest size with about 50 bedrooms.

Ireland's largest railway company was the Great Southern & Western Railway which had its Dublin terminus at Kingsbridge. Cork lay 165 miles to the south west, and Valentia Harbour, Co. Kerry, the most westerly point reached by any railway in the British Isles, lay 234 route miles from Dublin. Within the Company's territory lay the ancient Kingdom of Kerry and the beauty spots of Killarney, Dingle Bay and Kenmare River. The first hotel project undertaken by the company was a joint venture with the Killarney Junction Railway for the building of the *Railway Hotel* at Killarney. Opened in July 1854, the hotel had more than 150 bedrooms and was the largest provincial establishment in Ireland and proved to be consistently profitable. An added boost to the hotel's popularity came in 1877 when it was "Patronised by their Imperial Majesties the Emperor and Empress of Brazil, and H.R.H. the Duke of Connaught during their visits to Killarney."

In the last decade of the century, the GSWR increased its interests with the purchase in 1890 (and subsequent enlargement) of a castellated house on the shore of Caragh Lake. The railway, to Valentia Harbour was barely a half-mile distant. In 1893, a 22-miles railway was opened between Headford Junction (on the Mallow-Killarney line) and a terminus at Kenmare. Here, J.F.Fuller designed a substantial stone-built hotel, with 60 bedrooms. Opened in 1897 and named the *Southern Hotel*, the same architect who provided the design for the larger 83-bedroomed Southern Hotel at Parknasilla, set amid 180 acres of grounds on the Kenmare river.

Visitors bound for Parknasilla travelled the 15 miles from Kenmare by horse-drawn coach. Also, some considerable distance from the nearest railhead was the smaller *Southern Hotel* at Waterville, opened in 1893. Pleasantly situated on a narrow strip of land separating Lough Currane from the Atlantic Ocean, visitors could reach their destination either from Cahirciveen station, near Valentia Harbour, or by horse-drawn coach from Kenmare. The GSWR placed the management of its hotels in the hands of the Southern Hotels Company, a subsidiary formed in 1893, which merged with its parent eight years later.

Facing page, above: The Great Southern & Western Railway built a second hotel, the *New Hotel*, at Killarney, in 1908. The tariff was less than that charged at its more elderly neighbour.

Facing page, lower: The London & North Western Railway of England built the *North Wall Hotel*, at Dublin, in 1885. It is featured here on a tourist map published by the LNWR. *Author's collection*.

Below: The modest *Station Hotel*, Cork, was opened in 1894 by the Great Southern & Western Railway. *Author's sketch*.

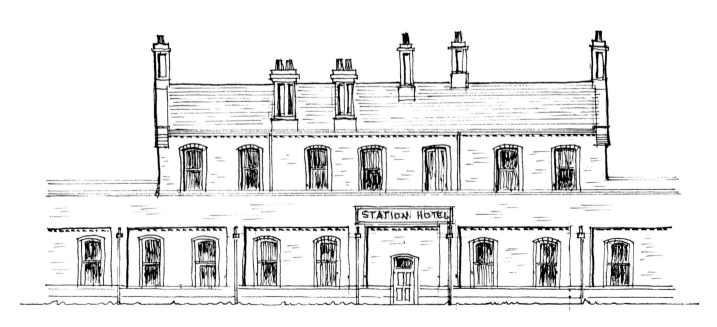

AN ILLUSTRATED HISTORY OF RAILWAY HOTELS

The New Hotel, Killarney. A.Burkart & Co. London E.C.

NORTH WALL HOTEL DUBLIN

Limerick Junction, the most important point on the GSWR system, like Swindon and Normanton in England, long served as a 'dinner stop', with all trains scheduled to call for at least ten minutes. For travellers requiring overnight accommodation, the company opened a small commercial hotel at the station in 1856. Similar accommodation was provided opposite the Kingsbridge station, Dublin, in the mid-1870s, and within the overall design of the new Glanmire Road Station, Cork, in 1894. For the less opulent holiday maker, the GSWR built two small unlicensed hotels, *Bishops House*, Parknasilla (opened in 1905) and the *New Hotel*, Killarney, opened in 1908. A week's board and lodging at the *New Hotel* cost £2.10 compared with £4.20 at its larger neighbour. The small Dublin & South Eastern Railway also had a brief stake in the hotel industry, with its *Station Hotel* at Rathdrum, opened in the mid 1890s and closed in 1911.

Ireland's fragmented and somewhat complicated railway history was rationalised following the establishment of the Irish Free State and the Province of Northern Ireland. The railways and the hotels within the Province passed through a process which led eventually to the establishment of the Ulster Transport Authority and the sale of the hotels in 1966.

In Southern Ireland the GSWR and the Midland Great Western Railway became two of the constituents of the new Great Southern Railways in 1925. Two years later the company commenced a new hotel at Sligo (the *Great Southern Hotel*) and on the debit side sold the hotels at Waterville and Caragh Lake.

In January, 1945, Great Southern Railways and its hotels passed into State ownership, under the now-familiar title CIE (Coras Iompair Eireann). Meanwhile, the Great Northern (Ireland) Railway, whose metals lay both in the Province and the Republic, was administered by representatives of both Governments. This arrangement survived until 1958, when the assets were shared between the Ulster Transport Authority and Coras Iompair Eireann. Under the settlement the Great Northern Hotel at Bundoran passed to the CIE and was renamed the *Great Southern Hotel*.

In the late 1960's CIE's wholly-owned subsidiary Ostlanna Iompair Eireann (OIE) embarked on a policy of expansion and built large new hotels at Rosslare (the *Great Southern Hotel*, 192 beds) Corrib (the *Great Southern Hotel*, 200 beds) and Torc (the *Great Southern Inn*, 96 beds) and purchased the 54-bedroomed *Russell Court Hotel* in Belfast. But expectations were not realised and a recession in tourism during the mid-1970s led to decisions to sell the hotels at Kenmare, Sligo, Mulrany, Bundoran and Belfast. The remaining six hotels, at Corrib, Galway, Killarney, Parknasilla, Rosslare and Torc are now owned by CERT the state-sponsored Council for Education Recruitment & Training, with the Hotel Catering & Allied Industries.

Below: The *Torc Hotel*, Killarney. Ostlanna Iompair Eireann (OIE) built several modern hotels in the years 1969-72, including this example. *Author's collection.*

AN ILLUSTRATED HISTORY OF RAILWAY HOTELS

Chapter 2

PLANNING AND AMENITIES
Style

Nineteenth century inventiveness, which produced steel and concrete, and the ingenuity to combine these new materials into new forms of construction, did not, unfortunately, extend to style!

To the early Victorians, the architecture of their Georgian predecessors appeared flat and insipid. In its place, an assortment of revived and mixed styles became the characteristic hallmark of the period between the 1830s and the early 20th century. Professor Thomas L. Donaldson, at the opening meeting of the Architectural Association in 1847 asked: "The great question is, are we to have architecture of our own period, a distinct, individual, palpable style of the nineteenth century?" It was not to be; Donaldson and other like-minded thinkers were paid little attention.

For the newspaper and magazine correspondents and staff artists, the task of describing the varied and sometimes flamboyant buildings to their readers, was a new challenge. In December, 1852, *The Illustrated London News* described the style of the *Great Western Royal Hotel* at Paddington, then nearing completion, as: "Imitating the French of Louis XIV and later, and the curved roof forms are a striking novelty here." In July 1860, the same journal found the *Grosvenor Hotel* at Victoria station more difficult to describe. "The architecture of the building is almost entirely of stone and white brick, and, as regards design and character, will shortly speak for itself more clearly than drawings can speak for it." This did little to enlighten the poor reader!

The Builder was more forthright in its description of the *Victoria Hotel*, Sheffield, in March 1862: "It is a simple design - a study from the works of Inigo Jones." Dominating French pavilion roofs, one of the most repetitive features of Victorian and Edwardian design, prompted *The Illustrated London News*, in its

Above: The *Great Western Royal Hotel*, London, designed by Philip Hardwick Jnr. The buildings aroused a lot of interest, but the twin towers appeared an unneccessarily high adjunct, in the already elaborate French classical facade. *RIBA Collection.*

Above: This was E. M. Barry's and Owen Jones' interpretation of French classical detailing for the restaurant at the *Charing Cross Hotel*, London, built in 1865. *Authors Collection.*

description of the *Charing Cross Hotel*, in June 1864, to observe: "The roof is of that form borrowed from the Louvre at Paris, which has lately come so much into vogue for our large public buildings, and which presents, we believe, some important practical advantages; though it has still a quaint appearance to an English eye."

For the Board Meeting of the Great Northern Railway held in May 1865, M.E. Hadfield and Son, Architects for the new hotel at Leeds, were at pains to explain the choice of style. "The general character impressed upon the design is an adaptation of the brick architecture of the 12th century. The numerous window openings and the absence of the opportunity to break the square mass the site presents, has led to the choice of this style; whilst its comparative cheapness and the picturesque effect obtained by the grouping of the chimneys and dormer windows, and pitching of the roof well up, will give the Hotel palatial character - strictly in harmony with its purpose". The Board duly recorded their satisfaction and approved an estimate of £22,500, which included £2,500 for fittings. (1)

The MR's choice of Sir George Gilbert Scott's Gothic design in the completion for its St. Pancras terminus and hotel provided the company with what *The Times*

Right: At the *Midland Grand Hotel*, much care was taken with interior decor, as shown in this contemporary illustration. Note the decoration applied to the wrought iron beams and their supporting brackets, the frieze above the door head height and the ceiling panels. *RIBA Collection*.

Above: At London's, Liverpool Street station, this heavily classical detailing was the theme employed by C. E. Barry for the dining room of the *Great Eastern Hotel*, in 1884. *Author's collection.*

described as: "The most beautiful terminus in London, remarkable alike for its convenience and its inspiring effect". *(2)* The competition, in 1866, came at the time of the so-called 'Battle of Styles' between Gothic and Classical. Gothic, championed by Pugin and described by Ruskin as the style that could "Shrink into a turret, expand into a hall, coil into a staircase, or spring into a spire with undegraded grace and exhausted energy". *(3)* For the architect, the

culmination of the St. Pancras scheme brought a measure of satisfaction: "Having been disappointed, through Palmerston, of my ardent hope of carrying out my style in the Government offices (the new Whitehall offices which Scott subsequently designed in the classical manner in 1856) I was glad to be able to erect one building in that style in London". *(4)*

In 1880, the LNWR and LYR decided to hold an open

AN ILLUSTRATED HISTORY OF RAILWAY HOTELS

Above: A bedroom at the *Midland Hotel*, Manchester, in 1903; note the wash stand with its china ewers and basins. Brass bedsteads were still in vogue and every bedroom had its own fireplace. *Author's collection.*

Right: The *Midland Hotel*, Morecambe, on the Lancashire coast, was one of the best designs from the 1930s. Oliver Hill's curving frontage is seen here from one of its first floor bedroom windows. From an LMS postcard. *Author's collection.*

competition for the design of an hotel at Preston. T. Mitchell, of Oldham, was judged to be the winner of the £200 prize for a design in the 'Elizabethan Style.' *(5)*

The beginning of the Edwardian Era saw no lessening of the search for historicism. For the extensions to the *Great Eastern Hotel*, Liverpool Street, Sir R. W. Edis "adopted one of the best examples of the work of the early part of the reign of Louis XV for the Hamilton Hall, and Egyptian for the Masonic Temple." *(6)*

In that same year, 1903, the MR presented Manchester with an hotel which *The Guardian* could only describe as: "A novelty among Manchester buildings". *(7)* Perhaps the flamboyant mixture of terracotta detailing, turrets, the pair of tunnel-like entrances, and its polished red granite plinth defied easy description. But in Liverpool, nine years later, the same company took its first, and as history proved, its last, step into the 20th century. Using for the first time a fully-framed steel skeleton, the new *Adelphi Hotel* was clad in Portland stone and had comparatively plain facades. The Liverpool Daily Post proudly described the nine-storey hotel as the "World's Greatest Hotel". *(8)* Internally, the Adelphi struck a less-modern note with Ionic columns, domed corridors and a Louis XIV style restaurant at ground floor level.

The interruption brought about by the First World War and the Grouping of the railways in 1923 led to a virtual end in hotel building until the 1930s. Financial restraints also led to hesitation on the part of hotel committees as to where best to locate new developments. Hotel design was poorer too for the loss of three important schemes: extensions to the *Midland Hotel*, Manchester, in 1930 (on an adjacent site); and in 1936 for a grand holiday hotel at Looe, Cornwall, for the GWR (both designs involving Sir Edwin Lutyens) and in 1939 for a modern hotel at Snow Hill, Birmingham, for the GWR.

The most important hotel to reach fruition in the 1930s was undoubtedly the rebuilt *Midland Hotel*, Morecambe. Completed in 1933, Oliver Hill's design was refreshingly modern in all its aspects. *The Builder* was enthusiastic, pointing out: "The building, decoration and general design will belong to no historical architectural period .... and will be British in design, materials and workmanship." *(9)* Built to conform to the curve of the new promenade, the long, low white-rendered elevations had continuous string courses, which emphasised the horizontality. To the west convex side (facing seaward) continuous bands of recessed sun lounges dominated the elevation. Indoor, traditional stone cladding and wood veneers were enhanced by polished aluminium and stainless steel finishes for the public rooms.

Enthusiasm for the rebuilt *Queens Hotel*, Leeds, in 1937 was not so forthcoming. The LMS commissioned W. Curtis Green, architect of the Dorchester (1933), to partner their own architect, W.H. Hamlyn, to carry out the work. "Cosmopolitan classic with a decided transatlantic bias" were the words used by *The Architect and Building News. (10)* With a white portland stone frontage and three-window wide end bays set forward, the building presented a plain, unembellished appearance, at least up to the seventh of its eight storeys. Its eight floor level was dominated by three pedimented kiosks each with twin Corinthian pilasters. Thirty years and the Second World War were to intervene before the last British Transport hotel was built at St. Andrews. Designed by Curtis and Davis, the 80-bedroomed building had both its principal facades dominated by projecting bay windows and balconies, which the local people quickly nicknamed the 'chest of drawers!'

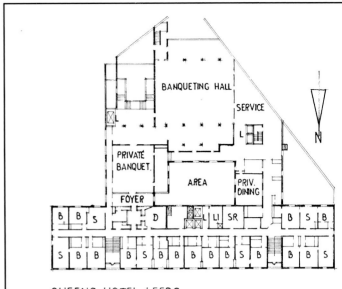

QUEENS HOTEL, LEEDS. REBUILT 1937. W. CURTIS GREEN & W. HAM
FIRST FL. PLAN. KEY: B= BED RM. EACH WITH BATH ATTACHED.
D: PRIV. DINING RM. L: LIFT. LI: LINEN. SR: STOCK RM. S: SITTING RM.
0 10 20 30 40 50   100 FT.

Above: At Leeds, the bedrooms at the *New Queens Hotel* had ensuite bathrooms, as shown by this floor plan. Full central heating and improved ventilation replaced the traditional coal fire in each room. *Author's sketch.*

Below: The *Old Course Hotel*, at St Andrews, of 1968, was the first and last railway hotel built by British Transport Hotels. Its balcony-dominated elevations earned it the local nickname 'The Chest of Drawers!' *Author's collection.*

AN ILLUSTRATED HISTORY OF RAILWAY HOTELS

Construction and Amenities

WHEN the London & Birmingham Railway Hotel & Dormitories Company embarked on its hotel building venture at Euston in 1838, the same foresight which had been applied to the promotion of the scheme was also applied to the planning of the accommodation. To suit the varying requirements of the passengers and visitors using the twin four-storey hotels flanking the approach to the Doric Arch, differing standards of comfort were provided.

Simple in style, and domestic in appearance, the stucco-covered *Victoria Hotel*, on the West side, was chosen for dormitories "divided into as many rooms of convenient dimensions as the allotted space would admit." On the ground floor, a coffee room for meals and refreshments was provided, but the house was not licensed. On the East side, the licensed *Euston Hotel* catered for first class passengers, boasting individual bedrooms and a spacious coffee room. *(11)*

At Derby, the magnificent station and adjacent hotel, both designed by Francis Thompson (1808-1895) featured as a coloured lithograph in the guide book *The Gem of the Peak*, published in the mid-1840s. The hotel is shown as an H-shaped building with a pair of brick and stone three-storey wings, linked by a single storey entrance vestibule. The kitchen and service accommodation was contained in a two-storey continuation of the wing nearer the station.

Another architect involved in hotel design was G.T.Andrews (1805-1855), who was responsible for the railway hotels at Gateshead (1844), Hull (1851) and York (1853) in which each displayed a different layout. The Gateshead terminus of the former Brandling Junction Railway had an imposing entrance frontage. The hotel, which had two floor levels and seven windows in width, was linked to the station by a single high arch, which gave access to the departure platform. First and second class refreshment rooms, a bar, a parlour, and a washhand room were sited at ground level, and "lodging rooms and sitting rooms" at first floor level. The kitchen was located in the basement. *(12)*

At Hull, the hotel built for the York & North Midland Railway formed a three-storey hollow rectangle, approximately 130ft by 120ft externally and approximately 60ft square internally. The enclosed courtyard had a crown glass canopy supported on cast iron columns, which gave protection to the kitchens and service rooms bordering the quadrangle. *The Hull Packet* for November 7 1851, described the accommodation as comprising "120 apartments, which included extensive coffee and commercial rooms, a cigar divan, separate parlours, drawing and sitting rooms with numerous suites for families, a billiard room, and every requisite for the comfort of a large number of guests." The hotel was constructed from Anston stone "the material used in the construction of the new houses of Parliament." The inclusion of a variety of public rooms enabled the hotel to offer a venue for large social gatherings and functions.

The inclusion of hotel accommodation within the station building at York was something of an after-thought. One of the architect's drawings featuring the station frontage shows the outline of the hotel pencilled in on the right-hand of the facade. *(13)* At Newcastle-upon-Tyne, John Dobson's design for the new station (1846-50) included an hotel as part of the overall street frontage. *(14)*

The years of the mid-century were increasingly busy with more and larger hotels being added to railway company assets. Provincial newspapers were quick to report on the opening of new hotels, especially those in London. In June 1854, *The Cumberland Pacquet* described the newly-opened *Great Western Royal Hotel* at Paddington as having "Fifteen sitting rooms, one hundred and three bedrooms, nine dressing rooms, a club room, an admirable coffee room measuring 59ft x 30ft x 27ft, and a retiring room. The *Illustrated London News* enlarged on the

Below: The Gateshead station and hotel designed by G.T. Andrews, opened in June 1844. The hotel is at the left, linked to the station by an arch. *Author's sketch*.

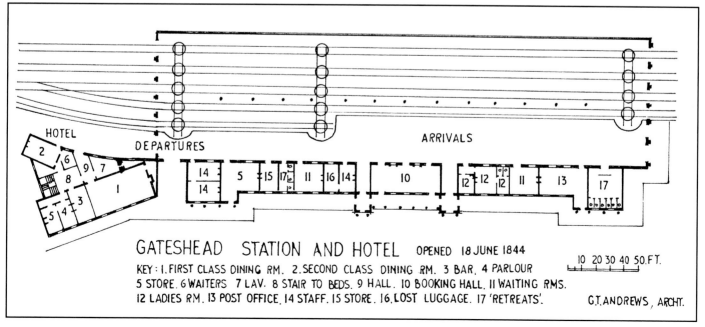

GATESHEAD STATION AND HOTEL OPENED 18 JUNE 1844

KEY: 1.FIRST CLASS DINING RM. 2.SECOND CLASS DINING RM. 3.BAR. 4 PARLOUR
5 STORE. 6 WAITERS 7 LAV. 8 STAIR TO BEDS. 9 HALL. 10 BOOKING HALL. 11 WAITING RMS.
12 LADIES RM. 13 POST OFFICE. 14 STAFF. 15 STORE. 16.LOST LUGGAGE. 17 'RETREATS'.

10 20 30 40 50 FT.

G.T. ANDREWS, ARCHT.

description, pointing out that several of the bedrooms were arranged en-suite consisting of a bedroom, dressing room and a sitting room "an arrangement found on the Continent but not common here." *(15)*

The accommodation was arranged on four principal floors, with the coffee room, club room and retiring room dominating the ground floor. The kitchens were sited in the basement, and staff and visitors servants were housed in the two attic storeys. The pair of flanking towers were not entirely ornamental and held water storage tanks and bedrooms. Running the length of the slender rectangular plan, on the upper floors, was not a narrow central corridor but what was described as "a gallery from which the various rooms open." Generously wide, these galleries and the staircases were built in "fireproof construction", which in mid-19th century terms usually consisted of flat brick arches or stone slabbing. No clue as to the number of baths and water closets is given, other than that at "convenient places on each floor, are bath rooms,etc."

The construction which was in the hands of Hollands of London, seems to have gone on apace; the whole of the work being completed within 14 months at a cost of a little under £44,000. *(16)* The same year, 1854, witnessed the completion of the *Great Northern Hotel* at Kings Cross. With five principal floors and an attic storey, the slender, curved building was tall for the period, when visitors were reluctant to pay so much for rooms above the first two or three floor levels. Some of its 69 bedrooms were similarly arranged to those at the Great Western Royal Hotel, with sitting rooms en suite. Vertical railways, ascending chambers and rising or lifting rooms, as the first passenger lifts were referred to, began to appear in America, following experiments by Henry Waterman and Elisha A. Otis. By 1854, Otis had perfected a safety lock to prevent the car from falling in the event of a broken rope occurring, and in 1857 installed his first passenger lift in New York.

The *Grosvenor Hotel* opened at Victoria station in 1861, had a steam-powered lift, one of the first to be installed in London. *The Illustrated London News* observed: "The height of the building will be upwards of 100ft from the pavement, but a lifting room adjoining the staircase will diminish this internally to zero, and suggest to sufferers of Parisian troisiemes a possible mode of uniting moderate room rent with comfort, which cannot easily be much longer lost sight of in hotels abroad or at home." *(17)*

The integration of hotel and station into the same building, which had its origins at Curzon Street, Birmingham, though an afterthought (and in the twin hotels on the platforms of Swindon station; and in the work of G.T. Andrews) was taken a step further during the 1860s. At Paddington, an intervening space known as 'the lawn' separated the hotel from the train shed roof, providing a barrier to smoke and noise. In contrast, for their design of the terminus stations at Charing Cross and Cannon Street, Edward M. Barry and John Hawkshaw allowed the hotel and train shed to merge into a compact space-saving layout, which nevertheless focussed noise and smoke into the back of the hotel. The single span roofs, designed by Hawkshaw, were greeted with disapproval by *The Building News*. "These enormous roofs are not required .... The necessity being disallowed, we regret the disfigurement and repeat that it must have been but a careless exercise of power which permitted their existence in their present form." *(18)* This was a visual, rather than utilitarian

criticism, it would seem. The hotels, which formed prestigious street frontages and effective closures to the large train sheds behind, differed considerably in the type of accommodation provided.

Charing Cross could accommodate about 250 beds, some of which were arranged in suites. A 'rising room' with comfortable seats served the five principal floors and two attics. The public rooms, decorated to the designs of Owen Jones, included (at first floor level) a general coffee room, ladies' coffee room and resting room, a reading room, a smoking room with a balcony which overlooked the station platforms, a committee room for meetings and a billiard room. The hotel frontage, set back about 120ft from the Strand, was protected by iron railings and a pair of police lodges. In total, the design presented one of the most varied assortments of detailing yet seen in London. Plain white brick, nail headed brick, terra cotta and artificial stone mouldings joined, with an uneasy assembly of arched and square headed windows, pilasters and string courses. *(19)* The marked horizontal emphasis created contrasted sharply with the slim elegance of the replica of the Eleanor Cross which the company erected in the forecourt. The original cross dated from about 1292 and occupied the site where the equestrian statue of Charles I now stands. The replica cross, designed by Barry and carved by T. Earp, of Lambeth, was provided at company expense as a gesture to remind passers-by that the site of the original Eleanor Cross was close by.

The *City Terminus Hotel* at Cannon Street employed similar materials and detailing but was a storey less in height (four in all, and an attic) and catered for public meetings and banquets. The article in *The Building News* which had attacked the "enormous roofs" of Charing Cross and Cannon Street, made a scathing attack on the ornamentation used by Barry at Cannon Street. Internally, the hotel's public rooms were large by any standards, the great hall at first floor level measured 114ft x 93ft and was about 36ft high at its centre. The hall had a recessed gallery, one for the ladies and the other for musicians. Lighting was provided by double glazed windows in two tiers, under the train roof. The first floor also housed the restaurant, coffee room, ladies' coffee room, reception room, and board room. A large meeting room, business rooms and anti rooms, three small dining rooms, and two other dining rooms were located at second floor level. This left space for only 84 bedrooms and dressing rooms, which included about 20 in the attics. Five bathrooms were provided in the hotel. *(20)*

The hotels at both Charing Cross and Cannon Street were colossal feats of engineering and construction. At Cannon Street, 25 million bricks alone went into the substructure, required for the series of groined arches to lift the platforms and hotel above the river level. Valuable cellars extending to almost 140,000 sq ft were created beneath the station.

For the hotel's guests, the noise of wheeled traffic on the granite setts in the forecourt, and train noise and smoke, seem to have been tolerated as necessary, but at St. Pancras the problems of noise and smoke later came under much scrutiny. When *The Illustrated London News'* correspondent visited St. Pancras in September, 1871, he observed that "there is nothing of the kind equal to this structure in magnitude, its size far exceeding that of the Cannon Street and Charing Cross stations." Scott's grand design provided

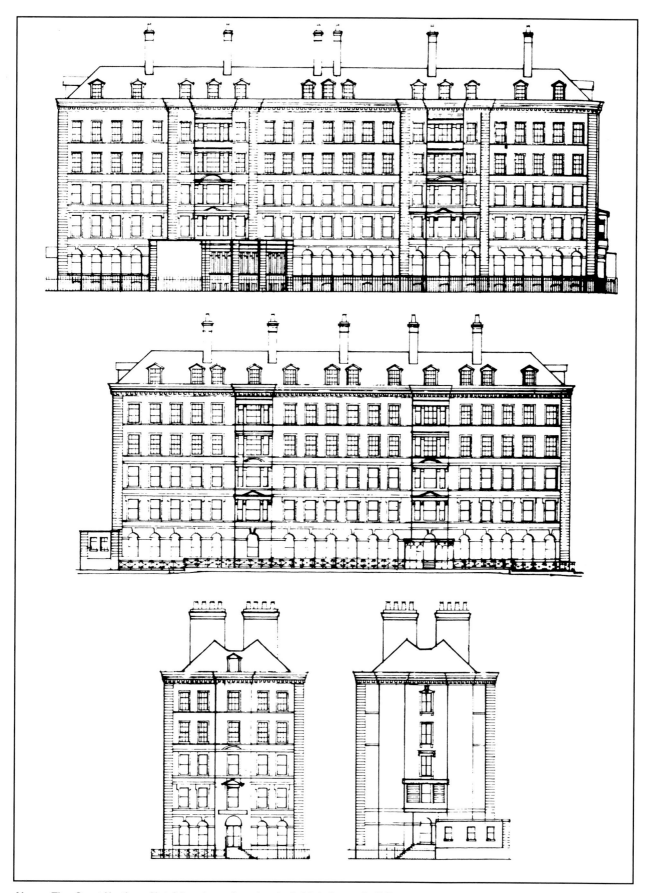

Above: The *Great Northern Hotel*, London, where Lewis Cubitt's house-building experience is evident. Guests had a lot of stair-climbing before a lift was installed! *Courtesy DEGW.*

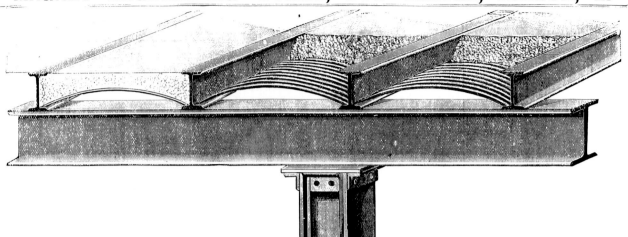
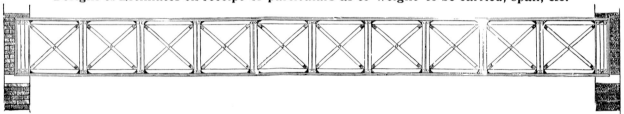
Above: Many 19th century public buildings claimed to be 'fireproof'. This illustration shows a typical 'fireproof' wrought iron beam and concrete infill floor. *RIBA Library.*

Right: By the end of the 19th century, lifts were an accepted feature in new and modernised hotels. This is a contemporary advertisement for hydraulic, steam and hand-powered lifts. *RIBA Library.*

for separate carriage entrances to the arrival and departure platforms. Within two years of the hotel opening, the noise of traffic beneath the eastern arch, serving the arrival platforms, caused the company to experiment with rubber setts obtained from Mackintosh. Not entirely successful, wooden setts with rubber strips placed in the joints were substituted and proved sufficiently effective to be adopted for the western entrance too. The *Illustrated London News* at the time of its visit in September 1871, also noted that the western tower was under construction but that the west wing "designed to sweep round in a slight curve forward" had not been started. When the west wing was completed, proximity to the granite surface in Euston Road re-opened the problem of noise. Eventually, in 1881, the St. Pancras Vestry agreed to replace the granite setts with wooden blocks and accepted a contribution of £1,000 from the MR towards the cost. To counter the noise from trains and the presence of smoke within the train shed it had earlier been decided to interpose a glazed screen

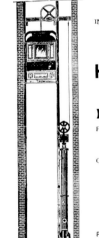

between the inner end of the roof and the hotel.

The grandeur of St Pancras' Gothic frontage and clock tower was apt to draw attention away from the accommodation within. The west wing housed the principal public rooms, including the grand coffee room at its first floor level, within the curved facade. There were also approximately 14 suites of rooms at the same level, and, in total, sufficient for about 150 beds. At the eastern end of the building, dominated by the clock tower, was a large room set aside as a Boardroom for the company.

In choosing the building materials for St. Pancras, much came from locations within the territory of the MR; facing bricks from Nottinghamshire; some of the stone from Mansfield; some slate from Leicestershire; and red granite from Shap. The whole of the building was 'fireproof', using Mulland's patent floor system, except within the attics. Economies which forced the MR to build four, instead of the five principal floors originally intended, was a considerable blow to prestige. Indeed, the sketches prepared for inclusion in timetables and brochures clearly showed the five-storeyed scheme, including an illustration used in the 1888 edition of *Whitaker's Almanac*. The passenger elevators referred to in this illustration were supplied by Sir William Armstrong, including a 10-passenger water-powered hydraulic lift supplied at a cost of £710. This lift became 'stuck' in June 1874, but fortunately no one was injured and the manufacturers accepted liability for the repairs, and also agreed to build another lift for use in the west wing. This was designed by Crossley's, in conjunction with S.W. Johnson, the Midland's Locomotive Superintendent. The final cost of the *Midland Grand Hotel* as disclosed by the Chairman to the shareholders in February, 1877, totalled £438,000, which included £304,335 for the fabric, £49,000 for the decoration and fittings, and £84,000 for the furnishings. *(21)* St. Pancras and its hotel had one close relative (in layout and appearance), the St. Enoch station and hotel, Glasgow, completed in July, 1879. the St. Pancras train shed covered a space of 700ft by 240ft and was 100ft high at its apex. The St. Enoch train shed was 550ft by 200ft and was 85ft. high at its apex.

St. Enoch had the distinction of being the first purpose-built railway hotel in Scotland. Its five-storey frontage to St. Enoch Square was approximately 260ft long and it was intended to extend this by further 100ft to Howard Street. The hotel contained 200 bedrooms, 22 private and 20

Above: A view of the splendid dining room, at the *North Western Hotel* Liverpool, Circa 1912. *Author's collection.*

Above: The railway hotels provided a wide range of facilities. This is the hairdressers saloon at the *Exchange Station Hotel*, **Liverpool. Note the overhead driving belt which powered mechanical hair brushes!** *National Railway Museum.*

public rooms, not counting the restaurants and 45 servants apartments. The basement, which housed the kitchen, was carried out in brick arch construction, and filler joists (steel joists bedded in concrete) were employed for three out of five principal floors. *(22)*

Matthew William Thompson, Chairman of the GSWR, was also Chairman of the MR and it was obviously no coincidence that the stations were similar in layout. The similarity extended to style as well and *Industries of Glasgow* (published in 1888) pointed out that the design "embodies leading characteristics of the Gothic order, and is indebted for the style of its mouldings to the Early English Period."

The pattern set by Charing Cross, Cannon Street, St Pancras and Glasgow St. Enoch, of an hotel abutting a single-span train shed, was used with variations elsewhere. the *North Western Hotel*, at Liverpool's, Lime Street station, designed by Alfred Waterhouse and opened in 1871, abutted a multi-span train shed. Nearby, the *Exchange Station Hotel*, opened in 1888, was separated from the train

shed by an interesting carriage concourse with its own glazed roof. The *Great Eastern Hotel* at Liverpool Street, London, opened in 1884 and extended in 1903, formed an irregular shaped closure to the train shed on three frontages.

Unusual in design was the solution adopted by the Caledonian Railway for its new terminus at Glasgow Central. The granting of powers in 1873 marked the culmination of a 30-years struggle by the company to gain a firm footing on the north bank of the Clyde. Crossing the river with a bridge at the Broomielaw, a large roughly rectangular site with four street frontages was developed. When the station opened in 1879 the corner abutting Gordon Street and Hope Street was seen to have palatial offices, rising through five storeys, plus a further two attics. But before completing what were intended to be offices for the Caledonian Railway a change of course was ordered. Following a further four years of work, the offices were remodelled into even more palatial hotel accommodation. The L-shaped hotel was indeed large, with room for 420 guests and 170 officials and servants. An immediate success, the demand for more room was met by additions which, by 1921, had raised the accommodation to 550 guests, nearly 300 staff, 50 lavatories and 40 bathrooms. Some idea of the size of the building can be gained from the fact that the principal corridors were a monotonous 343ft long. In addition to the usual public rooms, provision was included for a musicians' gallery in the dining room, a separate music room, a billiards room, a ladies' coffee room, a hairdressing salon and, somewhat unusual, an arbitration room with witness rooms and a retiring room en suite. From the inner windows of the first floor coffee room a view of the station concourse could be had, described at the time as "a spectacle of perpetual and astonishing fascination."

To maintain the hotel's six boilers and seven electric generators (hotels and large buildings frequently made their own electricity in those days), deliveries of coal were brought into the station by rail hopper wagons, and dropped through chutes into the basement. *(23)*

A move away from the fully integrated station and hotel, in favour of large hotels on their own 'island' sites was the solution chosen by the Board of Directors of the North British Railway, for their new hotels at Edinburgh. The construction of the *North British Station Hotel* between 1895 and 1902, supervised by a separate Construction Committee, was one of the largest hotel building ventures ever undertaken by the railways. Its architect, William Hamilton Beattie 1843-1898, had already designed three hotels in Edinburgh, the Central, the Clarendon and the Royal and was the original promoter of Edinburgh's cable tramway system.

When a souvenir of the opening of the hotel was published in October, 1902, it was observed that the architect had blended the "Old Scottish architecture of the Old Town with the rather severe classical architecture of the New Town." The task undertaken was formidable. Rising ten storeys, first by four levels from the Waverley

station platforms to Princes Street, and six storeys from street level to the eaves of the roof, the building was dominated by a squat clock tower rising about 90ft above the roof. The floor plan was simple, measuring approximately 190ft x 180ft and with a central light well approximately 70ft square. At street level, the well was glazed to form a Palm Court, or lounge. For the outward facing rooms, double windows were used to combat street noise. For the rooms facing into the white glazed brick light well, the loss of a view was compensated to some extent by a distinctly quieter environment.

The dining room, at street level, occupied a 112ft frontage facing westwards towards the Scottish National Gallery and could claim one if the finest townscape views in Britain. The four levels beneath housed, at station platform level, an entrance and coal stores; at the second level the boilers; at the third level kitchen preparation and stores; and at the fourth level billiard rooms, an American Bar and a smoking lounge. Space for shops (for letting) was provided on the east and west sides, the latter occupying the landing levels of the steps linking the station and Princes Street.

In total, the hotel contained more than 700 rooms, including more than 300 bedrooms, 52 bathrooms and 70 WCs; there were also hairdressing facilities, a commercial travellers' writing and stockroom, 1,000 windows, 2,000 doors, 5,000 electric light fittings, 25 miles of hot and cold water service pipes, fire hydrant service pipes and waste and vent pipes. 75,000 gallons of water were stored in tanks in the tower. *(24)*

This hotel was built in the transitional period, when load-bearing perimeter and cross-walls, used in combination with mild steel beams, were being progressively steered towards the fully-framed steel skeleton. In fact the hotel was the first building in Edinburgh to use mild steel joists, girders and stanchions. A total of 1,600 tons of steel was manufactured, drilled and rivetted by a local firm. *(25)* Concrete and steel filler joists

Left: Manchester. The *Midland Hotel*. Afternoon tea and music on the roof, Circa 1912. Note the art noveau styling in the wrought iron balustrading. *George Dow Collection.*

construction was used for the floors, and the use of as little inflammable material as possible led the company to claim that the building was "absolutely fireproof".

The hotel was heated by a plenum system, using large fans drawing in between 14 million and 18 million cubic feet of air per hour, giving four to six air changes per hour, and, by pre-heating, maintained a steady temperature of 60 degrees F. Also an innovation were the pair of electric elevators and a Van Kannel or 'turnstile' door at the front entrance. Staff and visitors' servants were, as was normal, accommodated within the attics.

Meanwhile, at the west end of Princes Street, the Caledonian Railway was bringing to fruition an impressive scheme which had its origins in the year 1867 but which had been shelved for lack of funds until 1890. The Architect chosen was John Dick Peddie (1823-1891) a dynamic businessman with high regard for his native city. His first important work was the Queen Street Hall, won in competition, followed by work for banks, insurance companies and hospitals. His design for the Caledonian Railway's Princes Street terminus provided for a triangular building, with its point removed to form a short entrance frontage. Still dogged by financial restraints, the contract was let in 1890 (shortly before fire gutted the existing station) and provided for the arcaded ground floor to enclose the platforms. The upper three storeys and attic storey (which provided the hotel accommodation) was not commenced until 1899 and opened in December 1903. *(26)* In spite of earlier delays, the finished station and hotel were built with the finest materials available. Red Locharbriggs sandstone was used for the facades, marble wall cladding and paving for the entrance hall, and a grand staircase lit by a huge stained glass window displaying the Coat of Arms of the chief towns served by the Caledonian Railway. One of the hotel's most famous rooms was the Louis XV drawing room. Under the regime of Arthur Towle, the room was converted into a French restaurant, the *Pompadour*, which survived until 1938. Re-opening following refurbishment in 1953, the restaurant resumed its role as one of the finest in Edinburgh.

In 1897, when the MR received Parliamentary approval to build an hotel at Manchester, William Towle had

Above: A rare 'behind the scenes' view at the *Midland Hotel* Manchester. Staff are seen here at work in the 'German Kitchen.' *George Dow Collection.*

AN ILLUSTRATED HISTORY OF RAILWAY HOTELS

completed 33 years' service with the company. By this time, his reputation was such that the Board of Directors gave him a virtually free hand in planning of the new hotel, the first major challenge since the completion of the *Midland Grand Hotel* at St. Pancras, 24 years earlier.

When William Towle retired in 1914, the *Railway Gazette* recalled the events which preceded the building of Manchester's 500-roomed *Midland Hotel*, and its accommodation. "Prior to its opening, owing to lack of good hotel accommodation, few people stopped at Manchester who could possibly help it, but in the nineties the Midland Railway decided to open a hotel there. Before the designs were prepared, Mr Towle and the Architect, Mr Trubshaw, travelled all over America and the Continent studying the most up-to-date examples of hotel design. This now famous hotel was finally completed and opened in September, 1903, and is unique amongst railway hotel both on account of its size and the number, novelty and luxury of its public rooms. The hotel has five public restaurants, a grand banqueting hall, winter garden, theatre or concert hall, Turkish baths and many other novel features which have made it the social centre of Manchester." *(27)*

Charles Trubshaw, *(28)* the company Architect, had earlier designed the *Midland Hotel* at the Foster Square terminus, Bradford. Opened in 1890, the four-storey hotel had one principal street frontage, and a dominating octagonal-shaped corner turret marking the set back to a recessed frontage, which enclosed a covered station forecourt and carriage entrance. Among the features which Trubshaw repeated in the design of the Midland Hotel, Manchester, were the angle turrets, the grouping of the windows in pairs, and a liberal use of Burmantofts tea-pot brown coloured faience. The warm coloured faience, red brick and matching Aberdeen granite plinth diverted criticism from the elaborate detailing used in the four street frontages. In 1924, Professor C.H. Reilly likened the "vast and disordered mass to an ant heap." By the 1960s, Professor Pevsner had mellowed the description to: "a vast and varied affair, red brick and brown terra cotta." The elaborate facades hid a more mundane layout of bedrooms which bordered mosaic-floored corridors. The rooms facing the streets had double windows to combat noise, and the

inner rooms overlooked white brick-lined light wells. Like the *North British Station Hotel*, Edinburgh, a proportion of suite accommodation was provided for residential purposes. The 800-seat theatre, which hosted England's first repertory company, fell victim to the increased popularity of the cinema and closed in 1922. Its auditorium had a level floor and was not entirely successful, preventing much of the audience from obtaining a satisfactory view of the stage. Constructionally, the *Midland Hotel* had a mild steel frame, used in conjunction with some load-bearing walls, filler joist-type concrete floors, polished granite cladding to the ground floor frontage, and an elaborate system of stub steel joists and bearers to which the moulded blocks of glazed coloured faience were fixed.

For the convenience of visitors arriving by train, a covered way with a glazed roof linked the back door of the hotel to the adjacent Central station. A feature of the covered way was the upward jump in the roof, provided to allow trams to pass beneath, along the Windmill Street frontage. For visitors arriving by cab at the front entrance, a covered carriage court, with separate entrance and departure portals, was provided. However, the increased use of the internal combustion engine, with its risk of carbon monoxide poisoning in the confined space, led to the abandonment of the court in 1936.

Above: Manchester's imposing *Midland Hotel*, opened in 1903 to the design of Charles Trubshaw. Now restored and modernised, this leading hotel once again serves the citizens of Manchester and its guests. *The Sankey Collection.*

Time has been comparatively kind to the *Midland Hotel*. Its popularity warranted the purchase of an adjacent site in 1930, for a large extension. However, the economic depression and war uncertainty intervened and the plans were abandoned. The hotel survived the Manchester blitz, thanks to the hard-working fire wardens. The hotel's Lloyds Bank branch closed in 1945 and the famous *Midland Hotel* postmark used by the hotel's sub-post office remained in use until 1949. Its winter gardens became a modern lounge whilst the theatre was converted as three levels of modern bedrooms. The grill room became the *Butty Bar*, the dining room became the Trafford Restaurant, and the German Restaurant the Goblet Wine Bar. One of the last changes to take place before the hotel was sold, in 1983, was the letting of self-contained accommodation to the Ladbroke company for use as a casino, for which the law required a separate outside entrance. As the railways gained more experience, most of their hotels and particularly those in towns and cities, were designed to cater for a variety of needs; for the overnight and longer stay visitors; for the commercial traveller and for those who chose to make an hotel their permanent residence; banquets and assemblies, music and entertainment; and sometimes a Masonic lodge. For the permanent resident, the closure of their place of abode was a sad occasion. Alderman W. Kelly and Mr Lionel Everett, Chief Constable of Liverpool, were both long-term residents of the *North Western Hotel*, Liverpool, at the time of closure in 1933, when the LMS decided to concentrate facilities at the more up-to-date *Adelphi* and *Exchange Station Hotels*.

By the time the *Midland Hotel*, Manchester, had been completed, the era of the large multi-function hotel was firmly established. The *Hotel Cecil,* in London, opened in 1896, had more than 800 rooms and claimed to be the largest in Europe. *(29)* The *Central Station Hotel*, Glasgow; the *North British Hotel*, Edinburgh, and the *Midland Hotel,* Manchester, kept the railways abreast of developments.

In April 1907, hotel planning was the subject of a paper read to the Royal Institute of British Architects by Stanley Hamp, ARIBA. *(30)* The paper contained several interesting observations on current design practice, some of which are still valid and some of which are now outmoded curiosities. Edwin Hall, Vice President of the RIBA, recalled that: "the hotel building boom during the past 25 years had been preceded by the opening of the Langham Hotel (1864), and that people had said it was madness to build such a large hotel, and that the boom could not last. In fact, many people who had town houses now live in hotels."

Stanley Hamp and his partner, T.E. Collcutt, had designed extensions to the Savoy Hotel, London, and hotels at Bournemouth, Jersey, Spain and East Africa. Hamp identified three types of hotels, residential, commercial and railway. The railway hotel used as an example, the *Hotel Great Central*, at Marylebone Station (1899) although fulfilling that role, was owned by Frederick Hotels, Ltd.

Hinting at the beginnings of modernism and a reaction against Victorian ornateness and decoration, it was suggested that hotels should present a pleasing exterior, avoiding the "usual tawdry and showy character, and have a simple architectural treatment, an inviting entrance, a well lit interior and bright and cheerful rooms... furniture should be substantial and not flimsy and stand wear and tear." The usual accommodation listed by Hamp comprised, at the ground floor, a lounge or winter garden, dining rooms, restaurant with an orchestra available, coffee room with adjoining service rooms, a reading and writing room, a small drawing room, a smoking and billiard room attached, a ballroom and reception room, an office and manager's room, a gentlemen's lavatory and cloakroom, and ladies' retiring and toilet rooms. The kitchen, staff dining rooms and servants' hall were earmarked for the basement. In addition, one or two private dining rooms were useful, and, in the provinces, a large hall for public banquets and meetings and separate service arrangements. A barber's shop, a bakery and a laundry were frequently included too. A hint of current practice was Hamp's reference: "it is becoming the fashion for each bedroom to possess its own bathroom with lavatory, WC, bath and heated towel rail." Fitted furniture was also beginning to replace movable items. For the health-conscious, Turkish, electric, medical and hot and cold sea water baths were recommended for inclusion.

On the siting of kitchens, Hamp recommended that: "space next to the dining rooms should be set aside for this purpose" (as had been provided at the *North British Station Hotel,* Edinburgh). Failing this, a basement location immediately below the dining room was suggested. Top floor kitchens (as used in the Holborn Viaduct Hotel, London, in 1877 and the *Exchange Station Hotel,* Liverpool, in 1888) were not recommended because of difficulties in maintaining a good draught for the oven flues. It was also difficult to keep the larder and food storage rooms cool in the summer. Servants' bedrooms were healthier sited at the top of the building, rather than the basement.

Electricity, which had made its debut in the early 1880s, was often cheaper to make, rather than buy. Thus, exhaust steam from the hotel's boilers could be used to drive

Above: The *Adelphi Hotel*, Liverpool, under construction in 1912. Fully-framed steel skeletons had become established building practice by this time and this hotel made the most of the technique. *The Builder.*

Right: The *Adelphi Hotel*, Liverpool. Compare this illustration with that of a bedroom at the *Midland Hotel*, Manchester (Page 59). The decade which separated the buildings saw the wider use of fixed wash hand basins, built-in wardrobes and wooden beds. But the still-important fireplace can be seen in the mirror. *Authors collection.*

AN ILLUSTRATED HISTORY OF RAILWAY HOTELS

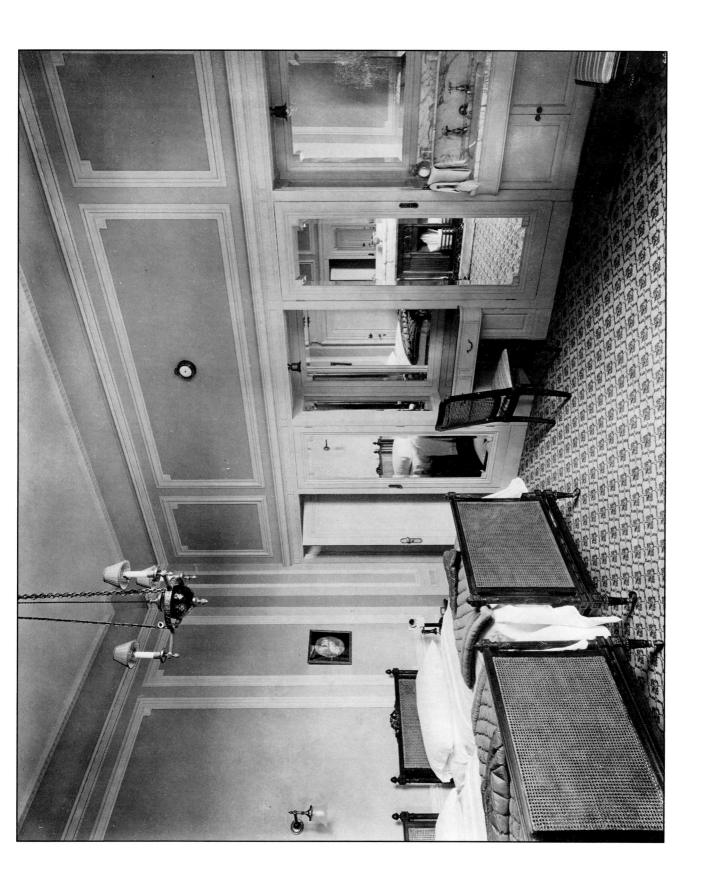

Above: The glazed veranda at the *Furness Abbey Hotel*, Barrow in Furness, where guests could relax in conversation, perhaps over a pot of tea, or read a newspaper. *Authors collection.*

generators. This was the method employed at the *Central Station Hotel*, Glasgow, utilising coal brought direct into the station in rail hopper wagons. The principal drawback was vibration and heat transmission to adjacent parts of the building. Home-made electricity nevertheless became common practice until the 1930s, when mains services became increasingly available and competitive. Electric lifts were also superceding hydraulic lifts by this time, making vertical communication for goods and passengers safe, fast and reliable. The telephone was further being recognised as being of inestimable value both for outside and inside communication and was consequently recommended as an "absolute necessity".

Vacuum cleaners, taken for granted today of course, were a recent innovation, but they were not electrically-driven as we know them now, in their early days. They required a circuit of iron pipes embedded in the walls and floors and connected to a vacuum pump by an electric motor. Flexible tubes were then connected to the room outlets.

Mechanical ventilation, and in particular the system used at the *Midland Hotel*, Manchester, was used as a good example of current practice. Two fans revolving at 180RPM introduced two and three-quarter million cubic feet of fresh air (cooled in summer and heated in the winter) into the building. The air was filtered through a screen of special material capable of extracting soot and chemicals. The screen was large enough not to cause undue resistance to the fans. The extraction of foul air was of equal importance, particularly in those areas generating heat, such as the laundries and kitchens. This was done with the aid of

ducting and suction-inducing fans.

To simplify the window cleaner's task, reversible windows (to allow inside cleaning) and the use of double windows facing on to busy thoroughfares, were both advisable. The Edwardian era was a period when coal fires were provided in every bedroom and sitting room, but central heating was used in all public rooms, staircases, corridors and landings.

Construction was outside the scope of Hamp's paper, but on the matter of fire precautions he recommended 'fireproof' construction, and the inclusion of one or more fire escape staircases, arranged with escape doors at each corridor and provided with fire hydrants, breaking glass alarms and sprung mechanical door-closers in all public corridors. Vigilance was kept in most hotels by one or more firemen and a team of trained staff. Night patrols by a fireman clocking-in to prescribed points in the building, accompanied by periodic fire drills, were designed to promote the efficient safeguarding of the building and its guests and staff.

The years which separated the completion of the *North British Hotel*, Edinburgh, and the *Midland Hotel*, Manchester, in 1902/3, and the rebuilding of the *Adelphi Hotel*, Liverpool, 1912/14, were years which witnessed considerable change in hotel planning and construction. The greatest advance was in the acceptance of steel-framed construction, although as early as 1879, the Royal Institute of British Architects had revealed the profession's disapproval of the new material. One contributor summed up the matter thus: "The mischief arises from the attempt to cramp and confine the use of the new material within the

AN ILLUSTRATED HISTORY OF RAILWAY HOTELS

lines of the old, with which it is altogether incongruous." John Ruskin added weight to the argument and condemned such horrific examples as the cast-iron spire recently added to Rouen Cathedral, along with his general opposition to iron and steel construction. The steelmakers themselves seemed content to wait for orders rather than go out and sell their new material to the world. (31)

The Edwardian era witnessed the final overcoming of the opposition to steel. the *Ritz Hotel* (1904/5), *Selfridges* (1906), *Inveresk House* (1907) and the *Waldorf Hotel* (1907), all in London, led a growing number of fully framed steel buildings. The 1909 London Building Amendment Act, often known as the 'Steel Frame Act', gave recognition to the new form of construction. R. Frank Atkinson, (32) architect for the new *Adelphi Hotel*, was experienced in steel construction, having been involved in the design of the first stage of Selfridges. For the *Adelphi* he used a six-storey skeleton formed round two light wells and planned to a 14 ft. 3 in. grid. The plan was modified before construction actually began, when the back wall of the inner rectangle was omitted for economy. Some of the "cramping and confining" of the new material within the lines of the old became apparent in the juggling and offsetting of the steel beams required to miss the massive brick-built chimney flues. A fireplace in every bedroom was still very much an accepted feature of the period.

Outwardly, the Portland stone clad facades struck Professor Pevsner as "stodgy," (33) but interior planning broke new ground. Each bedroom was provided with hot and cold water to a fixed wash hand basin, the majority of which were set in marble tops, linked to an attractive range of built-in wardrobes and a dressing table. Even so, the outmoding of the matching china wash hand bowls and water jugs placed on a marble-topped wash stand in each bedroom did not meet with universal approval. Oscar Wilde wrote: "who wants an immovable washing basin in one's room? I do not. Hide the thing. I prefer to ring for water when I need it." (34) You can't please all of the people, all of the time!

The *Adelphi* also took a further step towards full air conditioning for buildings. In the 19th century, coal fires and a limited number of radiators were used to heat public rooms. At the *Midland Grand Hotel* at St Pancras (1873) the radiators were housed in cast-iron panelled enclosures with marble tops. At the refurbished and re-equipped *Aberdeen Palace Hotel*, Aberdeen, (1890), an electrically-driven induction fan took air, passed it through a damp sieve or screen and over a heat exchanger of pipes, before ducting it into the public rooms. (35) Similarly, foul air was drawn into a separate extraction system. The design of a heating and ventilating system for a large building prompted the MR to publish a small book on this subject, entitled *A problem and its solution* in 1903.

The air conditioning system used for the public rooms at the *Adelphi* was Crittalls' balanced system of mechanical inlet and extract ventilation, used in conjunction with Carrier's air conditioning plant. Fine adjustment of the system was possible at the ducted inlets to the rooms because heater batteries with regulating valves were positioned at each of them. A separate extraction system removed foul air from the rooms and kitchens, by way of ducting which terminated at roof level. Each bedroom had its own coal fire, but for the visitor who preferred central heating, Crittalls' 'invisible' radiant panels were placed

beneath each window. To supply hot water, three Stirling-type automatically stoked water tube boilers were employed, each having a heating surface of 1.441 sq.ft.

The hotel was well-provided with lifts and staircases. The Otis Elevator Company installed two passenger lifts, one staff lift, and five goods lifts. Absent from the accommodation, however, was a Winter Garden or Palm Court sited in the lightwell. In its place, an elegant Fountain Court was provided, overlooked on four sides by dome-vaulted terraces, which in turn gave access to a pair of principal dining rooms and large ballroom.

A new note was struck by the accommodation provided in the basement: Turkish baths, a squash court, tennis court, shooting gallery, billiard room, and an essential feature in City centre hotels – a range of stock rooms for commercial travellers. The kitchens, sited beneath the Hypostyle or inner hall, were planned round an island unit containing 10 solid fuel ovens fired on the Fourneau system, together with other ancillary equipment. The laundry dealt with all the hotel's needs and also 'took-in' laundry from the *Midland Hotel*, Manchester, by way of a speedy rail link from Liverpool Central station to Manchester Central Station.

In order to provide a measure of variety in the furnishing of the *Adelphi*, five suppliers were employed. The main hall was furnished by Waring & Gillow; the dining rooms and drawing room by H.H. Martyn, of London; the French restaurant and smoke room by Hampton & Sons, of London; the lower lounge by Fryers Ltd, of London; and three of the sitting rooms by Liberty & Company. On a final note, the traditional brass bedstead was also ousted in favour of walnut and mahogany bed ends. (36)

The decision by the LMS, in 1935, to completely rebuild the 72-years old *Queens Hotel*, Leeds, provided the company with an opportunity to create the most most modern city centre hotel in the provinces. For Arthur Towle, Controller of LMS Hotels, it was the culmination of 37 years work in hotel management.

Engaging W. Curtis Green, RA, as consultant to assist W.H. Hamlyn, the LMS Architect, their design lived up to expectation. Outwardly scholarly, the eight-storey hotel occupied a roughly triangular site, set amongst a range of tunnels and a former canal. Each of the 206 bedrooms was provided with its own bathroom, fitted wardrobe, air conditioning and telephone. This was the first new hotel in Britain to have air conditioning and central heating in all its bedrooms as well as its public rooms. Coal fires were completely banished. Emphasis was placed on compactness, and space in corridors and other circulation areas was reduced to the minimum. The steel frame construction was used to advantage, forming compartments from which lightweight block partitions could be supported. Rubber-cushioning in the door rebates, sound-resistant floors, suspended ceilings, and insulation to the fans and duct work, all contributed to a quieter environment than had previously been possible. Double windows up to and including second floor level, and rubber paving bricks on the adjacent station approach also helped to minimise external noise.

Contrasting with the white Portland stone cladding of the facade, the interior was decidedly colourful. The French restaurant, almost circular in plan and served by its own entrance from the street, was decorated in cream, silver and gold, enlivened by red doors and furniture and a green carpet. For the banqueting hall on the first floor, goatskin wall linings in a soft grey-green complemented the green carpet. Furniture consisted principally of mahogany and walnut. Six passenger lifts and eight more lifts for goods and staff catered for vertical communication. The kitchens were sited in the basement, and the boiler plant found useful accommodation within the area formerly occupied by the canal. *(37)*

Hotels were provided for different types of customers, and just as the city establishments were aimed at business travellers and were accordingly equipped, so the seaside hotels were fitted-out more for the leisure market. Thus, when William Peachey, architect to the Stockton & Darlington Railway, designed the *Zetland Hotel* and terminus station at Saltburn-by-the-sea, several features were included with the holiday-maker in mind. The buffer stops and platform terminated virtually at the rear entrance of the hotel, and to keep visitors and their luggage dry, a glazed covered way was included.

To make the most of the fine sea views, spacious terraces and French windows, opening on to the first floor balcony, were provided. The photograph taken in 1863 of a visiting delegation from the British Association for the Advancement of Science shows the terraces and steps being used to good advantage. Towards the right of the photograph can be seen a semi-circular bay, which terminated above the roof level in a viewing chamber housing a telescope. For visitors wanting a more bracing

view, a spiral staircase led to a lead-covered viewing platform on the roof.

After dinner, guests who tired of conversation, piano music and songs in the lounge, could make their way into a detached building behind the hotel, accommodating a billiard and smoking room above and the hotel's kitchens beneath. Billiards had become increasingly popular following John Thurston's development of the slate bed in the 1830s and the introduction of rubber cushions, both of which revolutionised the game. Play, however, could not take place at will because the archaic Gaming Act prohibited resident guests from using the tables out of licensing hours! No games were permitted either on Sundays, Christmas Day, Good Friday and Thanksgiving days. Saltburn was blessed with a good water supply from springs, as well as sea water, which was available in the hotel's four bathrooms. An added luxury was rainwater, collected from the roof, for use in the wash bowls in the bedrooms. *(38)*

When the *Great Eastern Hotel* at Harwich opened nearly two years later in June 1865, views of the adjacent harbour and River Orwell could be had from the first floor balcony which ran the full length of the hotel's facade. On fine days, guests could climb to the roof and take a seat on the lead-covered viewing platform, protected by wrought-iron railings. For members of the Harwich Yacht Club, a

Below: The *Cruden Bay Hotel* was familiarly known as 'The Palace in the Sandhills'. The hotel is seen distantly, overlooking its golf course, which was laid out by Tom Morris. *Author's collection.*

private billiard room was available in the hotel.

To make the most of the British summer and provide protection on damp days, elaborate sun lounges were a feature often included in the design of resort hotels. At the *Sandringham Hotel* at Hunstanton, dating from 1876, guests could obtain views of the sea and beaches from large bay windows, or sit in wicker chairs in a large conservatory.

When James Brooks made a rare departure from ecclesiastical work to design the *South Eastern Hotel*, at Deal, in 1901, he provided glazed verandahs on either side of the entrance. A postcard published in 1906 remarked: "The verandahs are kept delightfully cool in summer by running water over the roof." At the Highland Hotel at Strathpeffer opened in 1911 roomy bay windows and verandahs with balconies above formed important features of the design. The verandahs were recommended for use "during the late summer and autumn months." *(39)*

The Glasgow & South Western Railway's decision to employ James Miller (1861-1947) to design its resort hotel at Turnberry provided the company and their successors, the LMS, with one of the most attractive of all railway hotels. Miller first gained recognition in 1901 with his designs for the Glasgow International Exhibition. He won several competitions, designed Cadbury's buildings at Bourneville, several hospitals, Glasgow Medical School, the BBC building in Belfast and railway stations in the Glasgow area for the Caledonian Railway. Turnberry's outward attractiveness was in its colours, chosen in Miller's words because: "Common brick with roughcast and a red tile roof will be much less than stone and be more effective for the situation and purpose. Red tiles will give colour to the landscape, and be valuable as non-conductors, making the rooms in the attics cool in the summer and warm in the winter."

Miller pointed out that the "principal traffic to and from the hotel will be by the station entrance" (provided with a revolving door). However, the year 1906 also saw the advance of the motor car and the accommodation of chauffeurs was a topic which required some thought. At first, a separate wooden-framed building to accommodate five beds and toilet facilities was considered, but was

The car and chauffeur at the *Cruden Bay Hotel*, Port Errol, circa 1900. Note the locomotive-type boilers used for the hotel's central heating plant, visible in the background. *Author's collection.*

abandoned in favour of more permanent quarters off the kitchen courtyard. *(40)*

It was also the architect's responsibility to prepare a specification for the furnishing of the hotel, and some interesting items were found in the dining room, where decoration was to be in Queen Anne style. The chairs were to be of first quality Tobasco mahogany or French walnut, with a dull finish, upholstered in hair and covered in Morocco, the colour to be chosen later. The tables were to be 36in square with club feet and birch framing, their tops of unpolished cypress and covered with baize. The carpet was to be Donegal or other hand woven at 15/9 (prime cost) per sq yd, and laid in five sections for ease of lifting. The curtains were to be of glazed chintz.

Principal bedrooms were to have wash stands measuring 4ft 6in by 4ft 3in, a bidet, and a pair of 3 ft. 6 in. wooden French bedsteads, with spiral box spring and hair filled mattresses. The bolsters were to be feather-filled and the pillows mixed down-filled. Other bedrooms were to have 3ft 6in by 6ft 6in. brass bedsteads. Bedroom carpets were to be of Brussels style. All windows were to be hung with wool challis at 2/8 per yd., complete with bronze rods, to cover the entire glass area. The bedrooms were to have, in addition, dark green linen blinds on spring rollers. All carpets were to be laid on heavy woollen felt underlay at 1/6 per sq yd.

The hotel was fitted with low temperature hot water radiators throughout and electric lighting powered by two 50HP oil-engined generators; in anticipation of the future a "house for motor cars" was also built. *(40)*

In contrast to Turnberry's manageable 78 bedrooms, arranged mainly on two floors, and its attractive colour and coastal setting, Matthew Adam's design for the *Gleneagles Hotel* was an example of solidly-built opulence and high quality craftsmanship, rather than a piece of outstanding architecture. Commenced in 1913, construction was halted during the First World War and completed by the Caledonian Railway's successors, the LMS, in readiness for opening on June 2 1924.

It was the solid bulk and setting of the *Gleneagles Hotel* which created such an impression. Within ten months, *The British Builder* wrote: "Gleneagles Hotel, which was completed last year has, owing to its size and unique situation, becoming one of the most famous hotels in the United Kingdom.... The interior is mainly designed in the Adam style, adapted for modern purposes.... The dining, room, for instance, has panelled walls painted in primrose colour, set off by curtains of blue-green brocade and a richly-coloured carpet. This is, perhaps, the keynote of the hotel decoration, which consists throughout of workmanship of a very high order in a conventional style adapted to equally conventional requirements." *(41)*

Major Muggeridge, Sir William Towle's son-in-law, took a hand in the planning of the decorative and furnishing schemes. His aim was to achieve variety, with practically no two bedrooms alike, and, for the suite rooms, gold and green or brown and gold were used. An interesting feature of the interior were the electric light fittings, carefully chosen, with shades to match the colour schemes. For guests taking a break from golf, or driven indoors by poor weather, the billiard room provided a welcoming colour scheme of grey-stained oak with panels bearing a pattern of dull gold on peacock blue, and silver-plated electric light wall brackets.

Above: The Grand Ballroom at the *Gleneagles Hotel*, Auchterarder, is seen as sketched for an LMS publicity brochure, of 1925. *Richard Casserley Collection.*

Huge quantities of carpet were required to furnish the hotel: 12 miles of 27in wide material for the corridors, and 10,000 yards for use in the bedrooms. The ballroom (large enough to accommodate 200 couples) was provided with Ionic pilasters and magnificent facet cut glass chandeliers. Ventilation of the room was effected by a domed opening at the centre, housing ducting and a powerful extraction fan.

The hotels at Turnberry and Gleneagles were the last of their line of resort hotels. Their traditional methods of construction using load-bearing walls, pitched roofs, and an increasing amount of steel for beams and columns, was soon to have a new competitor in a more versatile and exiting material – reinforced concrete.

Arthur Towle, now controller of LMS Hotel Services, had witnessed many changes and innovations during his career in the hotel industry. One of the most daring decisions made by the LMS in 1931 was the appointment of Oliver Hill to design a new hotel at Morecambe, to replace the ageing *Midland Hotel*. Using reinforced concrete and

skillfully prepared finishes, the hotel, completed in July 1933, was one of the most exciting hotel designs of the period. The site chosen for the hotel was acquired from Morecambe Corporation and bounded the recently completed curved sea walls and promenade. Hill allowed his plan to conform to this curve, and faced the hotel's exterior with glistening white rendering, composed of white cement and carborundum, polished to resemble marble.

The entrance and service areas were sited on the concave side, facing east, and the reception whilst most of the guests' rooms were on the convex side, facing west over the sea; they were provided with continuous balconies with obscure glass dividing screens. The plan was dominated at its centre by a graceful circular staircase, rising through three levels to a Solarium accommodated on the flat roof. On the right-hand side of the building, a circular cafe overlooked the site of the new swimming pool.

Though not new in concept, a curved facade having

been used for the *North Euston Hotel* at Fleetwood in 1841 and for the hotel at King's Cross in 1854, the new hotel at Morecambe made a useful contribution to hotel planning. The use of reinforced concrete, particularly for the construction of the staircase, demonstrated the versatility of the material, and the high quality finishes and decoration of the interior were the culmination of a successful partnership between architect, artist and sculptor. Eric Gill's contribution included a low-relief Portland stone panel for the entrance hall, to represent hospitality, a circular panel set in the staircase ceiling, with the coloured areas painted by Denis Tegetmeier, and a pair of carved Portland stone sea horses for the entrance facade. Eric Revilious painted the Frescos representing Morning, Noon and Night for the cafe. Marion Dorn designed the mosaic pavings for the entrance hall.

Blue and white were the colours chosen for the bedroom and sitting room curtains, and a wide range of wood veneers were used for the furniture and wall linings: Makore for the lounge; white ash burr for the dining room; mahogany for the writing room and cherry and orange woods for the tables; Nigerian cherry for the bed ends; Australian walnut for the floor of the cafe. The use of metals also took on a new look; polished aluminium was used, for example, for the horizontal baluster rails to the staircase.It was also used for the linings to the service doors between dining room and kitchen. Stainless steel tubular framing was used for the acid etched glass servery screen, while cellulose finished tubular steel chairs were provided for the cafe. *(42)*

Surprisingly, amidst all this excellence, not all the bedrooms had a bathroom en suite. Nevertheless, the total cost of £71,004 for the 40-bedroomed hotel represented good value for money. Unfortunately, the new *Midland Hotel* had a very short career. Barely six years of peace passed, before it spent nine years as a Royal Navy establishment. Following a poor recovery in peacetime after 1945, and the falling interest in Morecambe as a holiday resort, the hotel was sold for £50,000 in July 1952.

Thirty-four years were to pass before the next, and, as events proved, the last railway-owned resort hotel was built, at St Andrews. During that time, building costs had

Above: The grand staircase at the *Station Hotel*, Inverness. Pictures like this highlight the degree of craftsmanship and style incorporated into every aspect of the prestigious railway hotels. *Author's collection.*

PLANNING AND AMENITIES

Above: A very rare photograph indeed. Delegates from the British Institute for the Advancement of Science visit the *Zetland Hotel*, Saltburn by the Sea, in 1863. *Norman Bainbridge Collection.*

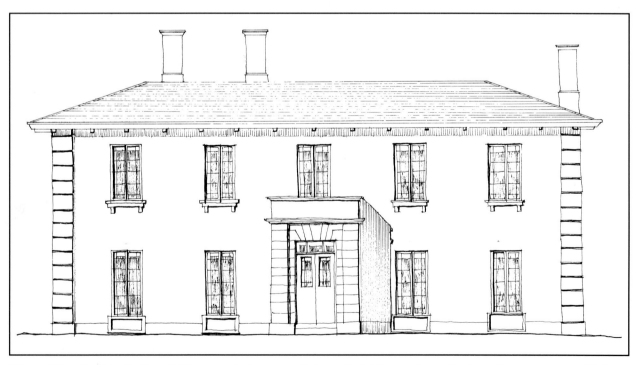

Above: Before the introduction of dining cars, trains stopped at selected stations where refreshment rooms were provided. the *Station Hotel*, Normanton, fulfilled this role, in its career. *Author's sketch.*

AN ILLUSTRATED HISTORY OF RAILWAY HOTELS

escalated many times. By way of comparison, the cost of the new Midland Hotel at Morecambe was approximately £1,775 per bedroom, whilst that of the new *Queens Hotel*, Leeds, opened in 1937 and provided with added amenities (including air conditioning) was £2,058 per bedroom. However, the cost of *The Old Course Hotel* at St. Andrews was approximately £8,750 per bedroom. Utilising a five-storey reinforced concrete frame and with the ends of the building clad in stone, a centre corridor layout was used to serve the bedrooms on each side. Each of the 80 bedrooms had its own bathroom and balcony.

More recently, the new resort hotels opened by the Great Southern Hotels group in Ireland at Torc (Killarney) in 1969, Rosslare in 1970 and Corrib in 1972, utilised flat-roofed two-storey steel-framed construction, and each provided approximately 100 bedrooms with bathrooms en suite.

Outbreaks of Fire

Fortunately, railway-owned hotels maintained a very high standard of alertness and only two serious outbreaks of fire are recorded. The first, involving the *Great Northern Hotel* in Leeds in 1906, originated in an adjacent warehouse. The cause of the second major fire, which destroyed the *Palace Hotel*, Aberdeen in 1941, has never been satisfactorily explained.

The risk of fire was an ever-present worry for managers. Open coal fires, candles and naked flames (albeit somewhat safer in the mid-1890s following the invention of the incandescent mantle) posed a constant hazard. To combat these risks, round-the-clock patrols by staff firemen were maintained. The use of 'clocking-in' points made sure that watchmen were maintaining due vigilance in all parts of a building. Staff were also trained in the use of water hydrants and hand-operated fire extinguishers. Owning companies were also at pains to familiarise their guests with fire escape routes and usually provided a plan showing the layout in each room.

The arrangement of insurance cover was a matter which hotel committees needed to review annually. The arrangement adopted for *The Welcome Hotel* at Stratford-on-Avon was typical. When purchased in 1931 the property was insured for £61,000, including £10,000 for the contents. The risk was spread between four insurance companies. Following purchase by the LMS, the cover was raised to £90,000 for the building and £10,000 for contents, the risk being spread among seven companies. The Royal, The Liverpool & London, The Sun Office, The North British Mercantile, The London & Lancashire, The Commercial Union, and the Alliance companies each taking an equal share and the LMS receiving 15% commission for the business. *(43)*

The circumstances concerned with the outbreaks of fire at Leeds and Aberdeen make horrific reading. *The Leeds & Yorkshire Mercury* for July 26 1906, recounted the events which had taken place during the night:

9.15pm: Fire alarm sounded at Messrs Hotham & Whiting's warehouse.
10pm: Sparks from the engulfed building carried by light wind onto the roof of the Great Northern Hotel. By this time fire brigades from Leeds, Bradford, Halifax and Wakefield were on the scene, but the appliances were unable to reach seat of the fire in the warehouse.

10.30pm: Hotel staff were using hoses from the building hydrant system to drench the roof with water, but the fire had gained a firm hold. Evacuation of the hotel was under way.
11pm: The greater part of the hotel's roof collapsed.
Midnight: The two uppermost 'Fireproof floors' collapsed.
1am: The Lancashire & Yorkshire Railway's Fire Brigade arrived from Newton Heath, Manchester, by special train. By this time the hotel's reduced height brought the 'top' of the building within the reach of the hose.
3am: Fire under control.
3.30am: Fire practically extinguished.

Two firemen working inside the hotel were badly burned by falling debris, and the scene at dawn was one of a partially 'gutted' building. Indeed, the *Leeds & Yorkshire Mercury* for July 26 described the hotel as "burned down". But it did survive, saved largely by its remaining fireproof floors and the destroyed upper floors were subsequently rebuilt to a less ornate design.

The fire which destroyed the *Palace Hotel*, Aberdeen, on the night of October 30/31 1941, was a disaster resulting in the death of six members of the staff. The night of terror started about 11.20 p.m. when a guest complained of smoke in his room. Unaware of the pending disaster, the assistant manager gave orders for the guest to be accommodated in another room. No sooner had this been accomplished than the automatic fire alarm sounded in the boot room and in the fire station. Prompt action by the fire brigade, who were on the scene within two minutes, and assistance from the staff, secured the rapid evacuation of the building. Even so, six of the 113 people in the building could not be accounted for. Great tongues of fire spread from the roof and windows of the upper floors, setting up a glare which could be seen for miles. In spite of the efforts and gallantry of about 100 firemen, the building was rapidly consumed. Later it was discovered that the six missing persons were female domestic staff, who had been trapped and overcome in their attic quarters. The cause of the fire was never conclusively proved and the cruel blow occurred only five months after the hotel had celebrated 50 years of railway ownership. Plans to rebuild the hotel in 1950 never came to fruition. *(44)*

Above: The Lancashire & Yorkshire Railway fire train, in the charge of a 2-4-2T, en route to a fire. It was with the help of the LYR's Manchester fire train and crew that the serious fire at the Great Northern Hotel, Leeds was brought under control on July 26 1906. *National Railway Museum.*

Chapter 3

MANAGEMENT AND STAFF
Management

When the railway companies entered the hotel business in 1838, they needed the consent of Parliament before they could build or purchase property. As their lines multiplied and the need for more hotels grew, companies found themselves with properties scattered in several and sometimes distant localities. The question arose as to whether it was wiser to rent-out an hotel to an approved tenant, to lease-out for a longer period, or to appoint a management company composed of railway directors and shareholders to keep a tighter rein on affairs. Later, hotel committees were appointed with the specific task of running hotels and undertaking the purchase or building of new properties. Ownership took two main forms; outright possession and shared ownership. The titles were sometimes owned jointly with another railway and sometimes with an individual or private company. Occasionally, railways lent money to finance non-railway owned hotel projects, simply with the intention of bringing traffic and trade into a given locality, where railway receipts would doubtless increase.

Not until the 1880s did the railway encounter hotel empires as large as their own. But the new hotel companies like Gordons, Spiers & Pond and Fredericks all sought railway business and tendered for hotel contracts from railways which chose not to pursue their own management. Unlike private hotel companies, the returns from railway-owned hotels were compounded in the general income of the company, though it is known that the lucrative income compared well with the 10-12% normally paid out by the principal hoteliers. *(1)*

Powers to Build or Purchase

Although the United Kingdom parliament expressly limited the railways to the business of carrying passengers and goods, it never held that the railways were barred from keeping hotels, provided that their actions were confirmed. Furthering the point, Sir William Towle said: "It seems only logical that if it is the duty of a railway to carry a passenger safely to his destination, it is equally its duty with its own resources to make due and reasonable provisions for his personal comfort, but experience teaches that this business cannot be limited to persons with railway tickets." (2) Once a company determined to build an hotel, the procedure was somewhat lengthy (up to 12 months) and required committee enquiries of both Houses, followed by three readings in each House before the necessary Local Act of Parliament was given the Royal Assent. European practice differed somewhat and on occasion resulted in legal battles, such as that which accompanied the case of the Paris-Lyons Railway's *Terminus Hotel* at Marseilles. Eventually, after much argument,

Above: An imposing portrait of the Midland Railway's Sir William Towle, undoubtedly the most famous personality in the story of Railway Hotel and Catering Services. *National Railway Museum.*

the superior court upheld the railway's right to own and manage the hotel. *(2)*

In the United Kingdom, hotel matters requiring approval were usually included with other business for submission under the heading of 'New Works' or 'Additional, Further, Various, or General Powers.' For an hotel about to be built, the local Act of Parliament granted the company power to "Erect or complete, furnish and maintain an hotel and appurtenances thereof at (named)".

For hotels already completed or purchased, local Acts granting retrospective powers "To hold, enjoy and maintain the hotels (named), now belonging to and held by them," were obtained. Alternatively, the prompt purchase of a desirable property on the open market was sometimes effected without applying for retrospective powers. The MR did this twice. First, in 1860 when a trustee of the company purchased the *Midland Hotel* at Derby and then transferred the property to the company by indenture in 1862, following the grant of powers to purchase, contained in the Midland Railway Additional Powers Act, 1861 *(3)*. Then, in 1890, controlling shares in the Adelphi Hotel Company, Liverpool, were purchased in the name of William Towle, manager of the Midland Hotels, pending the grant of powers to purchase contained in the Midland Railway Act of 1892. *(4)* Following the amalgamation of the railways in 1923, the four groups were subsequently given powers to build or subscribe to schemes virtually anywhere in the country. By the Great Western Railway Act of 1929, the Company was empowered to "Provide and maintain hotels and other like accommodation in any district in which a station on any railway owned and worked by them either singly or jointly with any other company, is situate and acquire by agreement and hold land for such purpose, and may furnish stock, equip, manage and conduct such hotels and accommodation and the business thereof and may subscribe to the fund of or advance money to any company, body or person providing, owning or leasing hotels in such districts." The only limitation of these powers was that development be restricted to a five mile radius of any station of the GWR, except by specific consent of the Minister of Transport. *(5)*

Like powers were granted to the LMS in its Act of 1933 *(6)* and to the SR and LNER in their Acts of 1947. *(7)* Nationalisation of the railways and the ensuing Transport Act of 1947 gave the British Transport Commission powers to build " .... in places in Great Britain where their passengers may require them to provide both for their passengers and for other persons, hotels, hostels and other living accommodation and places for refreshment." The 1962 Transport Act confirmed these powers but the 1968 Transport Act widened the powers to enable hotel development to take place anywhere in Great Britain and elsewhere. with prior consent of the Minister of Transport.

Leaseholds

Once powers had been obtained, it was time to decide if management of an hotel should remain firmly in the hands of the owning company, or should be offered either on the basis of an annual rent or lease to an approved tenant. When the railways were in their infancy it was usual to adopt the latter system of renting out or leasing. When the *Victoria Hotel* at Euston was opened during the last week in September 1839, Mr Robert Bacon, former steward

of the Athenaeum club, was appointed manager and Miss Fanny Heffer as housekeeper. For his services, the manager was to receive a quarter of the annual net profits after deducting £100 per annum for ground rent, 10% on the cost of furniture, plate, linen and the like and all rates and taxes. His staff was to total 24, including Miss Heffer who was to receive £45 per annum, ten maids, one cook who was to receive £25 per annum, and two assistants, four waiters and six porters. *(8)*

The letting of the *Euston Hotel*, on the opposite side of the road, proved more difficult. At the meeting of the London & Birmingham Railway Company held on August 25 1839, it was recorded that: "After repeated attempts by advertisement and other means to induce an offer for taking the lease on the hotel and that to undertake the furnishing, outfit and working of the hotel by the company, would require an outlay of funds never contemplated nor provided for," it was resolved to accept an offer made by Messrs Dethier and Vantini. The agreement was for a 21 year lease determinable by either party at the end of five or 12 years at the following annual rent: First year £600; second year £800; third year £1,000; fourth year £1,200; fifth-twelve year £1,600. The hotel opened for business in December 1839. *(8)*

Separate management of the twin hotels did not last long. On September 29 1841, the Hotel Committee resolved that Messrs Dethier & Vaniti: "should be charged with the exclusive management of both the Euston and Victoria hotels on a 21 year lease at £3,500 per annum." Four years before the lease was due to expire, the growth in rail traffic and the need for more accommodation prompted the hotel company to review development at its meeting held on July 10 1857. It was resolved that: "Since the formation of the London & North-Western Railway in 1846 and the absorption of the London & Birmingham Railway Company, the former has desired to extend hotel accommodation at London (Euston) for second and third class passengers. With this in view they had between 1850 and 1851 purchased various properties adjoining the *Victoria Hotel*. As a result, it is resolved to sell the interest of the proprietors of the London & Birmingham Railway Hotel Company to the LNWR for the sum of £55,000." With the ownership issue settled, the LNWR ran the *Euston* and *Victoria Hotels* and eventually linked the buildings in July 1881, with a new structure which bridged the road.

The twin hotels at Euston had been in business a little over ten years when the GWR obtained powers to build a new station and hotel at Paddington. It was written into the Great Western Railway Act of 1851 that: "It shall be lawful for the said company from time to time to demise the said hotel and premises when built for such rent and upon such terms and conditions as they shall think proper". The newly-built hotel, opened in June 1854, was let on a 42 year lease to a body known as the 'Great Western Royal Hotel Company', which was composed of company officers and shareholders. When the lease expired at Midsummer 1896, management was assumed by the GWR's Hotel & Refreshment Rooms Committee. *(9)*

Similar arrangements governed the running of the *Charing Cross* and *City Terminus* Hotels. Although formed as two companies, the Charing Cross Company and the Cannon Street Station and Railway Company respectively, both were formed largely from South Eastern Railway shareholders. The company which ran the hotel at Cannon

Street was named the City Terminus Hotel Company, and first met on January 25 1864, then, barely seven years later, was bought out by its parent, the South Eastern Railway. The company formed to build and manage the Grosvenor Hotel, at Victoria station (opened 1861) had the grand title The Grosvenor & West End Railway Terminus Hotel Company, and was absorbed by the LBSCR in 1893. *(10)*

Less orthodox was the way in which the *Queens Hotel*, Birmingham, was managed. When the hotel opened in May 1854, a Mr Scott was appointed as manager. Twenty months later he relinquished his appointment and successfully negotiated the lease of the hotel for a period of 14 years which was subsequently reviewed in 1868 for a further period of 14 years. The following year, owing to failing health, Mr Scott took on a Mr J. Williams as partner and in 1874 the lease was transferred to Mr Williams. In December 1881, Mr Williams surrendered the lease, and the owning company (the LNWR) regained both possession and

management. (11) Messrs Scott and Williams seem to have been capable and well-respected lessees, but the practice of continued letting frequently resulted in neglect and ensuing problems should re-possession by the owners become a necessity. Not far away, the *North Stafford Hotel* at Stoke-on-Trent had been let to various tenants from the time of its opening in 1848 until 1918. That year the NSR leased it to the Home Countries Public House Trust Ltd. (later Trust Houses Ltd.) for a 14 year term. In October 1931, shortly before the lease was due to expire, the LMS Hotel Committee found the hotel to be in lamentable condition. In the words of Arthur Towle, the Controller: "the worst hotel I have visited during the past 10-15 years." *(12)* The problems were remedied by the LMS and the hotel re-opened after modernisation and under their management in October 1933.

When the £11,900 contract for the building of the *Country Hotel*, Carlisle, was completed in 1857, the owning Lancashire & Carlisle Railway promptly let the hotel to

Pictured at the Hotel Managers' meeting held at the *Great Western Royal Hotel* in February 1962: Seated, from left — Messrs L.C. Pritchard, *Great Western Royal*; G.H .Watson, *Great Eastern*, Liverpool Street; J.W. Nelson, *Central*, Glasgow; A.H.L. Cuany (retired); E.J. Vacher, Chief Hotels Manager; F.G. Hole, General Manager; R.L.Turnbull, Hotels Superintendent (Scotland); J.W. Turpie, *Midland*, Manchester; W.S. Land, *Exchange*, Liverpool; V.P.R Woodcock, *Royal Station*, Newcastle upon Tyne; R.D. Duquenoy, *Midland*, Bradford; W. Wainwright, Turnberry. Middle row — J. Petre, *Royal Station*, York; F.H. Moulin, *Caledonian*, Edinburgh; D.S. McDermid, *Midland*, Derby; P.J. Harris, *Royal Victoria*, Sheffield; F.R. Collins, the *Adelphi*, Liverpool; A.J.C. Pardini, *Euston*; H.A. Berry, North British, Edinburgh; A. Hatfield, *Great Northern*, King's Cross; R.F. Jones, *Royal Station*, Hull; M.A. Curtis, *Tregenna Castle*, St Ives; J.F. McGuire, *Great Northern*, Peterborough; J.G. Reid, Lochalsh; E.O. Williams, *Station*, Perth. Back row — J.C. Reavley, *Welcombe*, Stratford-upon-Avon; W.J. Currie, *Station*, Inverness; R.J. Pearce, Dornoch; H.E. Irwin, *Zetland*, Saltburn; N.D. Blrrell, *Grand*, West Hartlepool; A.A. Short, *Queen's*, Birmingham; J.K.S Bannatyne, *Manor House*, Moretonhampstead; D. McLeod, *Station*, Dumfries; J. Forster, *St Enoch*, Glasgow; A.S. Bonthron, *Station*, Aberdeen; I.M. Jack, *Queen's*, Leeds; and A.E. Wilson, Relief Manager.

AN ILLUSTRATED HISTORY OF RAILWAY HOTELS

George Head, a local banker, on a 999 year lease at £60 per annum. The hotel was managed well both by Mr Head and the Country Hotel & Wine Company Ltd. which was formed to manage the business in 1864. The CR and the LNWR considered the repurchase of the hotel in November 1918, but declined. Ownership passed to Scottish & Newcastle breweries in 1970.

The First World War brought an abrupt end to the lease on the *Cannon Street Station Hotel*. Negotiated by the SR and C.R. Anson in 1931 for an 80 year term, commencing at £1,250 for the first year, £3,750 for the second year, and £5,000 for subsequent years, German fire bombs ended the hotel's career in 1941. *(13)*

Joint Participation

Outright ownership of a building without legal or financial ties was the aim of most developers, but some less-frequently encountered forms of ownership occurred. These included joint ownership by two or more railways, or by a railway and an individual, or between a railway and a private hotel company.

For example, when powers were obtained to build an hotel at Perth in 1865, the joint committee which administered the running of the station comprised two directors from each of the four companies using the station; the Scottish Central, the Scottish North Eastern, the North British and the Inverness & Perth Junction Railways. However, the powers to build an hotel were not implemented until 1888 and during that time the amalgamations of the SCR and SNER with the CR in 1865 and 1866 respectively and the absorption of the I&PJR into the Highland Railway in 1865, altered the distribution. Under the new order, the CR was represented by four directors, and the North British and Highland companies by two Directors each, who constituted the Perth Station Hotel Committee; it held its first meeting on February 16 1889. Following the opening of the hotel in June 1890, the joint committee sat until 1923 when its membership was altered to take into account the changes brought about by the amalgamation of the railways. The new committee comprised representatives of the LMS and LNER. In 1946, the LNER's share was bought by the other partner, for £25,000. *(14)*

Under the Lancashire & Yorkshire Railways (New Works and Additional Powers) Act of 1872 the company was authorised jointly with the LNWR to contribute towards the construction of an hotel, with all necessary buildings, approaches and conveniences at Preston. (15) Ten years passed until the new Park Hotel opened in 1882 and was administered by the LNWR's Hotel Committee, on behalf of the partners.

The railways also held stakes in the ownership of private and limited company hotels. The LNWR subscribed £5,000 to the Buxton Palace Hotel Ltd. (1868) and were represented on the Board until 1896, powers to do this having been gained in the LNWR (Additional Powers) Act of 1871. The same Company, under its Joint and Various Powers Act of 1877 was empowered to hold a two-thirds share in the ownership of the *Windermere Hotel* (1847). (16) At Keswick, the Cockermouth Keswick & Penrith Railway purchased a site for the construction of an hotel, in 1863. Three years later the company launched the Keswick Hotel Company, nominating their chairman in a joint role.

The imposing hotel, linked to the adjacent station by a covered way, opened in 1869. Ownership of the hotel company subsequently passed out of railway hands entirely.

Sometimes, more than one railway company participated in a hotel building venture. In 1859, the MSLR and the GNR each subscribed £2,500 to help float the Sheffield Hotel Company. The Duke of Norfolk was another subscriber, with £1,000. Amidst strong opposition to the choice of site, at the top of the carriage drive to the Victoria Station, a £10,000 contract for the building of the hotel, was awarded to Chadwick & Sons of Masborough in November 1860. In spite of its elevated and somewhat 'out of town' site the *Victoria Station Hotel* became a popular resort and in August 1875 played host to the Prince & Princess of Wales, during their visit to Sheffield. *(17)*

Financial involvement also extended to the lending of money to finance hotel projects. More holiday resorts with more hotels and more passenger traffic was business worth encouraging, but hoteliers new to the business often lacked the necessary financial backing and looked elsewhere for help. For example, the GWR came to the assistance of Cornish Hotels Ltd in 1891 with a £2,000 loan (repayable over 16 years) for the purchase of the *Atlantic Hotel*, at Newquay. *(18)* However, two years later, wary of competition on the doorstep of its own Tregenna Castle Hotel, the GWR declined taking a financial interest in the Carbis Bay Hotel Company. *(19)*

One of the largest financial involvements incurred by a railway company in the construction of a private hotel was that undertaken by the CR in the Gleneagles schemes. Promoted by a private company in 1913, the Caledonian Railway Order Confirmation Act of the same year authorised the company to construct, subscribe towards, or take shares or stocks in any company formed for carrying on such undertaking. The First World War curtailed work, by which time some £82,000 had been spent. Unable to resume work owing to insufficient resources, the Gleneagles Company's obligations were taken over by the CR, which considered the scheme to be a sound revenue-earning proposition. The company's action was confirmed in the Caledonian Railway Act of 1923 and by opening day (June 2 1924) more than £700,000 had been spent. By this time part and parcel of the CR, the original Gleneagles Company Ltd was wound up on November 15 1928.

Hotel Committees

As the railways grew and widened their interests to include steamship services and hotel keeping, the need for additional management committees arose. Unlike a private hotel company whose concern was the running of an hotel or a group of hotels, the Board of Directors of a railway company were not picked for their hotel-keeping abilities, nor had they sufficient time to devote to the day-to-day running of their hotels and catering services. The solution lay in the appointment of separate committees responsible for matters of policy and finance to the Board, but which had power to deal with the day-to-day affairs of hotel and catering management.

As the railways grew in experience, Sir William Towle declared that the earlier policy of leasing hotels to outsiders, was unsatisfactory, because of the different methods of management adopted and the impossibility of securing uniformity of quality of service to the customer. He therefore urged companies to establish their own catering departments and pointed out that the receipts from hotels and refreshment rooms should equal about one-tenth of the total passenger receipts and could be made profitable with the most moderately-priced, yet attractive fare. *(20)*

Hotel Committees usually met at monthly intervals or as required. Between six and a dozen members were appointed by the Board of Directors. Agendas covered many topics; to receive and approve managers' reports and balance sheets; to appoint staff and fix wages; to order foodstuffs, wines, spirits and fuel; to review tariffs; to order furniture and fittings; to consider complaints; and to generally carry out the every-day duties of management. The simple title 'Hotel Committee' was usually adopted. the LNWR's Hotel Committee first sat in 1860 and met at regular intervals until the Grouping of the railways in 1923. The NER's Hotel Committee first met in 1877, the GSWR's in 1880, the GNSR's and MSLR's in 1890, the CR's and NBR's in 1895, and the HR's in 1911.

Of the other railway hoteliers, the GER combined its hotel keeping with its shipping activities under a 'Traffic Continental Traffic and Hotel Committee' which first sat in March 1866. In 1881, in preparation for taking over the catering from the contractors, Spiers & Pond, the shipping and hotel activities were split and a separate Hotel Committee took up its duties. The LSWR likewise combined shipping and catering under a 'Docks, Steam Packet and Hotels Committee', established in 1900.

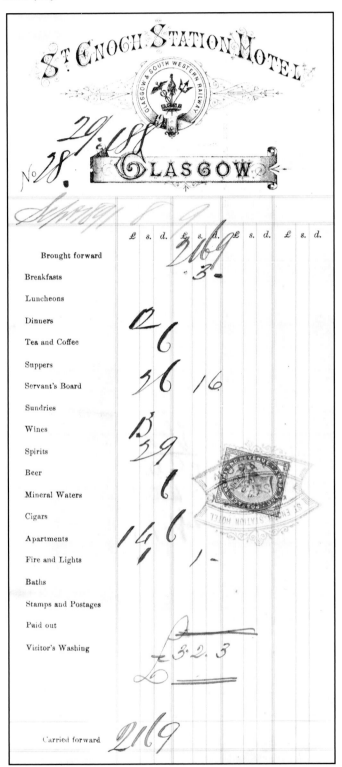

Above: An 1891 bill from the *St. Enoch Hotel*, Glasgow. *Author's Collection.*

Below: A bill from the *Station Hotel*, Inverness, circa 1900. *Author's collection.*

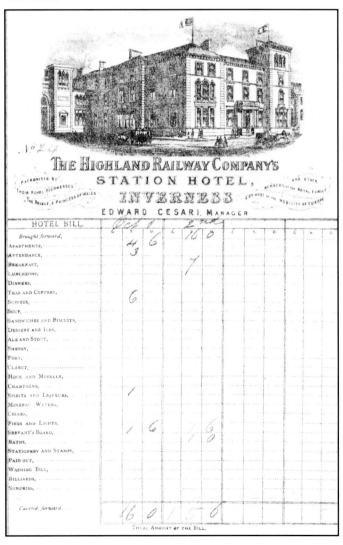

AN ILLUSTRATED HISTORY OF RAILWAY HOTELS

The GNR's 'Leeds and other Hotels Committee' sat in 1867 and was joined by the 'Kings Cross Hotel Committee' in 1874/5, which in turn was amalgamated into the Hotel Committee in 1876. The GWR's 'Refreshment Room Committee' was established in 1873 and was retitled the 'Hotels and Refreshment Rooms Committee' in 1881, but the Tregenna Castle Hotel had its minutes recorded separately during the years 1927-40. The MR whose catering and hotel service grew to occupy a position of pre-eminence in the industry, had several committees dealing with hotel building and management matters. The Leeds Hotel Committee sat from 1859-63. The St. Pancras Matters Committee sat from 1877-82. The Adelphi Hotel Extension Committee sat from 1910-16. Meanwhile a separate Hotel Committee was established in 1884.

Of the other hotel-owning railways, the small number of premises involved did not warrant the creation of a committee and the Board of Directors dealt with matters. The SER, which owned several hotels, departed from general practice by leasing most of its hotels to tenants. Following the amalgamation of the railways in 1923, the 'Big Four', the LMS, LNER, GWR, and SR each established Hotel Committees to take over the duties of their constituent companies. The headaches and duties of management varied little over the years. A century ago, the LNWR's Hotel Committee, meeting at Euston, recorded these notes concerning The *Lime Street Station Hotel* at Liverpool: *(21)* "19th November 1874. It was reported that hats and coats had been stolen from private and public sitting rooms, and it was resolved, to ask the detective police to be on the alert." The same month it was noted that a vegetable maid received sixteen shillings per week, a waiter fifty-two shillings, a housemaid ten shillings, and a housekeeper thirty shillings. In January 1875, a substantial gas bill was queried, but the manager reported that dark and foggy weather and the use of gas by workmen cleaning the hotel was responsible. Best coal ordered for the hotel cost eleven shillings and sixpence per ton.

In February 1875, the committee was given the task of disposing of visitors' luggage taken in lieu of cash settlement of accounts. At the same meeting it was reported that the second cook, who received £78 per annum had resigned because the work was too hard and the pay too little.

The *Central Station Hotel*, Glasgow, Committee minutes for March 1896, *(22)* revealed the customers had complained about the quality of the whisky. The Committee was told that Messrs. Greenless Bros. had supplied the whisky at seven shillings per gallon, less 5% proof strength. However, to make amends, the suppliers placed in bond 2,000 gallons of good quality whisky for the hotels forthcoming years consumption. During the First World War, embarrassment was caused to several hotel committees by their sale of German wines, and instructions were given to discreetly remove wines of German origin from sale.

The North Eastern Railways Hotel Committee, anxious to keep up-to-date with innovations and guests' safety, recorded these minutes at the turn of the century: *(23)*

"2 November, 1899. 336 electric light fittings purchased at £1 each for the Zetland Hotel, Saltburn.

9 March, 1905. Each room at the York & Newcastle Hotels

to be provided with a framed plan of the building showing the fire escapes, at a cost of 2/3d per plan.

9 December, 1909. Electric vacuum cleaner purchased at a cost of £220 for the Royal Station Hotel, York.

Dogs were frequent offenders, and their admission was usually a matter for the manager's discretion. Damage to a new carpet at the *Tregenna Castle Hotel* prompted the GWR to ban all dogs from the hotel in 1878. Similar problems encountered by the North Eastern Railway led to a ban from all its hotels as from October 1915.

The safeguarding of valuable items owned by guests and staff presented many problems. In 1917, when the second housekeeper at the *Euston Hotel* reported that jewellery valued at £74/13/6 had been stolen from her room, the LNWR decided that it was only partially responsible for safeguarding employees' valuables and made a contribution of £25 towards the loss.

Hotel Committees also had the task of recording the circumstances of deaths and accidents which occurred among guests. After hearing about a spate of thefts and bad debts at the *Charing Cross Hotel* in 1929, the SR's Hotel Committee was told that on Christmas Eve of the last year a guest had sustained fatal injuries after falling from the first floor landing into the hall below. On a happier note, committees sometimes authorised a visit abroad for a chief officer. In 1929, LMS Hotels Controller Arthur Towle was

Above: Afternoon tea at the *Euston Hotel*, circa 1912. *National Railway Museum*.

sent to Rome as a delegate to the International Hotel Alliance. In 1934, with plans for a new hotel at Leeds in mind, he visited New York, Quebec, Montreal and Toronto. *(24)*

Companies new to the hotel trade looked to their more experienced neighbours for help and advice. The GNSR, which became a hotelier in 1890 with its purchase and modernisation of the *Aberdeen Palace Hotel*, formed an Hotel Committee in December 1890. One of its first tasks was to send two representatives to Glasgow: "To get particulars of the mode of book keeping and generally the method of conducting the business of the hotels under the control of the railway companies there." They duly reported back in January 1891 and staff were engaged in readiness for reopening in August of that year. Miss McKilliam, who was appointed manager in December 1890, at a salary of £120 per annum, was paid £30 less than the chef, but her salary was subsequently raised to £350. The housekeeper was engaged at £45 per annum, the book keeper at £40 and pages in uniform received six shillings per week. For the benefit of guests, salmon fishing on the Dee was rented at £60 per annum on a five year lease.

The Company had a promising start, but was soon accused of pursuing unfair business practice. The trouble focussed on the hotels 'Boot-black' who was detailed to advertise the hotel on the platforms at the Aberdeen joint station. On September 2 1891, Mr Wieland, Secretary of the NBR, Mr Forshaw of the *Imperial Hotel* and Mr Scott of The *Douglas Hotel*, wrote jointly, asking that the *Palace Hotels'* 'Boots' be excluded form the platform of the joint station, or, alternatively, that all 'Boots' be admitted equally. Unruffled, W.M. Moffat, Secretary of the GNSR replied: "We understand you do not complain that the servants of your hotel have had any privileges hitherto by them within the joint station withdrawn or curtailed. But to extend the privileges further and admit your servants within the barrier would unquestionably lead to inconvenience and confusion. Whilst therefore this could not be allowed I am to say that no undue influence shall be used to get any of the travelling public to go to the Palace Hotel in preference to the other hotels in the city and instructions to that effect have been given and will be rigidly enforced." (25)

As might be expected, the letter was coldly received and hostilities continued until 1896, when an amicable settlement was reached, admitting all Boot-blacks equally.

Hotel Controllers

At a time when French and German names dominated the hotel industry, it was rare for an English family to rise to a position of importance. However, one of the most respected families in the business, and one which devoted a little over 150 years' service to the hotel and catering industry were the Towles. Sir William Towle (1849-1929) was raised in the territory of the MR at Twyford, near Derby. As a boy of 15 years, he was appointed as an assistant at the *Midland Hotel* at Derby. At the age 22 he was appointed Manager and also took control of the Derby refreshment rooms, following the retirement of Mr F.H. Plock. *(26)* In 1884, he was given the job of reorganising the management of the *Midland Grand Hotel* at St. Pancras. The following year he took charge of the *Queens Hotel* at Leeds. William Towle proved that railway hotels could be not only profitable undertakings but also a vital component

in the affairs of its surrounding community. His empire grew. The *Midland Hotel*, Bradford, opened in 1890; the *Heysham Towers Hotel* was purchased in 1896; the *Queen's Hotel*, Leeds, was extended in 1898; the *Queen's Hotel*, Keighley, was purchased in 1902; the *Midland Hotel*, Manchester, opened in 1903 and his last and biggest venture, the rebuilding of the *Adelphi Hotel*, Liverpool, was completed in the year of his retirement, 1914. He also improved the image of the station refreshment room, where the staple commodity had been beer and stale buns 'old enough to speak for themselves' whilst the soup was probably best described as 'warm water stirred with a candle' New fare included tea, coffee, and other attractive refreshments offered at lower prices than the intoxicants. He also introduced luncheon baskets and his experience was called on in the First World War when he sat on the Central Liquor Traffic Control Board, which dealt with the drink problem in the munitions and transport industries.

When the Board of Directors of the MR learned of William Towle's desire to retire, Company Chairman G. Murray Smith, observed "We regret to lose Mr Towle's services which have been of the very greatest value to the Midland Company, and have placed this company in the premier position among railways in the excellence of its hotels, dining cars and refreshment rooms. Mr Towle has, I feel sure, the best wishes of us all for a long life in which to enjoy his well earned rest." *(27)*

His sons, Lt. Col. Sir Francis William Towle (1876-1951) and Arthur Edward Towle (1878-1949) had both entered the service of the MR in 1896. Two years later they were appointed as Joint Assistant Managers of the Company's Hotels, under their father, and later succeeded him as Joint Managers in 1914. *(28)* The parting of the ways came in 1916 when Francis Towle became Controller of the Army & Navy Canteen Board. Later he re-partnered his brother for a brief spell and then became Managing Director of Gordon Hotels Ltd, in 1921. Between 1928 and 1930 he took part in the planning of the Dorchester and became its resident director. In 1921 he became an innovator, by staging the first big show (variety entertainment and singers) at an hotel - the Metropole. He believed in organised technical education for hotel staff and sat on the National Council for Hotel & Catering Education, which sought to provide facilities throughout the country at colleges and hotel schools. In 1949, he became first President of the Hotel & Catering Institute and, at the time of his death in 1951, 85 training establishments were in existence.

William Towle and his elder son were among the first members of the hotel and catering profession to receive knighthoods. Francis was thus honoured in 1919 and his father in 1920. This was in stark contrast to the recognition which Frederick Gordon (1834-1904) received, a six line obituary notice in The Times, beneath that of an obscure Major in the Indian Army. Meanwhile, Arthur Towle had become Director at the Ministry of Food in 1917 and in 1919-20 acted as Controller of Hotels for the Peace Conference in Paris. Returning to the MR in 1920 he became Manager of its hotel and catering services and five years later gained the same appointment with the newly created LMS. Now master of the largest group of hotels in Europe, he strove to keep the LMS in the forefront of the industry. He guided the rebuilding of the *Midland Hotel*, Morecambe, the new Queens Hotel, Leeds and, but for the second World War he would have implemented plans for a

Mr. A. E. Towle.   Mr. W. Towle.   Mr. F. W. Towle.

Above: William Towle and his sons Authur and Frederick, as featured in *The Railway Gazette*, in 1914.

new hotel at Euston. Much of the success which the Towle family achieved in their approach to hotel management lay in the personal touch, or, as the *Railway Magazine* termed it, "personality of direction". The Midland Railway's principal hotels were visited weekly, and the others a little less frequently, by William Towle or by his sons in their capacity as joint assistant managers. This allowed problems to be dealt with on the spot and often removed the need for correspondence. *(29)*

The method of servicing their hotels also proved efficient and was copied by other companies. The larger hotels were manned by a manager and a secretary, the former being in general charge and responsible for discipline, staff management and the reception of visitors, and the latter for business matters and the hotel licence where a resident licensee was insisted upon.

Headquarters staff numbered about 55 with 25 located at St. Pancras in the printing, clerical and stores department, and 30 at Derby who dealt with accounts. Supplies were purchased on the open market and selected by the individual managers. The stocking of the wine cellars at Derby and the selection and blending of the tea and coffee came under William Towle's personal scrutiny. The company's dining cars and refreshment rooms were serviced by the nearest convenient *Midland Hotel*, or by arrangement with other companies.

Arthur Towle perpetuated most of the well-proven Midland practices throughout his twenty years of service as Controller of the LMSR's hotels.

In due reward for their Controllers undoubted ability in hotel refreshment room and restaurant car management, the MR made regular salary reviews. Under terms agreed in January 1893, Mr and Mrs William Towle received a basic salary of £500 and a commission of 4% on profits calculated thus: "From the gross receipts from all sources, at each year ending 31st December, shall be deducted 4% on £80,000, being the estimated value of all the hard furniture, plate and machinery, to form a renewal fund for the same, cost of provisions, beer, wines, spirits, cigars consumed, salaries

and wages paid, gas, electric lighting, water, rates and taxes, fuel, stores, repairs of plant and buildings, renewals and all soft furniture, bedding, curtains, glass and perishable articles, painting, papering and decorating, carriage of all goods over Midland and other companies lines, except the distribution of stores etc., over the Midland system which are to be carried free."

The following gives effect to the proposed arrangement for 1893:

Gross profits as per balance sheet	£55,213.11. 6
* Add Manager's salary	£1,500. 0. 0
Add Capital expenditure out of revenue	£2,070.19. 7
Add renewals out of revenue	£1,929. 4. 9
Total	£60,713.15.10
Deduct: Midland Co's proportion of stores wines and carriage of goods and parcels and depreciation at 4% = £3200	£3180.16.1 £6,380.16. 1
Profits on which commission would be payable	£54,332.19. 9
Commission on this amount : plus salary of £500	£2173. 6. 5. £2,673. 6. 5.

* Mr. & Mrs. Towle earlier received a fixed salary of £2,000. the new arrangement which provided for a salary of £500 plus commission therefore required the addition of £1,500 to the calculation. *(30)*

In contrast to the £2,673 which Mr and Mrs Towle received for their managerial services in 1893, how did the Hotel Controllers of the other hotel owning railways fare? In 1904, the NER re-organised its hotel and refreshment room services and invited applications for the appointment of a General Superintendent. S.C. Howard, formerly Manager of the *Grand Hotel*, Brighton, was declared the successful applicant and took up the appointment in December 1904 at a commencing salary of £800 per annum without any

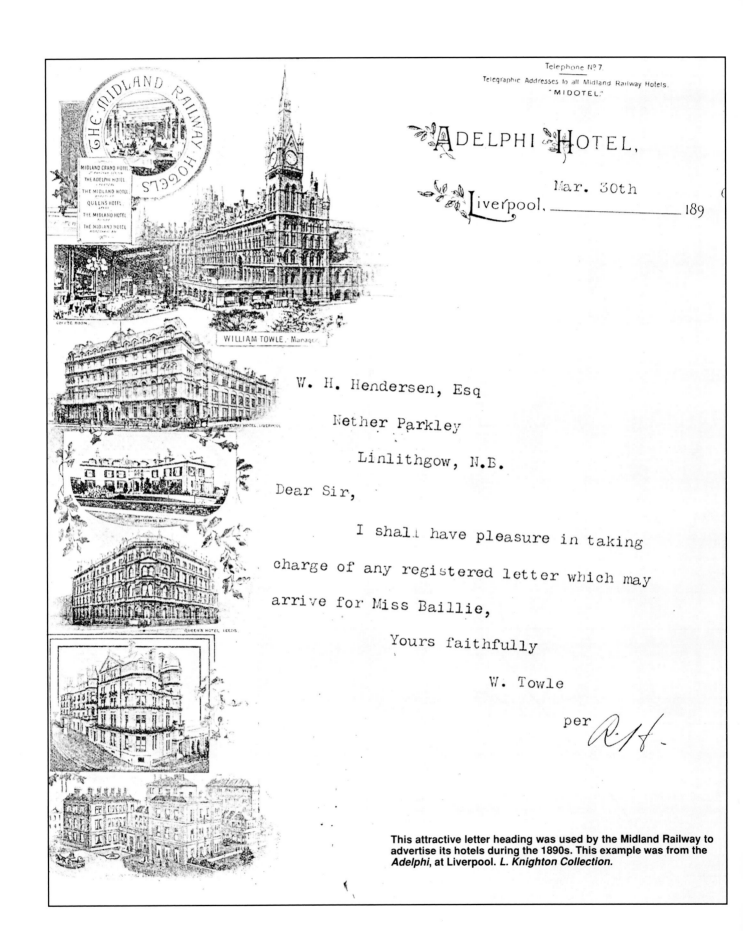

ADELPHI HOTEL,

Liverpool, _____ Mar. 30th _____ 189

WILLIAM TOWLE, Manager.

W. H. Hendersen, Esq

Nether Parkley

Linlithgow, N.B.

Dear Sir,

I shall have pleasure in taking charge of any registered letter which may arrive for Miss Baillie,

Yours faithfully

W. Towle

per R.H.

This attractive letter heading was used by the Midland Railway to advertise its hotels during the 1890s. This example was from the *Adelphi*, at Liverpool. *L. Knighton Collection*.

commission. Mr. Howard resigned, barely two years later and his successor, H. Gent commenced on a reduced salary of £700 per annum. The NER then had five hotels, compared with the MR's nine. In 1914, the Highland Railway, which owned five hotels and shared the running of the *Perth Station Hotel* with the NBR, paid its Hotel Manager, Mr. H.H. Ward, a fixed salary (without any commission) of £620 per annum. *(32)*

Constructions Committees

Instead of leaving matters in the hands of the Board of Directors, the construction of a new hotel was sometimes placed under the supervision of a separate committee. The Queens Hotel, Leeds, the MR's first venture into hotel building and one of the earliest and largest hotels in the provinces, was supervised by the Leeds Hotel Committee, which sat from 1859 until completion of work in January 1863. The running of the hotel was then placed in the hands of the Board until 1884, when a separate Hotel Committee was established. *(33)* Alternatively, hotel committees which had been established to supervise construction, later carried on to manage the completed building. One of the most illuminating sets of minutes concerning the building and management of a large hotel in the closing years of the 19th century are those dealing with the *North British Hotel*, Edinburgh. *(34)*

Powers to build an hotel at the Waverley station were obtained in the North British Railway Act of 1894 and on April 25 1895 the Board appointed an Hotel Committee of 11 members (Messrs. Boase, Carlow, Creighton, Grierson, Jordan, Pine, Parker Smith, Robertson, Robertson, Weymss and Wieland) to direct the work. The dominating personality was George Bradley Wieland (1838-1905), who had begun his career in the Managers Department of the LNWR, before moving to the NBR in 1873. He spent 32 years with the company, 19 years as Secretary, nine years as Director, and the final four years as Chairman. Not a well-liked man in Edinburgh circles, he had removed John Connacher, said to have been the best General Manager, the Company ever had, unseated the Chairman (the Marquis of Tweedale) and the Vice Chairman (Sir Charles Tennant) to make way for his own rise to power. Although hotel building was a new venture for the company, Weiland had earlier steered two costly projects, the Tay Bridge and the Forth Bridge to completion.

At the outset, some caution was exercised by the committee. William Hamilton Beattie (1843-98) a well known local architect, was chosen to design the hotel, following a limited competition in which six architects had been invited to submit sketches. But before confirming his appointment, the committee wrote to the NER, CR, and GSWR to enquire about architects remuneration in the design and construction of hotels. This settled, the MR's William Towle was consulted on several aspects of hotel design and Messrs. Carlow, Grierson, Jordan, the General Manager (John Connacher) and the architect were despatched to Paris, Brussels and Amsterdam to glean information about continental hotel design and management. By mid-November 1895 they reported that: "They had got some useful hints, but on the whole were satisfied that what they saw was no improvement on the hotels in this country." A visit to the new Gordon Hotel, the *Metropole* at Brighton, had also been planned, but the committee were rebuffed by the Gordon management, who feared that ideas might be 'poached.'

With preliminaries settled, the architect's plans were approved on November 22 and subsequently agreed by the Edinburgh Dean of Guild Court. During the following seven years, monthly and sometimes more frequent mettings of the committee were held to receive the architect's progress reports, appoint contractors and suppliers, and approve payments for works completed. The task ahead was formidable. With an average of 400 men at work and several expensive variations approved, it was likely that the cost would escalate beyond the £500,000 envisaged. But the hotel was a prestige job, occupying the only building plot on the south side of East Princes Street. Furthermore, it was the company's answer to the rival Princes Street Station Hotel being planned by the CR, at the western end of the famous street. The most significant variations approved were the substitution of fire resistant construction for all floors and the roof, and the omission of office space, apart from a limited amount at the upper mezzanine level and the shops on the east and west sides of the building.

The minutes reveal the committees varied trains of thought, about a whole range of issues. Wieland, the dandy and connoisseur of wines and tobacco, was anxious to see the hotel amply-stocked in advance of opening. As early as January 1898, nearly five years before the opening of the hotel, a letter was sent to the *Central Station Hotel*, Glasgow, an establishment of similar size, to enquire how much wine was consumed annually. When it was learned that three to four thousand quarts were used, Wieland was instructed to buy desirable wines and champagne on terms to be approved by the Committee. Following the architect's untimely death in 1898, matters got out of hand, when his associate Scott, omitted to gain Dean of Guild Court approval to alterations in the hotel's public house layout, before the work started. A rebuke and a £25 fine were duly recorded.

Management of the hotel had not been resolved, but enquiries from several companies, including Spiers & Pond, prompted the company to declare its intention to keep control of the building. Accordingly, applications were invited for the appointment of manager. Again the advice of William Towle, was sought and 20 applicants were short-listed for interview. F.J. Burcher, assistant manager at the *Carlton Hotel*, London, was declared the successful applicant in February 1902 and his salary fixed at £1,000 per annum. Burcher, aged 36 years, had assisted in the opening of the Carlton in 1899 for none other than Cesar Ritz (of the *Ritz Hotel* fame) and a reference from a leading name in the hotel industry no doubt carried due weight.

With the manager appointed, a licence for the hotel was applied for and promptly received in April 1902. In July, Burcher was sent on a continental visit to gain up-to-date experienced for his new managerial role. Other senior staff appointments were made including the head chef who received £364 per annum and the head housekeeper who received £120. The head hall porter, at the lower end of the scale, received twenty shillings per week.

Meanwhile anxiety was expressed at the ever-increasing cost of the hotel, now standing at over half-a-million pounds. Savings were suggested, which included the omission of as much sculptural detail as possible. In fact, the remaining work was limited to the series of masks at fourth floor level and four figures on the dormers. A necessity still required, was a good quality clock for the tower, and Messrs. Hamilton and Inches duly supplied a suitable timepiece at a cost of £168. To supplement the water supply, a separate bore hole, 30ft deep, beneath the tower was sunk. The hotel's laundry was sited not within the building, but in separate premises at Joppa. A separate hairdressing department was provided in the hotel and let to a Mr. Collins at £3/5/6 per week.

The Hotel Committee did not agree every request submitted to it. For example, permission was refused for the main contractor, sub contractor and suppliers to place advertising boards on the facades of the nearly-completed building. It was resolved not to provide telephone extensions into the bedrooms and erect a separate roof level dormitory for female staff. Plans for a piggery (to use the kitchen waste) and a hot house were postponed.

Naming and advertising the new hotel was the subject of much consideration. First named the *Waverley Station Hotel*, the title was soon amended to the *North British Station Hotel*. Advertisements were placed in the daily newspapers, Bradshaws guide, the ABC guide, Bradshaw's Manchester Guide, the Architect and Contract Reporter, and the Cairo and Egypt travel journal. Advertisements were also placed in the East Coast Joint stock trains and on the Atlantic passenger liners. An annual order for 20,000 sheets of notepaper and envelopes at 12/6 per thousand was placed with the stationer, to be taken as required. A contract was also placed for cleaning of the hotel's 1,000 windows. Insurance cover was taken out for the buildings, furnishings and other contents, including wines. Even after opening day on October 16 1902, many sundry items were still being ordered; more bedroom suites at £23.50 for single and £33 for double suites, fittings for the pneumatic tube vacuum cleaner system, rubber mats for the Van Kannel (revolving) doors, curtain rails and fittings, linen and crockery.

For the Hotel Committee, the emphasis turned to the everyday running of the hotel. The manager was instructed to keep a finance book and report thereon to the committee as required. A steady succession of embarrassing but not unusual situations were reported; claims for stolen luggage and jewellery, bad debts and deaths of visitors. The company also found itself in a compromising situation when the manager was summonsed in the sum of £500 by the reception clerk for slander and defamation of character. A cloud had developed around Mr. Burcher and although the company defended his actions, he resigned his appointment and was succeeded by Mr. Lord, at the same salary, on September 7 1905. Despite a rather shaky start, with working losses of £1,481 and £1,676 in 1903 and 1904 respectively, business improved and in 1906 17,484 visitors, and 349 visitors' servants used the hotel, with an average stay of 1.7 days each.

The 'Big Four' Period: 1923-1947

The system of management by separate hotel committees, which had been introduced by the LNWR in 1860, and subsequently adopted by most of the other companies, remained basically unchanged until the Grouping in 1923. That year, nearly 100 hotels, owned by 19 English, Scottish and Welsh Companies were redistributed among the new 'Big Four' companies, the LMS, LNER, GWR, and SR. In addition, some ten Hotel Superintendents or Controllers

found themselves in need of reappointment. Only the GWR escaped from the general upheaval. Here, as in many other aspects of its operations, the old order prevailed; even so, two small hotels, formerly owned by the Taff Vale Railway, were added to stock.

The LMS adopted an interim solution to its reorganisation problems by appointing four Area Controllers. Arthur Towle, former Controller of the Midland's hotels, was to be in charge of the former MR hotels and the new Gleneagles Hotel; S.W. Burleigh, Manager of the LNWR's hotels remained in charge of the former LNWR hotels between Euston & Crewe; G. O'Brian Hamilton took charge of the hotels between Crewe and Carlisle and those in Ireland; J.H. Thomas looked after his former charges in the old GSWR territory, while the other hotels in Scotland were to come under the General Manager for Scotland. Two years later, and effective from January 1 1925, Arthur Towle was officially designated Controller of LMS Hotel Services, with his headquarters in London. He was given three Assistant Controllers, one for the South of England, one for the North of England and one for Scotland. (35) As Controller, Arthur Towle assumed a position of strength and was responsible to the Chairman of the Board of Directors of the LMS. To deal with the day-to-day problems of management, the Hotels Committee met at regular intervals and was chaired by Sir Edwin F. Stockton.

The LNER viewed its responsibilities in a rather different light. Instead of giving overall control to one man, three areas were established; the Southern Area, North Eastern Area and Scottish Area, each with an Hotels Superintendent. However, instead of being responsible to the Chairman of the company, they were subordinated to their respective Regional General Managers. (36)

The SR, the smallest of the 'Big Four' companies, continued the policy of its constituents by placing the management of most of its hotels in the hands of contractors. This was carried out by the invitations of tenders. Although the *Charing Cross Hotel*, the nearby Craven Hotel and the South Eastern Hotel at Deal were kept under the control of the company and its Hotel Committee, the remaining hotels and refreshment room services were managed by several well known contractors. Bertram & Co. were successful, for example, in obtaining the contract for the Central section and signed a seven year contract, effective from the January 1 1927. The services included were the management of the *London and Paris Hotel* at Newhaven and catering on the Newhaven-Dieppe service.

In May 1930, Frederick Hotels Ltd, in competition with Gordon hotels Ltd, and Spiers & Pond , were successful in obtaining the contract for the Eastern & Western sections. Refreshment rooms, some of the refreshment cars on the Western Sections and the management of the *Junction Hotel* at Eastleigh were included. The terms agreed were 15% of the gross receipts, calculated on a minimum of £76,000 per annum.

Three years earlier, Spiers & Pond entered into a separate agreement to manage the Freemasons Arms public house at Lymington, a property which the SR had inherited from the LSWR. Spiers & Pond undertook to provide staff, stock and account for all receipts and outgoings and receive an allowance of 10/6 per month as a stocktaking fee and 5% upon the gross receipts to cover management and overhead charges. (37)

Above: BTH Chairman Frank Hole, and Chief Hotels Manager Etienne Vacher, at Mr Vacher's retirement presentation, in 1965. *Author's collection.*

Nationalisation of the Railways: 1948

The 'end of the road' for Britain's privately-owned railways came at the end of 1947, when under the provisions of the Transport Act, the railways and their assets passed into state ownership. The Act provided for a public authority known as the British Transport Commission, which was presided over by a Chairman and not less than four or more than eight paid members, all appointed by the Minister of Transport. To assist the Commission in the discharge of its functions five 'Executives' were established; the Railway Executive, the Docks & Inland Waterways Executive, the Road Transport Executive, the London Executive, and last but not least, the Hotels Executive.

Meanwhile, Frank Hole who had entered the service of the LMS in 1934 as Hotels Accountant and subsequently succeeded Arthur Towle as Controller of the LMS Hotel Services on January 1 1945, upon the latter's retirement, was appointed a full time member of the Hotels Executive. The next change came in 1953, when under the provisions of the Transport Act of that year, the Railway Executive was abolished. In its place, the British Transport Commission established, amongst other things, the British Transport Hotels & Catering Services with Frank Hole as General Manager. Five years later, in December 1958, a new Board of Management was established with Mr. Hole as Chairman, assisted by E.K. Portman-Dixon (Chief of Restaurant Cars and Refreshment Rooms); Etienne Vacher (Chief Hotels Manager); W. Harris Burland (Director of Accounts and Statistics BTC) and T.H. Baker as Secretary. *(38)*

The next change was in 1962, when the Transport Act abolished the British Transport Commission and established

in its place four public authorities, referred to as the British Railways Board, the British Transport Docks Board, the British Waterways Board and the London Transport Board. Under the provisions of the Act: "the Commission shall, as soon as practical, arrange for the Commission's hotels to be transferred to a subsidiary" - in effect an Hotel Company, which was to be a wholly-owned subsidiary of the British Railways Board. The new company, which came into being in 1963, was named British Transport Hotels Ltd, with Frank Hole as its first General Manager. Subsequent changes, announced at the Board meeting held in April 1969, provided for Frank Hole's title to be changed to Managing Director. George Hill and Ian Jack were appointed Directors at the same meeting. George Hill succeeded Frank Hole as Managing Director upon the latter's retirement on December 31 1969.

In November 1974, George Hill was appointed both Chairman and Managing Director. Fifteen Months later the responsibilities were separated, with H.L. Farrimond and Ian Jack becoming Chairman and Managing Director respectively. Succeeding Chairmen were R.L.E. (later Sir Robert) Lawrence, March-December, 1978, and J.M.W. Bosworth who continued in that capacity pending the disposal of British Transport Hotel's remaining assets. Peter Land succeeded Ian Jack in September, 1978, and held the appointment until April 1983, by which time the greater part of the Company's assets had been sold.

No review of the railway hotels period in public ownership would be complete without some reference to other people who served on the Board. Perhaps the most interesting was Col. Sir Louis Gluckstein, QC. He served with distinction in both World Wars, sat on the board of

Deputies of British Jews, was a Board member of the Albert Hall and was Chairman of the Army Kinema Corporation. Dame Isobel Graham Bryce, OBE was an Industrial Psychologist and a one-time member of the General Nursing Council. She and Sir Louis served as British Transport Hotels Directors from 1962 to 1978. Sir Alexander Glen, who was Deputy Chairman from 1978 to 1983, earlier had adventures as an Arctic explorer and served in the Mediterranean during the Second World War, before becoming Chairman of the British Tourist Authority from 1969 to 1977. Last, but by no means least among Board members, was the well-known hotelier Charles Forte who served from 1962 to 1966.

Profitability

Considering the speculative element in the choice of locations for the first railway hotels, surprisingly few schemes failed. The *Royal Hotel*, Slough, opened by the GWR in 1841, was expected to attract patronage from travellers alighting for nearby Windsor and Eton. In the event, business was poor and the hotel was sold; it became a school. The same fate befell the *Victoria Station Hotel*, Colchester; it opened in 1843 but by 1850 the building had found a new use as the Essex Hall Asylum.

Plans made by Peter Fleetwood Hesketh and the Preston & Wyre Railway for a new port (to be called Fleetwood) and sea route, to link London and Northern Ireland, Western Scotland and the Isle of Man, developed slowly. The North Euston Hotel, opened in 1841 as part of the overall development, was forced to close in 1859 and became a War Office School of Musketry. By the 1890s, Fleetwood's fortunes as a port and resort had improved sufficiently to warrant the *North Euston Hotel* reopening. Thomas Savin, of Oswestry, had ambitious plans for developing Cardigan Bay with a series of seaside resorts, equipped with ample hotel accommodation and served by the Cambrian Railway, which in turn would link the region to the rest of the railway network. In 1866, the financial collapse of Overend & Gurney's great discount house in London brought Savin's plans to an equally abrupt end. *(39)* On a brighter note, most hotel building ventures had a good start. When the Great Western Royal Hotel Company, of which Brunel was a director and shortly afterwards chairman, completed its first half year in business, a 10% dividend was declared. *(40)*

As the railway companies became more experienced in hotel management, they also became more reticent when the subject of profitability happened to be raised by enquiring shareholders. It was held, perhaps rightly, that in the hotly competitive business of hotel management, as little as possible ought to be given away. On the other hand, hotel companies were obliged to publish at least some information, if only declaration of dividends. When the MR shareholders were debating their Directors' recommendation to proceed with the building of the *Midland Grand Hotel* at St. Pancras in 1869, their Chairman, W.E. Hutchinson, was able to point out by way of comparison that the hotel company which ran the *Grosvenor Hotel* at Victoria Station was paying a dividend of 8% and the company which ran the *Charing Cross Hotel* were paying 10%. *(41)* But no information of this nature was disclosed about the Midland's hotels. When a shareholder tried to extract some figures at the half-yearly

meeting in August, 1889, he was told that the hotel paid, but that the Chairman was not prepared to disclose any details on their working and management.

Sir William Towle, in true partisan fashion, gave due emphasis to this point when he recommended that: "the system of inter-departmental accounts will enable the balance sheet to be prepared, without disclosing any of the details of working, which it is obvious in the interests of the company should not be printed in the formal accounts presented to shareholders." *(42)* The LNWR's subscription of £5,000 to the Buxton Palace Hotel Company Ltd proved to be a consistently reliable investment, with a 10% dividend declared during most of the railway's period of representation on the Board 1868-96. *(47)*

Some of the earlier secretiveness which obscured the financial aspects of the railway hotel and catering activities from public gaze was lifted in March 1914, by the publication of a detailed article which appeared in The Railway News. The previous year 23 railway companies in England, Scotland, Wales and Ireland controlled 107 hotels having a total capital cost of nearly £8m. Receipts totalled £3,155,385 and expenses to be deducted totalled £2,601,970, leaving a net profit of £553,415. Income derived from rented hotels added a further £35,377.

By the 1890s, a steadily increasing demand for accommodation frequently found the railways as the owners of profitable, but undersized hotels. Sometimes, additional bedrooms could be added, but the acquisition of larger premises or rebuilding was better in the longer term. The Great North of Scotland Railway bought the *Palace Hotel,* Aberdeen, in 1890, and to alleviate the problem of increasing demand added two more storeys in 1894 and then purchased a second hotel in the City, the *Station Hotel,* in 1910 *(43)*.

The North Eastern Railway exercised considerable caution when it decided that the time had come to find a larger hotel in West Hartlepool. Its first acquisition, The Royal Hotel, was sold in 1913. Before this, 12 months of negotiations took place with Mr Duxbury, the builder and owner of the larger Grand Hotel. Opened in 1901 at a cost of £15,000, the North Eastern Railway bought the Grand as a going concern for £27,036 in January 1912, but insisted that Mr Duxbury should sign a clause agreeing not to establish himself in competition elsewhere in West Hartlepool. *(44)* The acquisition of the Grand proved to be a sound move and the hotel eventually became Lot No.10 in the sale of British Transport Hotels in 1982.

The purchase of a dwelling house for conversion into a holiday hotel was a gamble which the GWR undertook twice, and proved to be highly profitable ventures. The Tregenna Castle at St. Ives was first taken on lease in 1878 and then purchased in 1895. *(45)* When Lord Hambleton's North Bovey Manor, Moretonhampstead, came on the market in 1929 the railway acquired it for £14,500, including 200 acres of land. £2,900 was spent on new bathrooms, £5,207 on furniture from Maples, and £6,650 on an 18-hole golf course to the design of Mr Abercromby. *(46)*

Following the First World War a few more hotels were added to the railway's company's stock. The Great Eastern Railway bought the magnificent *Felix Hotel* in June, 1920, for £150,000 *(48)* and the Gleneagles scheme, the most ambitious holiday hotel ever built, was completed in June 1924.

Of the 107 hotels listed in 1914, all but 15, which were

owned by the Irish companies, were redistributed amongst the 'Big Four' new companies created at the Grouping of 1923. The LMS was the largest of the four with 37 hotels, followed by the LNER with 32, the Southern with 12 and the GWR with 11 hotels. In spite of the wartime controls, reorganisation and uncertainties during the 1920s profits remained at a satisfactory level. In 1925, LMS hotel services, for example, had receipts totalling £1,984,990 and expenses totalling £1,611,449, which left a net profit of £373,541, representing an 18.82% profit to receipts. Incidentally, these figures approximated to the £314,500 earned by the eight future constituents of the LMS in 1914. Refreshment room and dining car services were also profitable undertakings in those days and added a further £257,903 to the LMS hotel, refreshment room and dining car receipts for 1925. *(48)*

Information available for 1933 shows the LMS with 32 hotels, whose receipts totalled £2,636,945. Expenses totalled £2,350,237, leaving a net profit of £286,708. This included refreshment room and dining car receipts. *(48)* Individually, some hotels had a far better record of profitability than others. Some, like the *Station Hotel* at Inverness, were consistently profitable. During its period of ownership by the LMS between 1923 and the outbreak of the Second World war, its percentage profits over receipts ranged between 20% and 30% and in 1931 rose to 35%.

At the upper end of the scale, the *Midland Hotel*, Manchester, one of the most successful of all railway owned hotels, had one of its busiest years in 1925. Receipts for that year totalled £369,196, from which expenses totalling £284,189 were deducted to leave a profit of £85,007, representing an 8.21% profit to receipts. The Adelphi Hotel, Liverpool, also had its busiest year in 1925, when profits topped £49,000. The Central Station Hotel, Glasgow, had its best year in 1938 when profits exceeded £39,000. In spite of its somewhat outdated amenities and high running costs, the *Midland Grand Hotel* at St Pancras still made a respectable profit of nearly £16,000 in 1925, but trade declined to reduce profits to a mere £2,781 in 1934, its last full year in business. *(48)*

Of the holiday hotels, the *Gleneagles* establishment had its best year in 1928, when receipts totalled £133,872, from which expenses totalling £100,322 were deducted to leave a profit of £33,550, representing a 4.16% return on the capital cost (£805,567) and a 25% profit to receipts. The hotel remained open all year during the period 1927-30 inclusive, and then reverted to a season which extended from April

Manager James Ballantyne and his staff at the *Gleneagles Hotel*, **assembled to mark his award of his MBE in 1980.** *The Gleneagles Hotel.*

to October (48). In addition to income from the bed and breakfast business, dinners and banquets, a lucrative income was also derived from letting accommodation for conferences, lecture courses, trade shows and exhibitions. In recent years the *Gleneagles Hotel* formed an attractive setting for occasional antique sales organised by Sotheby's. Several hotels have featured in film and television productions, including MGM's Hound of the Baskervilles, starring Basil Rathbone, filmed at the *Manor House Hotel*, Moretonham-pstead. The Second World War and its aftermath posed many problems. Hotels suitable for use as service hospitals and accommodation for personnel were requisitioned. The *Gleneagles Hotel* which showed a profit of a little over £17,000 in 1938 received £10,500 per annum for the duration of its war service between October 1939 and May 1947. The *Midland Hotel*, Morecambe, requisitioned for Navy use from September, 1939, until September, 1947, received £1,900 per annum for the period of its war service, which compared with its profit of £304 for 1938. Before life returned to normal it was apparent too that an increasing number of people were looking to the Continent and beyond for holidays, and once-favoured British resorts were declining in popularity.

To meet the cost of post-war modernisation and refurbishment, a reappraisal of the total hotel stock followed Nationalisation of the railways in 1948. The *Lord Warden Hotel,* Dover, and the *South Western Hotel*, Southampton (which had been converted as offices immediately after war service) and the *Seabrook Hotel*, Hythe were all sold in 1946. Other sales followed. Resort hotels, including the *Sandringham,* at Hunstanton (subsequently demolished); the *Cruden Bay Hotel*, Port Erroll (subsequently demolished); the *Station Hotel*, Ayr; the *Midland Hotel*, Morecambe; hotels at ports, including the *Fishguard Bay Hotel*, Fishguard; the *Yarborough Hotel*, New Holland; the *Royal Hotel* and the *Yarborough Hotel*, Grimsby; and town hotels including the *Park Hotel*, Preston; the *Crewe Arms Hotel*, Crewe; the *North Stafford* Hotel, Stoke-on-trent; the *Great Northern Hotel*, Leeds; and the *Great Northern Hotel*, Bradford were all sold between 1948 and 1953, and realised a little over £700,000. A small price in the days before costs soared in the 60s and 70s.

A post-war venture by the SR, the purchase of the *Knowle Hotel* at Sidmouth in October 1947, was disposed of in 1953 and realised a further £36,000. Following these sales and earlier closures, the hotel stock stood at 38, and a gradually improving operating profit could be discerned. By 1972, with stock adjustments having reduced the number of hotels to 31 (but with the new *Old Course Hotel* at St. Andrews added in 1968) the operating profit reached a record peak of £1,416,000. The number of visitors using the hotels also passed the one million mark in five successive years, between 1969 and 1973. However, the final ten years of operation (1973-1983) showed a steadily worsening situation, brought about largely by the growing rumours of privatisation and a consequential loss of morale and declining numbers of visitors. 1977, 1980, 1981 and 1982 were all loss-making years. Also with privatisation moves on the horizon, Travellers Fare (train and station catering) became a free standing division of the British Rail Board as from January 1 1982, with its own Board of Directors. Travellers Fare had earlier been launched in the Autumn of 1973, controlled by British Transport Hotels Ltd.

Staff

To look after the comfort of their guests, the hotels provided a trained specialist staff under the jurisdiction of the manager. The staff to guest ratio (the number of staff required to look after each visitor) has varied considerably over the years, and from hotel to hotel. When the *North Western Station Hotel*, Liverpool, opened in 1871, Mr & Mrs Edward Bisserot, who were appointed Manager and Housekeeper respectively, had a staff of 82 to look after approximately 300 guests. *(49)* In the 1970s, the *Midland Hotel*, Manchester, the largest of the British Transport hotels, had 195 staff to look after 425 guests. The General Manager had five assistant managers, a restaurant manager, head waiter, banqueting head waiter, 30 waiters and banqueting waiters, a chef de cuisine and six cooks, 30 kitchen assistants and apprentices, a head porter, head night porter, carriage attendant, ten porters, a head housekeeper and four assistants, 35 chambermaids, eight barmen, 15 receptionists (who worked in the Cashier's department, enquiry and bill office), 30 linen room and laundry assistants, ten maintenance staff and a hotel detective, seconded from British Transport Police. Additional casual labour was engaged for banquets and special functions.

Largely an itinerant race, hotel staff frequently gained in practical experience and promotion by moving from hotel to hotel. Staff trained in the railway hotels usually moved from railway company to railway company, but a free movement of labour between the railways and privately-owned sector also existed. There were advantages to be gained from employment by a railway, too. Staff were entitled to privilege tickets and free travel passes according to seniority, and for those railways owning resort hotels, work could be combined with pleasure during time off.

Before the Second World War, German, French and Italian nationals occupied many of the managerial and kitchen appointments, but the establishment of hotel management and catering courses at technical colleges and universities has led to a growing interest in the industry. Nevertheless a survey of staff at the *Midland Hotel*, Manchester, in 1959 revealed that employees from 17 countries were at work there. *(50)*

Some of the most apt and humorous lines written on the subject of hotel managers and their duties came from the pen of Sinclair Lewis. A young man is thinking of joining the profession. His parents run a small hotel, and he asks an old commercial traveller for advice:

"You will have to learn manners, learn to be poker-faced with people that would take advantage of you. You will have to know all about china and silver, glass, linen, brocades, and the best woods for flooring and furniture.

"A hotel manager has to be a combination of a hausfrau; a chef; bar-room bouncer; a doctor for emergencies; a wet nurse; a lawyer that knows more about the right and wrongs of guests and how far he dare go than old man Supreme Court himself; an upholsterer; a walking directory that knows off-hand without looking it up just where the Hardshell Baptist Church is; what time the marriage licence bureau opens; and what time the local starts for Hick Junction.

"He's got to be a certified accountant; a professor of languages; a quick-action laundry man; a plumber; a heating engineer; a carpenter; a swell speech-maker; an authority on the importance of every tinhorn state senator or one-night stand lecturer that blows in and expects to have the red carpet already hauled out for him; a fly cop that can tell from looking at a girl's ears whether she's married to the guy or not; a money lender, only he doesn't get any interest or have any security.

"He's got to be dressed better than a Twenty-third street actor,even if he has nothing in his pocket. He's got to be able, just from hearing a cow's moo, to tell whether she will make good steaks.

"He's got to know more about wines and cigars that the fellas that make them. They can fool around and try experiments, but he's got to sell them.

"All the time he's got to be a diplomat that would make Thomas Beyard look like John L. Sullivan on a spree. He's got to set a table like a Vanderbilt, yet watch the pennies like an Arab pedlar.

"If you can do all this you'll have a good time. Go to it ." (51)

Sometimes, the manager's duties assumed a decidedly sporting angle. At the *Manor House Hotel*, Moretonhampstead, the manager was also Chairman of the Golf Club, a member of the Rabbit Clearance Association and a member of the Upper Teign Fishing Association. (52) If salmon fishing was to be had, who better that the manager to negotiate terms. In 1896, the GNSR was pleased to record that the manager of the *Palace Hotel*, Aberdeen, had landed a five- year lease on the Dee for £60 per annum. (53)

Sometimes, resort hotels went into hibernation for the winter season, during which time the head hall porter usually acted as caretaker. As, the new season approached, maintenance staff moved in to service the electrical, heating and hot and cold water services. With the manager appointed, staff were earmarked from other hotels to set about cleaning and drawing groceries and stores, in readiness for opening. If the hotel happened to be newly-built, it was normal practice to appoint the manager well in advance of opening. By so

Staff at the railway hotels were usually attired in very smart uniforms - certainly those who had to deal with the customers. This is a porter at the *Station Hotel*, Holyhead, in his best uniform. *Ted Higgs Collection.*

doing, the careful ordering of wines, furniture, fittings and the appointment of staff could be dealt with properly. Sometimes, a new manager might come in from close at hand. When the *Langham Hotel* opened in Portland Place in 1865, Charles Schumann moved in as manager from the *Great Northern Hotel* at King's Cross. (54) Sometimes, much longer journeys were needed to find the best manager. Robert Etzensberger, the first manager of the *Midland Grand Hotel* at St. Pancras moved from the *Victoria Hotel*, Venice. (55) Brothers frequently moved too. Ernest and Albert Theim, from Thuringia, made their way to Scotland via France and America. Earnest became the first manager of the *St. Enoch Station Hotel*, Glasgow, and Albert became manager of the *Peebles Hydro*. (56)

Sometimes a bright young man was destined for greater heights. As we learned earlier Sir William Towle (1849-1929) received his first job as a fifteen-year-old as an assistant at the *Midland Hotel*, Derby. In 1871 his talents were recognised and he was appointed manager. Thirteen years later he was given the job of reorganising the management of the *Midland Grand Hotel* at St. Pancras, and soon became one of the best known names in the hotel industry.

But however well a hotel was administered, it was on the skill and reputation of the chef de cuisine that a hotel's reputation was made or marred. French or Swiss rule in the kitchen was a fact once taken for granted. Several chefs employed by the railway hotels had been trained by Escoffier, who had joined the *Savoy Hotel*, London, in 1889. Dubbed by the Kaiser as the 'Emperor of Cooks', Escoffier relied principally on aroma and seldom tasted a dish. He held firm principles and deplored the British and American habit of taking tea and cakes, or cocktails before meals, both of which he believed ruined the palate for his exquisite dinners. (57) For aspiring chefs de cuisine, it was a long training requiring proficiency in the several principal sections of the kitchen, as sauce cook, fish cook, larder cook, pastry cook, breakfast cook, butcher, and in management of the

Above: Golf at Turnberry. Frank Hole, the Controller of British Transport Hotels presents the Amateur Challenge Cup to Michael Bonallack, on 17 June 1961. *Author's Collection.*

stillroom. The most important section was that of sauce cook or saucier, because with the required standard reached here, the chef could be recognised as second-in-command, able to take over when the chef de cuisine was absent. A Royal visit or an inaugural dinner presented the greatest challenge to a chef's experience. Two menus preserved by the MR, for a visit by Queen Victoria to the *Midland Hotel,* Derby, in 1849, and the inaugural banquet at the *Adelphi Hotel*, Liverpool, in 1914, are reproduced on page 98.

Housekeeping was essentially a department run by a female head, and it became normal practice for a railway company to appoint a man and his wife as manager and housekeeper respectively. In fact, Sir William Towle and his wife were both employed in this capacity by the MR. Housekeepers were usually young women interested in the work and learned the job by acting as hotel assistants, giving all-round assistance in several departments, until they became assistant housekeepers. A head housekeeper required a strong personality, able to correct, organise and control staff of not only chambermaids and house-porters, but cleaners, charwomen, linen staff and all the other female staff. On her efficient management depended the

cleanliness and attractiveness of the rooms and their furnishings. She was directly responsible to the manager and her day was likely to be long, commencing at around 7am, her work frequently occupying her until around 10pm, but with time off in the afternoon. Usually, an efficent housekeeper managed up to about 70 bedrooms single-handed, but larger hotels had assistant housekeepers who worked under the direction of a head housekeeper.

The inspection of rooms, both empty and occupied, was the afternoon work of the housekeeper on duty. Beds were checked for correct making, carpets and upholstery examined, bathrooms inspected for cleanliness, and any dust, especially on tops of cupboards, removed. Defects were also noted, such as loose screws, squeaky beds, broken light bulbs, dripping taps and other routine minor repairs. With efficient maintenance, most minor faults could be remedied on the day of discovery.

Recalling the last years of the Victorian era, Mrs Jean Robertson, then a housemaid at the *Cruden Bay Hotel*, Aberdeenshire, said: "all the chefs were French or Italian, and any delicacy called for could be provided. Staff had to behave and look exactly right. Each evening waitresses received the head waiter's inspection. Each girl wore a

AN ILLUSTRATED HISTORY OF RAILWAY HOTELS

navy-blue crepe de chine dress, small apron fastened at the waist with buttons, a little white cap, stiff collar and cuffs. General appearance was checked, but special note was taken of finger nails and shoes. No make up was allowed. This over, the head waiter sounded the dinner gong and into the blue and gold dining room trooped lords, ladies and gentlemen.

"During dinner, the housemaids in their blue print dresses, large white aprons and white caps had to slop out the rooms, attend to wash bowls and ewers and remove the hot water cans that had been taken up to each bedroom before dinner." *(58)* Her day had started at 7am, as on every other day of the week, and continued with a two hour afternoon break, if work permitted, until 6pm. Her pay was seven shillings a week, and to such girls, tips, like a box of chocolates or as much as £10 from a guest who had stayed a month, were real luxuries.

The manager happened to be a lady, Miss Duffus, who received the princely sum of £100 per year. When she left, her successor, Miss Frater, failed to come up to her employers' expectations and she was sacked in 1901. In need of a new manager and a housekeeper too, the owners, the GNSR, advertised the jobs in October 1901, and selected ten applicants for interview. Mr Trenchard and Mrs Armstrong, both from the Claremont Hydropathic establishment, Rhyl, were appointed as Manager at £130 and Housekeeper at £80 respectively (59).

The hotel and its staff had their moments of excitement. For example, on a Saturday afternoon in August, 1902, the Marquis and Marchionness of Headford read a telegram to the assembled guests and villagers to announce that King Edward VII had been crowned amid scenes of great splendour.

Few members of a hotel's staff came under public scrutiny as much as waiters. Unfortunately, waiting-on has been a weak spot in the general scene ever since the days of the first hotels. In 1969, Egon Ronay was prompted to record: "Their skill is almost non-existent. Foreign waiters are loud, undisciplined and ignorant of simple courtesies, partly because of their scant knowledge of English. Witnessing their uninhibited arguments in public, struggling to make ourselves understood, ducking from physical dangers of their 'silver service' we often repent having criticised the poker-faced stiffness of English service; at least it was disciplined."

It was precisely this poker-faced stiffness which prompted Charles Dickens to write in 1860: "You repair to the nearest hotel, and arrive agitated in the Coffee room. It is a most astonishing fact that the waiter is very cold to you... He is not glad to see you, he does not want you, he would rather you had not come. He opposes to your flushed condition an immovable composure." *(60)*

Criticism apart, the affairs of a well-run dining room were watched over by the maitre d'hotel or head waiter, who had one or more assistants according to the size of the department. Below the head and his assistants were the station waiters who serve the orders, and below them were junior assistants or "commis de rang", who collected used

Above: Mr Charles Bamford (in the chef's uniform) spent more than 40 years as a chef with Midland and LMS Hotels. His last spell of duty was on the Manchester (Central)-London (St Pancras) expresses in 1928. *Author's collection.*

HER MAJESTY'S DINNER.

MIDLAND HOTEL, DERBY,
September 28th, 1849.

POTAGES.
Crême de riz
A la Julienne.

POISSONS.
Le turbot sauce homard
Les rougets al Italienne
Les soles frites.

RELEVES.
Le janbon
Les pouléts au riz.

ENTREES.
Les pigeons aux pois
Des riz de veau panés
Des cotelettes de mouton
Vol'au vent de ragoûs.

ROTS.
Poularde   Perdreaux
Les sarcelles.

ENTREMETS.
La tartelettes de comfitures
La gelú de fruits
La charlotte depommes
Le pudding de biscuits.

SIDE TABLE.
Roast beef
Roast mutton.

Bouillie gratiner.

INAUGURAL BANQUET.

MIDLAND ADELPHI HOTEL, LIVERPOOL,
INAUGURAL BANQUET,
March 14th, 1914.

Caviar D'Astrakan aux Blinis
Bénédictines roses.

Pot au feu côte D'Azur
Crème Reine Margot.

Suprême de sole Mercédes.

Zephirs de jambon de Prague aux Xérès.

Selle D'Agneau à L'Infante
Petits pois à la Française
Pommes Suzette.

Granite grande Chartreuse.

Pousin de Hambourg Belle Meunière
Salade des Gobelins.

Asperges au Beurre D'Isigny.

Timbale de pêches Mireille
Delices Parisiennes.

Fruits Serre Chaude.

Moka.

Examples of special menus supplied at Midland Railway Hotels: 1849 and 1914.

Right: An example of the special menus supplied at Midland Railway Hotels in 1849 and 1914 . *Author's collection.*

plates and brought dishes from the kitchen to the station waiters. It was a tradition that head waiters were good handwriters because misunderstood or misinterpreted orders caused confusion and delay. It is not easy to single out any one famous waiter for a word of recognition, but Luigi Balzaretti of the *Central Hotel*, Glasgow, earned an international reputation in the hotel's Malmaison Restaurant. Maurice Chevalier dubbed him 'the Prince of Head Waiters.' As a boy anxious to follow his brothers into hotel life, Balzaretti left his village near Lake Como and arrived at the age of 17 years at a boarding house in Brighton. From there, he moved to the *Adelphi Hotel* in Liverpool in 1915, promptly performed four years war service and then returned to the same hotel. He gained his black tie in 1923 as assistant head waiter and then moved to the *Central Hotel*, Glasgow, in 1930 as head waiter. Shortly before he retired, in 1964, he received the Italian Cross of the Republic. *(61)*

Guests saw only the service side of waiters' duties. Once the dining room emptied, tables were laid up, table cloths were changed, plate and silver were cleaned, cruets filled, carpets vacuumed and furniture dusted. Soiled linen was taken to the linen room, counted and replaced. A large function or banquet sometimes proved beyond the capacity of normal staff resources, and extra waiters were drawn from an agency. During the Edwardian era, one of London's most elite corps of extra waiters was commanded by a German named Boden. He used to line up his men at 6.30 pm in any hotel where he happened to have a team working. He went through them like a sergeant major - checking carefully for clean white gloves, clean white shirt and cuffs, neat haircut, clean fingernails not stained with nicotine (although they wore gloves), polished boots and general deportment. Any waiters not passing the scrutiny were not re-employed. But it paid to conform, because Boden and his smart teams of waiters commanded the attention of hotel managers. The usual fee for extra waiters at this time was 6s 6d per night until 2am or 3am – but Boden's men commanded a fee of 7s 6d. *(62)*

Many of the staff who performed the more menial

duties were, nevertheless, conscientious servants of the companies which employed them. P.W. Smith, of Bedford, who as a boy of 15 years in 1898, answered an advertisement in the local paper which read: "Wanted - boys for Railway Refreshment Rooms and Hotels. Apply Head Office, Midland Grand Hotel, St. Pancras Station, London." Back came a letter and a free pass which took him to London for a (successful) interview and the beginning of a hotel career which lasted 58 years. He served five employers, the MR, Frederick Hotels Ltd, the LMS, the LNER and finally Trust Houses Ltd. His first job, that of a page boy at the famous *Midland Grand Hotel* left the greatest impression. He was fitted with a chocolate-coloured uniform, with three rows of brass buttons, worked a 13-hour day, took meals when there was a little time to spare, and received the princely sum of half-a crown (12.5p!) per week. There was little time off, one half-day one week, alternating with all Sunday off the following week.

The Head chef at the *Midland Grand* was called Albert, one of the leading French chefs of his day, and to assist guests to enjoy the marvellous meals which he served, a small orchestra, an unusual feature at that time, played each evening in the French restaurant. An Italian tenor, whose favourite renderings were *O Sole Mio* and *Il Bacio* often accompanied the orchestra. Adjoining the French restaurant was the ladies' Smoking Room, a rarely found apartment, equipped with an Electrophone, via which guests could be 'tuned-in' to live performances from the Queen's Hall and other London halls and churches. Another of the rooms had a column printer, an electric tape machine which relayed news from the Stock Exchange, and racing results from the news agencies.

There were sometimes occasions when a young pageboy could rise temporarily to a position of

considerable importance. In 1899, the Van Kannel Door Company of America, which was trying to interest the British market in its new revolving door, sold a doorset to the *Midland Grand Hotel* for use at the main entrance. The London Fire Brigade, however was not happy about the performance of the door, should the rapid escape of guests become necessary in the event of fire. With fire officers and railway officials present, Page Smith was given the job of demonstrating how the door could be folded in a flash and slid flush to the wall to give an unimpeded exit. Everyone

Above: A century of service between them! Friends Stan Humphrey (left), Head Night Porter and Reg Squires, Head Hall Porter, at the *Euston Hotel*. Both began their service at the *Midland Grand Hotel*, at St Pancras. *Chronicle, Summer 1964.*

Left: A characteristic 1964 study of Luigi Balzaretti, the famous head waiter from the *Central Station Hotel*, Glasgow. He began his service at the *Adelphi Hotel*, Liverpool in 1915. *Chronicle, Summer 1964.*

was satisfied and the efficient young demonstrator was showered with tips – especially by the American salesmen, no doubt!

Treats, and particularly a day's outing, were events worth waiting and saving up for. The National Sunday League organised outings which were very good value; a ten shillings trip to Boulogne drew a capacity crowd. Departure was from Charing Cross at 8am and Boulogne was reached at 1pm A midnight departure for home, arriving at Charing Cross at 5am, was followed by a brief 'nap' and then duty at the hotel at 7am.

Staff discipline was strict on the MR during the Towle regime. Page Smith recalled two written reprimands: "Please note that you will be fined 3d. for eating an apple while on duty", and "Please note that you will be fined 6d. for being in your bedroom when on duty." Junior staff also had very little 'say' in the duties they were expected to perform. One morning, the head porter called Smith over and said: "Take this note to the Dining Car Conductor on the 9.30am Scotch Express and wait for an answer." No sooner had he boarded the train than the Conductor said: "You have been transferred to the Dining Cars and you are my new pantry boy." Soon the train was moving, with the first stop at Nottingham, 120 miles away!

A pantry boy's job included the cleaning and refilling of the cruets from the previous day, washing lunch plates, followed by a spell cleaning cutlery, then washing the tea plates, then the dinner plates, and so to a night at the railway hostel at St. Enoch, Glasgow - tired out - and a similar return to St. Pancras the next day, and every day except Sunday, for the sum of five shillings per week. After a month's work and nearly 10,000 miles of travelling, pantry boy Smith plucked up courage to ask for his old job back at the *Midland Grand Hotel*. The request was granted and after a spell of duty as a porter, receptionist and liftman, he was transferred to the *Queens Hotel* at Leeds. His first job there was night watchman, which required him to 'clock-in' at 16 different points in the hotel, with a recording clock, meet night expresses and look after two locomotive type hot water boilers in the basement. Then came promotion to the hotel switchboard, followed by a move to the enquiry office. A change in the licensing regulations in 1914 permitted ticket holders to use the station bar until 12.30am –but only under the supervision of a member of the hotel staff. So, a 14 hour day, from 8am to 8pm in the hotel and then from 10pm to 12.30am, checking ticket holders on the refreshment room door, became a daily routine. This continued until early 1915, when he joined the Leeds Rifles and spent nearly five years of active service.

Following his war service, he joined Frederick Hotels at the *Hotel Great Central* in London. Here, he learnt how to become a Toastmaster and was instrumental in arranging the Annual Dinner of the Railway Guards Friendly Society at the Hotel. On one occasion, when about 150 guests of the society were assembled, an hotel resident enquired:

The PLAYGOERS'
Theatre Company

Programme : Price Twopence

MIDLAND THEATRE

MANCHESTER

MIDLAND THEATRE.

General Manager: W. Towle. :: Sole Owners: Midland Railway Company.

The PLAYGOERS'
Theatre Company.

September 30th :: :: 1907.

EVERY EVENING AND MATINÉE ON SATURDAY.

Herr Robert Drescher's Viennese Orchestra.

❡ Overture at 7-30 prompt, when the audience is respectfully requested to be seated.

❡ Late arrivals would oblige by waiting for the fall of the curtain before taking their seats.

❡ It would add to the comfort of all if ladies would kindly remove their hats.

❡ Copies of Charles McEvoy's "His Helpmate," 6d., and "David Ballard," 1/-, may be obtained from the attendants, and leading booksellers.

❡ Chocolates on sale.

PRICES—Boxes (to seat 7) 25/-
5/- & 2/6 Reserved 2/- & 1/- Unreserved

Box Office open daily . . . . 10 to 5-30

A September 30 1907 programme from the Theatre at the *Midland Hotel*, Manchester. The entertainment was by Herr Robert Drescher's Viennese Orchestra. The auditorium had a flat floor, hence the request for ladies to remove their large hats! *Author's collection.*

AN ILLUSTRATED HISTORY OF RAILWAY HOTELS

"who are the distinguished people?", Whereupon Smith replied: "The Royal Association of British Scientists!" The guest said that he was not surprised and remarked on the presence of Viscount Lascelles. Apparently Insurance Companies at this time considered railway guards to be a bad risk, so the guards formed their own Friendly Society, and made it a custom to invite a member of the Royal Family to their annual dinner.

Restless at the sleepy atmosphere at Marylebone, Smith secured a job with the LMS and moved first to the new *Adelphi Hotel*, Liverpool, and then to Gleneagles in time for the opening of the new hotel on June 2 1924. Winter closing of the hotel in mid-October meant a move back to Liverpool. More moves followed back to London, then in 1938 to the *Great Northern Hotel*, Leeds, as night porter, and finally a change of employer, to Trust Houses Ltd, for nine years until he retired in 1956 at the age of 73. (63)

P.W. Smith's reference to music at the Midland Grand was a feature of hotel life which the Midland Railway recognised as warranting the services of a full time officer. Their best known name in entertainment was undoubtedly Henry Hall. Beginning as a stand-in pianist at the *Midland Hotel*, Manchester, in 1922 his talents were quickly recognised. On July 4 1924, he made his first broadcast, from the *Gleneagles Hotel*. The programme of dance music was relayed from the BBC's Glasgow station. On August 26 1924, he was heard on the London station for the first time, when the Gleneagles orchestra became the first to break the monopoly of the Savoy Hotel bands. Henry stayed with the LMS for nearly eight more years and built his railway hotel orchestras up to a formidable total of thirty-two, before moving to the B.B.C as their Dance Orchestra leader in succession to Jack Payne. *(64)*

Reprimands *(65)*

To maintain staff efficiency and culinary standards, periodic reminders in the form of circulars were issued by the Manager. During Sir William Towle's regime on the MR, recipients of more important circulars were required to sign in due acknowledgment. In 1900, problems with the soup promoted the following:

CIRCULAR NO. 13

I have lately been very disappointed with the quality of the thick soup supplied at our Stations and Hotels, and I shall be glad if you will pay special attention to this in the future, taking care that the soups are not made too floury, and that very strong herbs and spice are not used too freely. Please see that the calves head and oxtail are well cooked and that a nice piece of the meat is given with each basin of calves head, and a nice succulent piece of oxtail with this soup. I am sure if you pay a little more attention to the cooking of the soup you will improve the quality of the soup, and also please our customers.

I have also noticed lately that the Scotch Broth is often washy and that the stock is not sufficiently good and the barley is not cooked enough. I hope to see an improvement in these matters.

(Sd.) W. TOWLE.

Sometimes, instructions on the correct way to mix drinks required a little written advice:

CIRCULAR NO.34

COLD BOVRIL & SODA. August 21st 1900.

In case Cold Bovril & Soda is asked for, the way to make the drink is to put a teaspoonful of cold Bovril into a tumbler, and then add the Soda.

Acknowledge receipt.

(Sd.) W. TOWLE.

and on a matter of safety:

CIRCULAR NO. 33

GAS IN KITCHENS.   August 14th 1900.

Please note that no gas is to be left burning either in the stove or for lighting purposes in the Kitchen when it is closed for the night.

Acknowledge receipt.

(Sd.) W. Towle.

Instant dismisal awaited staff guilty of serious misdemeanours.

IMPROPER USE OF WASTE STOUT, BEER, etc. 30 June, 1903

It has come to my knowledge that in certain of the Bars the attendants have been in the habit of pouring dregs from the stout and beer bottles into another bottle kept under the counter for the purpose, and when the same is filled, corking it up, and serving it to the customers.

You must please understand that should any case of the kind come to light in future, the attendant found guilty of the practice will be instantly dismissed, as also the attendant in charge of the Bar.

Please read this letter to all your staff and acknowledge receipt on enclosed form.

(Sd.) W. Towle .

Chapter 4

PUBLICITY

Above: Naming styles differed considerably. The Great Northern Railway's Hotel at King's Cross had its name spelled out in large individual letters immediately beneath the top floor windows. *Author's collection.*

Naming

Amongst the customs and practice which the 19th century hotel inherited from the inns and coffee houses, was that of displaying a sign or name board. This practice dated back to Roman times, but unlike its predecessors, hotels rarely displayed a hanging sign which projected from the building. In its place a more permanent method of advertising was adopted. At the *Crewe Arms* Hotel (1836) the arms of the family, date of building and name were cut in stone, and formed a distinctive feature in the gable above the front entrance. At the *Great Northern Hotel*, Kings Cross (1854) the name was applied in large letters which were spread out to occupy the full width of the building. Sometimes the hotel name took second place to what were considered to be more important advertisements. For example, at the *Royal Station Hotel* at Hull (1851) a sketch prepared of Queen Victoria's visit in 1854, which appeared in the Illustrated London News, showed no name board but drew readers' attention to the fact that the hotel offered 'Commercial Rooms and Coffee Rooms', and was a 'Family Hotel and Commercial House.' *(1)*

In place of the colourful heraldic renderings which were a feature of so many inn signs, hotel companies used instead their own emblems. The MR used the Wyvern (a dragon-like animal) as its badge. The London Chatham & Dover Railway looked further afield by embellishing the facade of its *Holborn Viaduct Hotel* (1877) with heraldic shields, cut in stone, portraying the arms of the different towns through which the railway passed. *(2)* Sometimes, earlier names were coupled with more up-to-date names. the *George and Railway Hotel* at Bristol, and the *Lovat Arms* and *Station Hotel* at Fort Augustus, reminded visitors that the 19th century was also the railway age.

The name 'Royal' was held in special favour if the Queen or a member of the Royal family had visited the establishment. The *Great Western Royal Hotel* at Paddington owes its designation to a visit made to the hotel by Prince Albert, the Prince of Wales, and the King of Portugal in June 1854. *(3)* Other genuine 'Royals' included the *Royal Victoria Hotel* at Sheffield (1862) so named following a visit by the Prince and Princess of Wales in August 1875. The owners, the Sheffield Hotel Company, had the following minute recorded at their meeting of February 7 1876: "The need for such a hotel as yours in Sheffield was demonstrated on the visit of the Prince & Princess of Wales to the town in August last. The hotel was then used by their Royal Highnesses and their suite. Success attended every phase of that memorable visit and your

An attractive official Postcard issued by the North British Railway, circa 1910, promoting its station hotels at Edinburgh, Glasgow and Perth. *John Alsop Collection.*

board are glad to say that all the hotel arrangements on that occasion were good and gave great satisfaction." *(4)* The *Royal Station Hotel* at Hull and *Royal Station Hotel* at York both owed their designations to visits by the Queen in 1854. In 1930 the LNER decided that it was time to recognise earlier Royal visits to their hotel at Newcastle and changed the name from the *Central Station Hotel* to the *Royal Station Hotel. (5)*

In 1865, M.E.Hadfield, who had designed the Royal Victoria Hotel at Sheffield (1862) and later designed the Great Northern Hotel, Leeds (1869) adopted a novel way of spelling the name of the Royal Dock Hotel, Grimsby. In the keystones above the windows he had carved a rabbit, an owl, a Yorkshireman, an ape, a leopard, a duck, an otter, a cat, a kangaroo, a horse, an owl, a tiger, an elephant and a lion.The first letters of each of the animals spelled out the name! The hotel greeted its first royal visitors, the Prince and Princess of Wales, in July 1879, when they opened a link between two adjacent docks and unveiled a statue of Prince Albert in the gardens opposite the hotel.

Some railway hotels changed their names several times. When the North British Railway began to think about names for its new hotel in Edinburgh, the *Waverley Station Hotel* had been the first choice. *(6)* This was soon changed to the *North British Station Hotel*, and since the 1920s the shortened name, *North British Hotel*, has been used. At the western end of Princes Street, the CR's new hotel was named the *Princes Street Station Hotel*, then the *Caledonian Station Hotel* and finally by its shortened name, the *Caledonian Hotel*. The *Station Hotel* was too plain a name for the GSWR's magnificent resort hotel at Turnberry and it later took the name of the resort. When the MR purchased the *Adelphi Hotel*, Liverpool, in 1892 the name was prefixed the *Midland Adelphi*.

Sadly, most of the attractively named railway owned hotels are now just a memory, having fallen under the demolition contractor's hammer or have seen a change of use. Once the list included fine-sounding names like the *London & Paris Hotel* at Newhaven, and interesting names like the *Felix Hotel* at Felixstowe; the *Sandringham Hotel* at Hunstanton; the *Lord Warden Hotel* at Dover; and the *Royal Pavilion Hotel* at Folkestone; and one of the most famous names of all, the *Euston Hotel*.

Advertising

Anyone with a service to offer, whether it was a railway, steamship or hotel company, depended on advertising as one of the most reliable ways of keeping in touch with the public. Companies published their own timetables and guide books and often included whole page advertisements devoted to hotel and general matters. Publishing houses were quick to realise that the new travelling public needed reliable guide books, which could inform the stranger what to look out for in town or country – and where accommodation could be found.

Railways had useful free advertising space of their own in their carriages and on station platforms. One of my earliest railway memories was seeing the 'Stay at LMS Hotels' advertisements in the suburban compartment stock on the trains from Stockport to Manchester Central Station.

Black and white and coloured postcards were another well-tried medium. The LNWR.and MR in particular were prolific issuers of postcards featuring scenery, famous buildings, hotels and items relating to the territory through which the company's routes passed and to the company itself. Post cards have become sought after items nowadays. Bryant and Mays, the match manufacturers, also provided useful publicity in the form of printed tin plate match boxes and book of matches.

Above: A book of matches issued by the Great Central Railway, promoting the company's hotels at Sheffield and Grimsby. *Glyn Waite collection.*

Guide Books

Although Murray's Handbooks and Baedekers red-bound guides became the most sought after books for travellers, several other publishers were well-known for their guide book series. Guides as we know them date back to the mid-17th century. One of the first, Instructions for 'Forreine Travel' by James Howell was published in 1642, and though philosophic, does affirm that one eye-witness is worth ten travellers tales.

Adam Black (1784-1874) founder of the famous Edinburgh publishing house of A.& C. Black, can claim to be the first compiler of the modern guide book, at least for the British Isles. *Black's Economical Tourist, Scotland*, was published in Edinburgh in 1839, and was companioned that same year by *Black's Economical Guide through Edinburgh*, and, *Black's Economical Guide through Glasgow*. Black's interest spread to England in 1841 with *Black's Picturesque Guide to the English Lakes*. By the mid-1850s, *Black's Guides* were dealing with numerous English counties and a separate *Guide Book Advertiser*, usually containing about 100 pages of hotel, railway, steamer, and general advertising matter, was bound into the back of each volume. In 1878 the *Guide Book Advertiser* contained just over 180 hotel advertisements many of them illustrated and included entries from all parts of the British Isles.

Right: The *Adelphi Hotel*, Liverpool and the LMS Hotels Monogram (as used for a new series of brochures designed by Cross Courtenay) during the 1930s. *Author's collection.*

Below: A pair of facing pages from an LMS brochure promoting the *Adelphi Hotel*, in Liverpool. This was during the era of trans-Atlantic liner travel and the company naturally made much of this aspect of Liverpool life, now sadly long gone. *Author's collection.*

LIVERPOOL
AND THE
ADELPHI HOTEL

The Adelphi Hotel
Liverpool

PROLOGUE

*f*T may happen that the Liner comes into Liverpool on the Mersey's racing tide out of a great sunset of crimson and gold; and over the burnished waters flash the multitudinous white wings of gulls.

And then the minds of those who tensely cluster along the taffrails, and of those who tiptoe and stare from the landing stage, are being stamped with an undying memory.

To some of those along the rails the word "Home" is like a bugle calling. To others "Liverpool" means the Gateway to the Old Country, the second port of the British Empire, or maybe, just the hand held out for all the millions of bales of Cotton which the Southern States can sell.

As the eye of the returning exile sweeps along the Front he sees that his city's outlines are changing—new buildings thrusting upwards their harmonious mass of stone and steel. He remembers that beneath those surging waters men are tunnelling a great artery of transport.

Above: A rare survivor indeed. This paper bag advertised the Great Eastern Railway's hotels at Liverpool Street, Harwich, Parkeston and Hunstanton, circa 1914. *Glyn Waite Collection*

Another Edinburgh worthy, John McMurray (1745-1793) moved to London in 1768, to take over a book business in Fleet Street. His son, John Murray II (1778-1843) bought the publishing business of William Miller (1769-1844) in 1812 and moved to the latter's office at 50 Albemarle Street. Five years later, in 1817, John Cam Hobhouse (1786-1869) friend and travelling companion of Byron, wrote to Murray and spoke of the lack of useful guide book information for travellers and foresaw a 'field of glory' for the publisher who could produce useful guides. John Murray's son, John Murray III (1808-1892) adopted the idea and published the Guide to Belgium in 1836, followed by companion volumes covering Holland and North Germany. Murray's first guide to the British Isles appeared in 1859/60. At first, the guides lacked

advertisement pages, then like Black's guides, began to include an advertising section.

Books which dealt primarily with journeys and holidays that could be accomplished by rail, were also early comers to the guide book library; published in 1837 were the Grand Junction and Liverpool and Manchester Railway Companion by J. Cornish; the Grand Junction Railway Companion to Liverpool, Manchester and Birmingham by A. Freeling; and The Newcastle & Carlisle Railway, by H. Scott.

George Measom, who wrote a successful series of illustrated railway guides during the 1850s and 1860s, made scant reference to hotels, but included a list of: "the Chief Hotels, recommended from personal knowledge." His *Illustrated Railway Guide to the Bristol & Exeter, and South*

Wales Railways published in 1860, included a list of 34 hotels in places as far apart as Brighton and Aberdeen and in less frequented locations such as Stockport and Maidstone, but omitted any reference to London.

Some railway companies adopted the practice of publishing guides, in particular, the GWR, NER, GNR, and SER, who issued their first guides during the period 1857-63. One of the most comprehensive illustrated travel guides was that published by the LNWR in 1876. Containing 660 pages and intended for the use of American tourists, the book also included descriptions of the locomotive works at Crewe, and the carriage department at Wolverton. Details of excursions into England, North and South Wales, Scotland and Ireland were accompanied by 50 coloured plates, 63 woodcuts, and 42 pages of steamship and hotel advertisements. Not unnaturally, there was a bias against mention of too many rival railway hotels; for example, the list of London hotels omitted any reference to the brand new *Midland Grand* at St. Pancras, and the *Great Western Royal Hotel*, at Paddington. The *Euston & Victoria*, *Langham* and more distantly situated *Charing Cross* and *Cannon Street Hotels*, did, however, receive a mention!

Karl Baedeker (1801-1859) whose publishing house became world-famous for its gilt-lettered, red-bound guide books, placed its first copies on sale in 1854. *(7)* Baedeker's success came as a result of systematic and personally-supervised field work. his son, Fritz Baedeker, usually travelled incognito and noted the smallest particulars of management in the hotels which he visited. On geographical and historical topics he engaged experts, and it was little wonder a Berlin court in 1900 ruled that the word 'Baedeker' meant guidebook. A.P. Herbert, impressed by the publisher's passion for accuracy, wrote: "Kings and Governments may err - but never Mr. Baedeker." Baedeker was also the first guidebook published to award 'ratings' to objects, views and hotels. Two stars were granted only to such masterpieces as the Louvre, St. Peter's, in Rome, and the Pyramids. But praise where it was due was always freely-given. In 1926, publication of the English 'Baedekers' was transferred to George Allen & Unwin. Sadly, all this thorough and meticulous research is not available to us today, for almost all the Baedeker records were destroyed during the Second World War.

A sample of Baedeker's attention to detail and up-to-date information comes from the *London Guide* (18th Edit.) for 1923; a particularly interesting year, when 20th century amenities were becoming more widespread; it was also the year that the railway hotels passed from the ownership of more than 20 companies into the hands of the 'Big Four'. Modern luxuries included: "electric light, lifts, central heating, ample bath accommodation, telephones in bedrooms and, in many cases, private orchestras." There was a shortage of bed spaces in London during the season and: "it is therefore advisable to apply in advance by letter or telegram." Transport for the guest and his luggage could be obtained on previous application from the railway omnibus operators. Six or more passengers could be accommodated and fares were calculated at nine shillings up to four miles, then two shillings for each additional mile.

In central London and its Environs, Baedeker listed nearly 130 hotels and awarded stars to 28 of them. Of the railway hotels, only the *Midland Grand* at St. Pancras, and the *Great Eastern Hotel* at Liverpool Street were starred. In the city, the railways held command with the *Great Eastern*

and the *Cannon Street Hotels*, the latter "much used for company meetings etc."

Timetables

The other principal outlet for hotel publicity came from the timetables issued both by independent publishers and by the railway companies themselves. By coincidence, Karl Baedeker and George Bradshaw whose names became synonymous with guide books and timetables respectively, were both born in 1801. Unlike the Baedeker family, who were already well established as publishers, George Bradshaw, a native of Pendleton, Lancashire, was largely a self-made man. First apprenticed as an engraver in Manchester, he later set up in business on his own account, principally in the production of maps. He soon gained a reputation as the publisher of Bradshaws Maps of Inland Navigation; aware of the growing importance of the railways, he published his first timetable in 1838. His next venture, *Bradshaws Monthly Railway Guide*, appeared in December 1841 and was followed in June 1847 by *Bradshaw's Continental Railway Guide*. Hotel advertisements did not appear in the first 'Bradshaws', but by 1848 a growing number of entries were included. In the 'Golden Age' of the railways during the 1890s and in the Edwardian era, Bradshaws monthly General Railway and Steam Navigation Guide for Great Britain and Ireland contained more than 900 pages of timetables, over 50 pages of shipping information and about 150 pages of hotel advertisements, listing more than 700 hotels, hydropathic establishments and boarding houses.

Among other publishers who followed in Bradshaw's footsteps was Thos. Skinner, who issued his first 'ABC' railway timetable and hotel guide in 1853. The well-known Glasgow publishing house of Thomas Murray & Son, founded in 1820, also adopted the title 'ABC' for its series of railway timetables, which first appeared in 1873. Like Bradshaws, who published a local timetable for the Manchester area, Murrays local 'ABC' guides were designed to fit easily into the pocket. Nevertheless, each guide was a mine of information and was profusely filled with hotel advertisements, lists of local holidays, early closing days. times of high tides and an assortment of other useful data.

The MR, LNWR and GWR each had very comprehensive timetables, but the smaller companies, particular the NER, GER and the Scottish companies availed themselves of the advertising space offered by private publishers. During the Edwardian era the LNWR and CR issued an attractive tourist map, this time with the LNWR.s hotels portrayed round the map of the latter's territory and the Caledonian's hotels bordering a large map of Scotland. The LNWR's sketches appeared as black and white line engravings, but the MR used attractively-reproduced coloured sketches of its hotels for inclusion on the back cover of its timetables and guides, during the same period.

Advertisements were designed to catch the readers eye and bring to notice the latest innovations and attractions. When electricity was making its debut in the 1880s, the GWR timetables for October 1884 announced that: "The General Coffee Room, Drawing Room, Smoking Room and Reading Room, at the Great Western Hotel, will shortly be lighted with ELECTRIC LIGHT." Ten years later, the official guide to the MR announced that its hotel had: "Electric light everywhere." For the guest anxious to ensure his personal

THE GREAT NORTHERN RAILWAY STATION HOTEL, LEEDS,

A FIRST-CLASS HOTEL FOR FAMILIES & GENTLEMEN.

AN ELEGANT COFFEE ROOM.

SPACIOUS COMMERCIAL ROOM & LADIES' COFFEE ROOM.

BILLIARD AND LARGE SMOKING ROOM

Has a covered approach from the Central Station, and is situated in the most healthy quarter of the town.

It contains every convenience for the comfort of Visitors, at a moderate scale of charges.

TARIFF.

SITTING ROOM	..	..	..	..	..	per day, from	4/- to 8/-
BED ROOM, 1st Floor	..	..	..	..	..	..	3/6
„ 2nd Floor	..	..	..	..	..	..	3/-
„ 3rd and Upper Floors	..	..	..	..	..	..	2/6

Visitors have the option of Boarding as per Tariff, or at a fixed price of 10/6 per day.   Servant's Board and Lodging, 5/- per day.

HOTEL PORTERS ATTEND THE TRAINS, ALSO THE NIGHT MAIL

Price List forwarded on application to Mr. Meyer, the Manager.

Above: An advertisement from the GNR's 1870 timetable for the Great Northern Hotel, *Leeds, which opened in 1869.* **Stephenson Locomotive Society Library.**

hygiene, the SER offered: "Baths with sea water, fresh from Folkestone" at the *Charing Cross Hotel* (SER Guide, 1889-1915). Seawater tanks at the hotel were replenished by rail tanker.

Telegraphic addresses were printed out in bold type. The LNWR's 'Bestotel', later passing on for revival by British Transport Hotels. The Midland's 'Midotel', and North Eastern 'Nerotel' were other well known tags.

With the coming of the motor car, the HR (Timetable 1909) advised patrons that the: "Station Hotel, Perth, is provided with a large motor garage, inspection pit and resident engineer.

Brochures

A star rating or word of praise in Baedeker was something which every hotel-owning company wanted, but larger organisations like Gordon's Hotels produced a brochure entitled *Where to Stay* and invited other hoteliers to advertise their accommodation. The NBR was at first wary

of Gordon's friendliness, recalling an earlier rebuff when permission to visit the *Hotel Metropole* at Brighton was refused. The animosity was, however, forgotten and the NBR began to advertise in *Where to Stay* in 1906.

Souvenirs of official openings called for a special effort by printers and publishers. In October 1902, the NBR published a magnificent green and gilt lettered volume called *Souvenir of the Opening of the North British Station Hotel, Edinburgh, 15 October, 1902*. The contents, prepared by John Geddie, Author of Romantic Edinburgh, included a description of old and new Edinburgh, the new hotel, and its owners. The advertising space was devoted almost entirely to the builders, sub-contractors and suppliers of equipment and fittings, who had worked for more than six long years to bring the project to fruition.

Among the publicity issued for the opening of the *Midland Hotel*, Manchester, on September 4 1903, was a

Facing page: One of the most attractive timetable advertisements produced for the railway hotels, was this example, used by the MR at the turn of the century. *David Tee collection.*

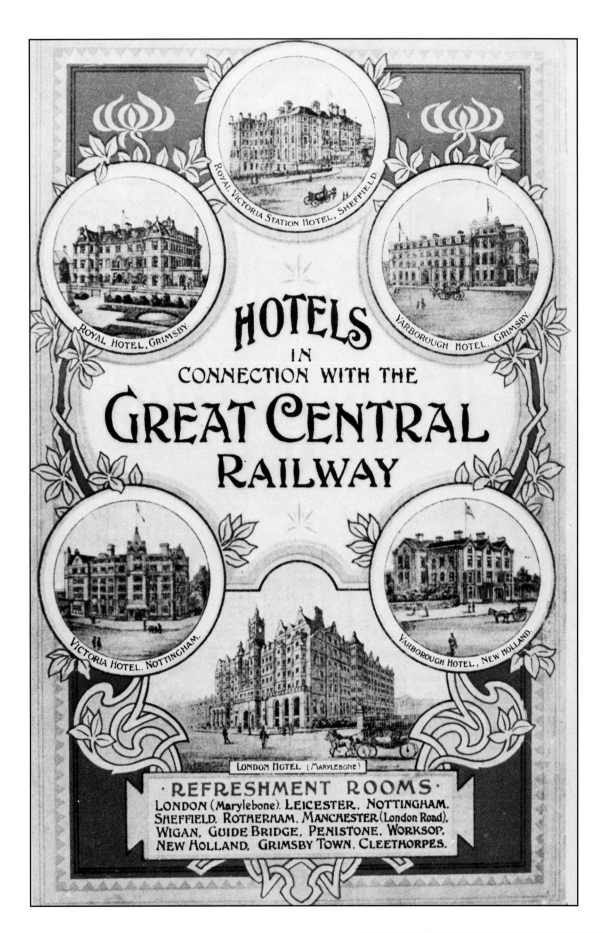

ROYAL VICTORIA STATION HOTEL, SHEFFIELD.

ROYAL HOTEL, GRIMSBY.

YARBOROUGH HOTEL, GRIMSBY.

HOTELS
IN
CONNECTION WITH THE
GREAT CENTRAL
RAILWAY

VICTORIA HOTEL, NOTTINGHAM.

YARBOROUGH HOTEL, NEW HOLLAND.

LONDON HOTEL (MARYLEBONE).

· REFRESHMENT ROOMS ·
LONDON (Marylebone). LEICESTER. NOTTINGHAM.
SHEFFIELD. ROTHERHAM. MANCHESTER (London Road).
WIGAN, GUIDE BRIDGE, PENISTONE, WORKSOP,
NEW HOLLAND, GRIMSBY TOWN. CLEETHORPES.

special presentation book. Music played an important part in the celebrations and the book records that the orchestra from the *Midland Hotel*, Leeds, would play in the Ladies' foyer; the orchestra from the *Midland Grand Hotel* at St. Pancras would play in the Concert Hall; the orchestra from the *Midland Adelphi*, Liverpool, would play in the Roof Garden; and the specially recruited Roman Orchestra which had been engaged for the season would play in the Winter Garden.

When the rebuilt *Adelphi Hotel*, Liverpool, opened in March 1914, the event was marked by the publication of *The History of a Great Enterprise*. A souvenir of a great extension scheme MDCCCCXIV, priced at five shillings (25p). Page three proclaimed: "Be it known also by all modern visitors to our township, whether from overseas or elsewhere,that we, the Midland Railway, have erected a most sumptuous residence in the said Township, where you may have all the liberties and luxuries of hotel and social life of the highest order." A smaller companion volume *Undeniably Perfect* was also issued to mark the opening.

Small pocket-size guides were issued by several railway companies, in order to familiarise their hotel guests with their surroundings, the tariff and sometimes details of the places of entertainment in the locality. Few early guides survived and these usually contained small print and line drawings. The LNWR was at pains to inform visitors to the *Queens Hotel*, Birmingham, that the hotel was the only one in the railway ownership in the city. By 1917, the same company was able to point out that the extension opened that year had more than doubled the accommodation and that new rooms were replete: "with every convenience, a constant supply of hot and cold water, together with synchronised clocks, and a post office telephone in each room." At this time, Birmingham had six theatres to choose from, and a Saturday afternoon visit to "One of the City's three celebrated Associated Football teams, Aston Villa, Birmingham and West Bromwich Albion" was strongly recommended.

Following the Grouping of the railways in 1923, LMS Hotel Services enlisted the help of Cross Courtenay Ltd, of Manchester, to produce a new series of colourful brochures. One of the first important events was to mark the opening of Scotland's wonder hotel at Gleneagles with *The Story of Scotland's Great Caravanserai*, which described a story which had begun in 1912 and which was completed by the LMS in June 1924. The new hotel's first brochure proclaimed: "Scotland without Gleneagles is unthinkable. The hotel of the heart of Scotland. A great caravanserai for the lovers of Burns, Scott and Barrie. A noble work of art. A lovely home centre for a thrilling holiday. A mecca for the sportsman." Interspersed among the 58 deckle-edged pages were attractive pencil sketches of the hotel and its surroundings and a reminder that the building was "Fireproof". The Smoke Room: "dedicated to my Lady Nicotine, has a colour scheme of stippled stone grey panels with olive green margins, and a blue, black and brown carpet of Spanish pattern".

Golfers were recommended to read the *Gleneagles Golf Book*, but for the general reader, the story of Jimmy Braid's visit to the site and verdict that it was: "A natural golf course" was told in some detail. A smaller brochure published shortly afterwards by McCorquodale pointed out that Gleneagles was also a place for music and dancing and that: "the Gleneagles Dance Band is one of the best in Europe", and referred to a separate booklet *The Gleneagles Collection of Scottish Dance Tunes*.

In 1929, Cross Courtenay used sepia printing and brown suede leather covers for a new guide to the *Adelphi Hotel*, Liverpool. The City had just welcomed the opening of the new Mersey road tunnel and the construction of the East Lancashire Road was the subject of much discussion. The hotel's sports facilities received special mention, together with the room telephones, hot and cold water in every room, and the bathrooms which were: "a masterpiece of sanity engineering."

The purchase of Welcome House, Stratford-Upon-Avon by the LMS in 1930 and its conversion into an hotel prompted the publication of an attractive brochure designed by J.P. Sayer. Printed in sepia, the simulated parchment covers had a colourful map of Stratford-Upon-Avon and the countryside as far as Kenilworth to the north and Evesham to the south. William Shakespeare featured a great deal in the text, and a photograph of the late President Teddy Roosevelt was a reminder of a famous visitor of more modern times. The 1930s were becoming recognised as the age of the motor car, and the new hotel was provided with hire cars to tour this famous corner of England. For the ardent train traveller, a new service was inaugurated on July 1 1931 (the hotel opened that day) leaving Euston at 4.35pm and arriving at Stratford at 7.10pm, and a return service leaving Stratford at 4.8pm and arriving at Euston at 6.40pm.

No reference to hotel brochures of the 1930s would be complete without reference to the very high quality work of S.P.B. Mais and the artist Chas. Mayo. Their collaboration for the brochure published by the GWR for the *Manor House Hotel*, Moretonhampstead, Devon, in 1939 was particularly successful. Mais' wrote: "Some hotels are noisy and barrack-like. The Manor House is so cleverly constructed that even in the largest rooms where you are awed at first by the magnificence, you soon find nooks and comfortable corners... many hotels expect you to live on the view and fob visitors off with dull, unappetising, unimaginative meals. Here you will find infinite variety and a delightful sequence of surprise on the menu." And on sport: "How many hotels in England posses a private full size squash court? A dozen? I doubt it. And what a glorious game. Immediately outside the hotel in the private grounds is one of the jolliest and certainly one of the most picturesque 18-hole courses I ever played on."

Following the Second World War in 1945 and the Nationalisation of the railways in 1948, brochures assumed a more utilitarian look, in the form of folded sheets containing photographs, a brief description of the hotel, and a separate tariff. Sometimes a map of the town centre and its outlying area was included, and when folded inside out the sheet revealed a location map of all the British Transport hotels. Colour printing was used for a new small brochure for the *Gleneagles Hotel*. Jock McLean was the golf professional and could: "cure the thickest slice and supply anything but silver spoons." For the less active, hire cars (with or without chauffeurs!) were available to explore the Ochils and the Grampians. A hairdresser, a bank, a post

Facing page: An illustration from the GCR timetable of 1908. The GCR did not, of course, own the hotels at London Marylebone and Nottingham, hence the careful description "Hotels in connection with...." *Author's collection.*

office and a shopping centre were also back in business, following the hotel's period of war service. A useful brochure of recent years has again been the folded sheet which, when opened, included coloured photographs, a location map of all the hotels, and a list of the hotels, giving the number of rooms, bars, conference and banqueting facilities, sports facilities and the nearest railway station and airport.

Postcards

One of the most popular collectors items nowadays is the picture postcard. From small beginnings at the turn of the century, postcards were issued in increasing numbers and in a variety of mediums. For railway-owning hotels, postcards were a very useful item of publicity. Several

companies used postcards featuring their hotels as pre-printed forms of acknowledgement of letters and orders. Postcards frequently carried an eye-catching sentence. The *Slieve Donard Hotel*, Newcastle, Co. Down, was: "Where the mountains of Mourne sweep down to the sea." The Queens Hotel, Birmingham was the: "only Railway Hotel in Birmingham." The *South Eastern Hotel* at Deal provided: "Every accommodation for anglers" and the hotel's glazed verandahs: "are kept delightfully cool in summer by running water over the roof". the new *Gleneagles Hotel* was described as: "Britain's premier sports hotel." Telephones were becoming an important means of communication in the Edwardian era, and numbers were often printed on postcards as useful aids de memoire. The *Euston Hotel* had an easy number to remember, Museum 3000. The *North British Station Hotel*, Edinburgh's telegraphic address was

THE ENTRANCE GATES

MANOR HOUSE HOTEL
NORTH BOVEY
MORETONHAMPSTEAD, DEVON

Telephone: Moretonhampstead 355 & 356
Telegrams: Manorotel, North Bovey

"British", Edinburgh, and the telephone number was Central 6130-34.

Postcards sometimes provided a rare insight of staff uniforms. A very attractive coloured card showing the grand staircase at the *Caledonian Station Hotel*, Edinburgh, includes the hall porters wearing red jackets with black collars edged in gold, black trousers and black and gold braided peak caps. Another member of the staff is wearing a black jacket with gold lapels and matching hat. A dining room scene at the *Great Eastern Hotel* at Liverpool Street, features smart waiters helping guests with their coats, showing guests to their seats and taking and delivering orders.

Unfortunately, many of the postcards do not feature the name of the publisher. But among the most attractive coloured cards ever published were the 'jotter' series by A. Burkart, of London. Prepared from original watercolours the series featuring the Great Southern and Western and the Midland Great Western railway hotels in Ireland included a view of the hotel and sometimes one or more small roundels showing a fishing, sailing or golfing scene.

Tucks published several attractive cards for the GSWR, including a fine coloured view of the company's hotels, the coat of arms, telegraph address 'Southwestern' and the Managers name, J.H. Thomas. Following the opening of the *Midland Hotel*, Manchester, in 1903, the MR issued a set of coloured postcards prepared from watercolours, of the interior and exterior of the building. The company's other hotels were also featured, in the same series and by the same artist. The most prolific issuer of postcards was undoubtedly the LNWR, which used McCorquodales on many occasions. Cards were issued in sets of six cards for 2d per set, and featured old and new locomotives, steamships, bridges, royal trains, places of interest, old railway views, stations and many other subjects, and not forgetting the company's hotels.

The Furness Railway issued sets of postcards of Lake District scenes by Tucks, and included a set of six photos for 4d of the *Furness Abbey Hotel*.

Modern post cards, though well produced and comparatively cheap, nevertheless lack much of the nostalgic content of their predecessors. The LNWR summed it up in a sentence which appeared on many of its cards: "The LNWR is noted for punctuality, speed, smooth riding, dustless tracks, safety and comfort, and is the oldest establishment in the railway passenger business."

Tariffs

When the *Victoria Hotel* at Euston opened in September 1839, the charges agreed by the Directors varied according to floor level. Accommodation on the first floor cost five shillings (25p) per night, four shillings (20p) for the second and third floor, and three shillings and sixpence (17.5p) for the fourth floor. Breakfast cost half-a-crown (12.5p) per head. When the hotel closed 123 years later, in 1963, a single-bedded room cost about £1.17.6 (187.5p) and £2.17.6 (287.5p) with a private bathroom. Breakfast cost from four shillings (20p). (8)

When the *Great Northern Hotel* opened at Kings Cross,

Facing page: The title page of a brochure issued by the GWR for its hotel at Mortonhampstead. The sketches were by Chas Mayo, and note the imaginative typography of the title - it would not be out of place in a similar publication today. *Richard Casserley Collection.*

in 1854, the charges were a little less; three shillings (15p) for the first floor; half-a-crown (12.5p) for the second floor; and two shillings (10p) for the third and fourth floors. Plain breakfast cost one shilling and sixpence (7.5p). Guests, however, had to watch carefully for 'extras' because a coal fire in the bedroom cost a further shilling (5p), waxlights one shilling and sixpence (7p), and a hot bath two shillings (10p) – more than doubling the bill for the unwary patron! (9) 135 years later, a single bed without bathroom at the Great Northern Hotel costs £50, or £65 with a bathroom, both inclusive of full English breakfast *(9)*.

The Great Western Royal Hotel Company endeavoured to be honest with patrons, and the charges for 1854/5, the hotel's first year in business, were explicit that the hotel servants were not allowed to receive fees or tips, but in lieu one shilling and sixpence (7.5p) was charged for the first day's attendance and one shilling (5p) per day thereafter. This charge included handling luggage and for all services in the hotel. "The prices charged per day for sitting and bedrooms and suites are all specified in the tariff, as well as for wines, ale stout, by the pint. Thus a person is able to calculate his expenses to a shilling and is relieved from anxiety as to the amount of charge during his stay". (10) Terms were always strictly cash and: "No cheques taken in payment of Hotel accounts" was frequently to be seen printed on account forms.

An attractive sketch of the GNR's *Station Hotel* at Leeds, published in the Great Northern Tourist & Excursion programme for 1874, advised visitors that bedrooms were available at first floor level for three shillings and sixpence (17.5p) and half-a-crown (12.5p) on the third and upper floors. Visitors had the option of boarding at a fixed price of ten shillings and sixpence (52.5p) per day.

When Charles Dickens Jnr., published the Dickens Dictionary of London in 1879, foreign visitors were advised that: "the Continental custom of taking all or the great majority of meals out of the hotel does not obtain in England, and that a London hotel keeper under such circumstances will consider himself ill-used. Attendance is now usually included in the bill. When this is the case, the servants invariably expect very much the same gratuity as when it was not included."

For the day's charges per person, for bedroom, breakfast with coffee and cold meat; dinner with soup and joint, attendance, etc., the prices included eleven shillings (55p) at the *London Bridge Terminus Hotel*, eleven shillings and sixpence (57.5p) at the *Euston*, twelve shillings and sixpence (62.5p) at the *Grosvenor*, thirteen shillings and sixpence (67.5p) at the *Great Western Royal Hotel*, and fourteen shillings (70p) at the *Midland Grand* and *Great Northern Hotels*. By way of comparison, hotels in the non-railway sector included twelve shillings and sixpence (62.5p) at the *Westminster Palace Hotel* and fourteen shillings and sixpence (72.5p) at the *Langham Hotel*.

Although prices were usually quoted by the day, visitors contemplating a longer stay were granted en pension terms for periods of three or more days, which meant a reduction of several shillings over daily terms. Another attractive proposition was the 'hotel-coupon' introduced by Thomas Cook (1808-1866). Like Karl Baedeker and George Bradshaw, whose names have become household words in the field of guide books and time-tables respectively, Thomas Cook was the first great name in the world of travel and tourism. Cook made the headlines in July 1841, when his first publicly-advertised excursion train made the comparatively short journey from Leicester to Loughborough. Later, he helped 165,000 visitors to attend the Great Exhibition. Cook did a great deal to popularise train travel and hotel usage and the railway copied his example. Cook's object was to offer the traveller a fixed charge ticket to cover the cost of the journey and bed and breakfast at a reliable hotel. Other 'travel agents' to emulate his ideas in the 1870s were Norton and Shaw, of Carrick Street, London, who specialised in circular tours of Great Britain and Ireland; and Henry Gaze & Son who extended their interests to Europe and the Middle East. For their part the railways offered a variety of 'Hotel Coupons' In the 1880s, the GER issued thirty shilling (150p) tickets which included first class travel from Liverpool Street to Harwich every Saturday, and board and lodging at the *Great Eastern Hotel* on Saturday and Sunday, and the return fare to Liverpool Street on the Monday morning. In the 1890s, a whole week's board and lodgings at the *Ayr Station Hotel* and first class travel to and from Glasgow St. Enoch cost only £3.10.0 (350p). The railway also entered into working arrangements with private hoteliers, and issued coupons to cover travel and three or more days' hotel board and residence.

Baedeker was very precise in his advice on selection and tariffs. In 1923, the visitor to London was told: "Charges for rooms vary according to the floor; and it is advisable to make enquiry as to prices on arrival. When a prolonged stay is contemplated the bill should be called for every two or three days, in order that errors may be detected. In some hotels the day of departure is charged for unless the rooms are given up by noon. Many hotels receive visitors 'en pension' for periods of not less than three days. The prices of rooms are raised at many of the West End Hotels during the season. The charges for attendance and light are almost

invariable included in the price of the room, but fires are an extra. Gratuities (tips) amounting to 10-15% of the bill (less for a prolonged stay) should be divided between the head waiter, the waiter who has specially attended to the traveller, the chambermaid and the 'boots'. To produce the best results they should be distributed weekly. Attendance at meals is not obligatory .... Ordinary charges for a hot bath are 1/- (5p) or 1/6 (7.5p); in many instances baths are now included in the charge for bedrooms or for pension. the servants of visitors are accommodated at cheaper rates. Many hotels refuse to receive dogs, but provide suitable quarters for about 2/6 (12.5p) per day."

Of the railway hotels, the *Cannon Street* establishment was the cheapest at nineteen shillings and sixpence (97.5p) for bed, breakfast, lunch and dinner; followed by the *Great Northern* and the *Great Western Hotels*, both at £1; the *Midland Grand* charged £1.2.0 (110p) and an additional seven shillings and sixpence (37.5p) for a room with its own bathroom. The *Euston Hotel* charged £1.2.6 (112.5p). When the *Gleneagles Hotel* opened in 1925, a single bedroom cost twelve shillings and sixpence (62p) and £1.5.0 (125p) with a bath en suite. Inclusive terms were from £1.10.0 (150p) per day. Green fees were half-a-crown (12.5p) per day or twelve shillings and sixpence (62.5p) per week.

Even after the upheavals of the Second World War, tariffs did not rise very appreciably. In 1950, the *Great Northern Hotel* at King's Cross was charging £1.13.0 (165p) a day which included bed and breakfast for nineteen shillings and sixpence (97.5p). lunch at six shillings (30p) and dinner at seven shillings and sixpence (37.5p). The *Great Eastern Hotel* at Liverpool Street was a little cheaper at £1.9.0 (145p) for bed an breakfast and lunch..

It is worth noting that these charges represent only a three-fold increase in the space of 100 years; in the

Above: Combined hotel and rail tickets issued by the LNWR, circa 1900. The company hotels are advertised on the ticket. Seven days inclusive travel and accomodation at the *Highland Railway's Hotel*, Strathpeffer, cost £14.11.10. for the first class passenger travelling from Liverpool The third class passenger paid £9.17.9 *Glyn Waite Collection.*

following 30 years charges have risen out of all recognition. In 1970, Egon Ronay said: "Customers seem to have accepted higher prices with remarkably little resistance." A single room with its own bathroom is now an accepted fact, but good Grade 2 hotels all charge between £35 and £40 for this facility, before the cost of lunch and dinner is even considered

Recent Trends in Classification

Several publishers sought to emulate Baedecker's reputation for accuracy and up-to-date information, including the Egon Ronay organisation. Dating from 1957, this organisation employs about a dozen trained inspectors to visit more than 1,300 hotels and a little over 1,000 restaurants annually. Ratings are based on a percentage system awarded after due consideration of 22 factors concerning cleanliness, comfort, state of repairs and general impression of the public rooms; the size, comfort, cleanliness and decor of the bedrooms; private and public bathrooms; efficiency of reception; conduct and appearance of the staff and the room service.

British Transport Hotels received numerous compliments. In 1969, Egon Ronay gave the *Midland Hotel*, Derby, (Britain's oldest surviving railway hotel) a 61% rating. It referred to: "commendable efforts to improve an old building, which now has excellent beds in well-fitted, tastefully decorated rooms......service is good and the hotel is well maintained." The *Gleneagles Hotel*, fully modernised with a bathroom for each of the 210 bedrooms, earned a 90% rating as: "One of Britain's most palatial and gracious hotels.....Chef Cottet is one of the great chefs, a genuine artist who creates masterpieces." Gleneagles received the *Egon Ronay Hotel of the Year* award in 1974. The *Midland Hotel*, Manchester, earned a 68% rating and was noted for its exemplary service. The Old Course Hotel at St. Andrews, the last hotel to be built by British Transport Hotels, earned a 75% rating and had "memorable individual service."

Of the *Great Southern Hotels* in Ireland, the hotel at Galway "a railway hotel on the grand scale" earned a 64% rating, fully modernised with a bathroom to each of the 130 bedrooms. The equally large *Great Southern Hotel* at Killarney earned a 65% rating for its "old world charm and modern comforts" each of its 181 bedrooms being upgraded with a bathroom. *(11)*

Openings

Hotel opening ceremonies were very grand affairs. Typical of the ceremonial which accompanied these events were the preparations made for the opening of the *Great Eastern Hotel* at Harwich on Thursday June 1 1865. The Royal Standard was flown from the roof, and the front of the building and the adjacent quay were decorated with flags of all nations, arranged under the supervision of Captain Chevallier, the GER's Marine Superintendent.

When the special train arrived at about 4pm with the Directors and guests, a 21-gun salute was fired, the church bells rang and the Harwich Artillery Volunteers played triumphant music. Dinner for the 200 guests was planned for 6pm and the interval before was set aside for a tour of the new building. Charles Lucas, the builder, carried out this duty for Thomas Allom, the architect, who was

seriously ill at the time. *(12)* The day was windy with strong gusts from the east, which meant that guests who visited the viewing platform on the roof had to hold on to their hats!

The furnishing of the hotel was not fully completed, but among the items which the press correspondent noticed was the silver plated table ware and cutlery supplied by C.J. Meadows, of Ipswich, and bearing the crest of the GER and the words 'Great Eastern Hotel'. The hotel was also well provided with clocks, which were to be wound and regulated by their supplier, Mr Parsons, of Harwich. The builder also let it be known that he was making a gift of a large illuminated clock for the pediment at the centre of the building.

When dinner was served, James Goodson, Chairman of the GER, presided and Charles Lucas, the builder, took the vice-chair. Among the more notable guests were Captain Jervis, MP, Deputy Chairman of the GER, Sir Morton Peto, MP, the Mayors of Harwich and Ipswich, Thomas Brassey and Thomas Brassey Jnr. When the health of the Queen and the Prince and Princess of Wales was proposed, reference was made to Sandringham and the journeys which the Royal Family made over the GER. Music accompanied the dinner and songs were provided by a group of professional vocalists. Time then ran out on the proceedings and guests had to make a hasty departure, in order to catch their waiting special trains to London and Ipswich. (13)

Royal Visits and State Occasions

Queen Victoria's journeys to Balmoral and Osborne and her visits to distant parts of Great Britain and Ireland, led the royal family to frequent many hotels. The Regent Hotel at Leamington Spa, which opened in the same year as her birth (1819), also happened, 11 years later, to be the first public building in which young Princess Victoria slept. Derby, Normanton, Doncaster and York, which were useful 'stages' en route for Balmoral, also claimed several royal visits. The menu for 'Her Majesty's Dinner' at the *Midland Hotel*, Derby, in September 1849, is one of the keepsakes preserved. The Royal Station Hotel, York, became an annual stop for the royal family in the 1850s.

Arrangements, however, were not always to Her Majesty's liking. At Perth, where the Queen frequently took breakfast or dinner, a flight of steep stairs had to be climbed to reach the committee rooms which served as a temporary dining room. But in June 1890, the new Station Hotel came to the rescue when it was arranged for a level gangway to be laid from the platform, directly into the hotel. (14)

Hotels frequently played their part in state occasions. In February 1848, the ignominious flight of the 74 years old Louis Philippe, King of the French, to London by way of Newhaven entailed a brief pause at the recently-opened London & Paris Hotel. In contrast, the state visit of Napoleon III seven years later was an extremely grand affair.

All was made ready at Dover on April 16 1855, including a royal suite at the *Lord Warden Hotel*. In spite of Channel fog which delayed the arrival of the Pelican and its royal cargo by one and a half hours and exhausted the repertoire of the welcoming Royal Bucks regimental band. A well-served luncheon at the hotel more than made amends for the delay. Then, moving into the grand saloon

LAST CALL FOR EUSTON HOTEL 1839 — 1963

PIONEER RAILWAY HOTEL CLOSES AFTER 124 YEARS

GENERALLY IN LIFE THE TRAIN OF PROGRESS TRAVELS ON AN ERRATIC COURSE. Its timing is as unpredictable as an English summer. Frequently, it is checked by signals of conflicting interests. Changing circumstances cause it to be shunted into a siding. Delay rusts the wheels.

It starts off again, runs smoothly for a time, and then brakes sharply as financial blizzards block the way ahead. Economic snow ploughs get the train into motion only to find it

The hotel died on May 13, 1963. How did it come to be born? Look back through the corridors of Time to 1825, the year when John and Edward Grantham tramped the fields to convert a dream into reality. They were making surveys for a proposed railway from London to Birmingham.

Three years later, a company was formed for making a railway from London to Birmingham ..."and the opening of new and distant sources of supply to the Metropolis by easy, cheap and expeditious travelling, and a rapid and economical interchange of the articles of consumption and commerce between the midland and northern

first railway-owned hotels in the world.

In April, 1838, a prospectus was issued to shareholders of the L. & B. Railway offering shares at the nominal value of £25 in a new company to be called "London & Birmingham Railway Hotel & Dormitories". A piece of ground in front of Euston station, acquired from Lord Southampton, was earmarked to erect an hotel and dormitories.

It's a reasonable assumption that two types of accommodation were introduced to cater for 1st and 3rd class passengers. The building on the east side of the station approach, christened "Euston Hotel", was

Messrs. Dethier & Vantin. A Mr. Bacon, "late of the Athenaeum Club House", was engaged to manage the Victoria. They opened in September, 1839.

Together but Apart

The establishments remained "together but apart", for many years. There was a full-page advertisement in the 1875 edition of the L. & N.W.R. "Official Tourists' Picturesque Guide". The editorial content sets the scene:

Euston Station, at once the great starting-point and terminus of this great system, is approached from Euston Square between two lodges,

Left: Early days — the view from Euston Road. The Victoria Hotel is on the left, then comes the famed Doric Arch (entrance to Euston station, and Euston Hotel. Above: Similar viewpoint but a close shot of the central building which united the hotels in 1881.

...all aboard with one way tickets, unaware of their destination until Fate jerks them off, are delighted, dismayed or uncaring —depending largely on their personal stake in the particular section of the journey.

The modernisation of Euston station has been on the stocks for many years. Schemes of magnitude were evolved and shelved. The green light lamp looked to be out of oil. British Transport Hotels, and its predecessors, while earnestly supporting the principle of progress could hardly view this

line, from London to Boxmoor, and the whole line from Euston to Birmingham on September 17, 1838.

(*In 1846, the Company amalgamated with the Grand Junction and Manchester and Birmingham Railways to form the London and North Western Railway.—Editor.*)

The directors had vision, harnessed by an acute instinct for the commercial possibilities. Before the line was completed they had decided to provide hotel accommodation for rail travellers. Euston Hotel was the pioneer—one of the very

particular project with particular enthusiasm for it could mean the lethal blow to the oldest hotel in the group . . Euston. It has.

When the final plans of this sweeping scheme were approved it was apparent that neither the earning capacity of the hotel nor the wine of sentiment could avert its closure and early demolition.

Mr. A. J. C. Pardini, Resident Manager.

Day Porters: Percy Loveless, Jack Grant, Reg. Squires, John Godwin, Stanley Walker, Arthur Swann, Wally Stiff, Bill Boyton.

Mrs. Mary Sinnott, Head Housekeeper, is seated on the left. With her are Miss Fiore Falco, Assistant (standing), and Miss Kay O'Reilly, 2nd Head Housekeeper. Mrs. Sinnott began at The Adelphi, Liverpool

the square and passing between the two great railway hotels, the "Euston" and "Victoria". . . .

The puff for Messr. Norton and Shaw was a trifle brash....they published the guide!

There were three other railway-owned hotels advertised in this issue: London & North Western Hotel, Lime Street, Liverpool; Royal Hotel, Holyhead, and the Station Hotel, Greenore.

rooms in excess of . . . as the allotted space would admit".

A coffee room for breakfast and refreshments was included in the Victoria schedule but the house was not licensed for the sale of wines and spirits. However, guests at the Victoria were allowed to use the Euston coffee room.

Philip Hardwick was the architect. Euston Hotel was let to

From left: Standing: Savvas Kaltinices, Michael Yiasoumi, Joseph Chaboteaux, Bill Birnie, Pat O'Callaghan, Andre Garino, Gracia Ruiz, Andrew Zacharia and George Papazacharia. Seated: Costas Lybouris, Charlie Hartley, V. C. N. Stanbury, Rusty Russell, Angelika Berthold.

A special article in the British Transport Hotels staff magazine *Chronicle*, issued in 1963 to mark the closure of the *Euston Hotel*, which had been Britain's first railway-owned hotel. *Author's collection.*

and in the presence of the Emperor, Empress and Prince Albert, an address of welcome from the Mayor and Corporation of Dover was read, prior to the guests' departure by train for London. (15)

In 1871, an unusual 'royal' occasion was held at London's *Grosvenor Hotel*, at Victoria station. (16) Following Napoleon III's capitulation at Sedan, in September 1870, which plunged France into ten months of political uncertainty and civil war, a group of royalist exiles decided to proclaim the Duke of Orleans as King of France, from the hotel, in opposition to the Third Republic.

Closures

The closure of a famous hotel was also an occasion for nostalgia and sometimes spirited protest. Amid the hurried bustle of London life, the passing of an hotel went largely unnoticed. The closure of the giant *Hotel Cecil* in 1930 and the *Euston Hotel* in April 1963 drew only brief comment in the press. It was a period in which the country was seemingly prepared to let historic buildings be demolished with abandon; witness also the unforgivable loss of Euston's Doric Arch, despite some popular protest. It would never be allowed today!

In the provinces, however, the loss of a hotel was more keenly felt, none more so than the closure of the *Queens Hotel*, Birmingham, on New Year's Eve 1965 after 111 years of valuable service to the city. The Chairman of the Birmingham and District Hotels & Restaurant Association claimed that the plans to demolish the hotel, to make way for the rebuilding of the adjoining station: "would mean a loss of 220 beds at a time when the city will be receiving an influx of visitors for the World Cup football competition", and that: "it seems sacrilege that a popular hotel which has an excellent staff should be closed." Undeterred, the Ministry of Transport allowed the axe to fall, claiming: "the demand for hotel accommodation will fall as a result of the expanding motorway network and a new high speed inter-city rail services."

The *Queens Hotel*, Birmingham, had experienced a full and eventful life. It had opened without undue ceremony in May 1854, replacing the small Victoria Hotel which opened in 1839. Its accommodation grew as a result of extensions in 1911, 1917 and 1925, increasing its capacity steadily from 60 rooms to 220. Its life was faster, racier and more cosmopolitan than its rivals, the *Midland* and the *Grand. Hotels.* To the Queens came Kings and heads of state, aristocrats and actors, statesmen and salesmen,

businessmen and beauties. It was the principal stopping place for visiting businessmen from all over the world. Its suites catered for board meetings and assemblies of all kinds. To its bars came Noel Coward, Ivor Novello, Nijinsky, Max Baer, Gracie Fields, Jack Buchanan, Laurel and Hardy, and Danny Kaye. The Queens had one of the world's best barmen, 'Flash' Battersby whose speciality it was to send cocktails skimming down the 20ft counter, to come to rest precisely in front of each waiting customer!

Queen Victoria came to the hotel, so did King George V and Queen Mary; and the Emperor Haile Selassie slept there, protected by armed body guards. Nikita Kruschev and Marshal Bulganin were also closely guarded, but a more relaxed atmosphere greeted General de Gaulle. Some guests were remembered by their special requests, such as comedian Will Fyffe, who expected to see a bottle of whisky waiting on the table. Others were remembered by their dress, author Edgar Wallace, for example, who went everywhere (even the bathroom!) in his bowler hat, because it helped him to think. Very famous people came to the Queens; Mae West, Primo Carnera, and the 27-stones Teddy Brown, the Xylophonist who had to step sideways into the lift and regularly broke the barber's chair. One of the most unusual guests was Trigger, (yes, that's correct, Roy Rodgers' horse!!) who climbed to the first floor to see his master's room, before moving to a stable!

For the unwary guest, a bedroom ordered with an even number was on the noisy railway side of the building. Of course, some guests loved the sound of trains, particularly Jack Teagarden, the Jazz trombonist who also gained permission to have a footplate trip on a locomotive. War brought change and anxious moments. For three days, Dunkirk survivors passed through the station and were served with refreshments by the hotel staff. In 1941, the hotel was evacuated until an unexploded bomb was made safe. Between November 1942 and March 1946 the old wing served as an American Red Cross Hostel. War service and the need for overdue modernisation sometimes brought rebuffs. In 1951, an unrecorded Conservative MP described the *Queens*: "a particularly bad example of a thoroughly disgraceful railway hotel."

Like all hotels, the *Queens* had its service entrances, through which debtors sometimes made their escape. The door to Platform 1 was the handiest and an alternative route lay through the basement and a tunnel to Platform 14. The basement also held the remains of four police cells reminiscent of a scene from *The Count of Monte Cristo*.

For the staff, closure meant transfer to another hotel, retirement or looking for another local job. the *Queen's* longest serving member of staff at the time was its pastry chef, Mr. Sutter, who had moved as a boy, from his first job

Below: Examples of specially made uniform buttons, worn by staff at many hotels. *Sketches by Angela Meredith*

at London's famous Savoy Hotel in 1918. A Swiss by birth and master of his trade, he had joined the Queen's at £4 weekly and left it with £25 a week. The crowning glory of his 47 years at the *Queen's Hotel* was a magnificent replica of the Birmingham Town Hall, created in cake and icing for the visit of King George V and Queen Mary.

The last guest to leave the hotel was Michael Argyle, Recorder of Birmingham, who had been living there with his family for three months. For him, as a member of the fourth generation of his family to use the hotel, the occasion was indeed sad. The Manager, Mr. Masser, performed his own gesture to mark the end of the hotel's career by personally drawing back the curtains in every room and switching on every light - the Queen's did not close without a final dazzling display!

Disposal of the contents was a feat in itself. Some of the best items were transferred to other hotels, including the eight crystal glass chandeliers which returned to their original home, the *Adelphi Hotel*, in Liverpool. The remaining contents, 1642 items in all, were sold in a three day sale in February 1967. *(17)* Now, the *Queen*'s is a memory, which can be made more vivid by a glance through a faded brochure or travel guide.

When the *Euston Hotel* closed after more than 122 years service, a coincidence became apparent. The hotel's first lessee and the hotel's last manager were both born in Corsica. Zenon Vantini, who with Mr Dethier had been accepted by the Hotel Committee for a 21 year lease on The Euston Hotel in 1839, acted as a courier for Napoleon before settling in England. Finding favour with the London & Birmingham Railway, he established the first railway refreshment room at Wolverton, then widened his horizons in 1841 by becoming proprietor of the *North Euston Hotel* at Fleetwood, and in 1844 proprietor of the SER's Pavilion Hotel at Folkestone. *(18)*

Mr A.J.C. Pardini took over at Euston in 1957 and was to see it die more than five years later. Leaving Corsica as a boy of 14 years, he worked at the *Grand Hotel* and the Regina at Marseilles. Life was tough: "I worked for the first six months without wages, relying on a share of the tips allocated by the Head Waiter. He was an odd character. If a 12-hour day had been worked for long spells without a break and time off was asked for, the unfortunate plaintiff was told that it was not a nursery and to get on with the job. Yet, if you said nothing he would suddenly stop and say that you could have time off, and even give you two or three francs." After arriving in England he spent three years at the Carlton, Cafe Royal and the Berkley. He joined the railway in 1922 first with a spell at the *Midland Grand Hotel* at St. Pancras, before moving to the *Central Hotel*, Glasgow; the *Caledonian Hotel*, Edinburgh; and then back

to St. Pancras before graduating to Head Waiter at the *Queen's Hotel*, Birmingham, in 1933. More moves followed before his first managers appointment at the *Midland Hotel*, Bradford, in 1937. *(19)*

Another member of the *Euston Hotel* staff who had started his service at the *Midland Grand* at St. Pancras, was Reg Squires, the Head Porter. As a page in 1912 he received three shillings and sixpence per week and slept in the basement. A Sunday morning duty was a trip to Finchley Road, and the residence of Sir William Towle, where young page Squires was required to deliver letters to the chief, and wait at his bedside in case replies were needed.

When the *Midland Grand Hotel* closed in 1935, three of the Euston porters were detailed to meet the St. Pancras expresses and try and steer the former *Midland* guests to the *Euston*. To make the job easier, a bus was made available to carry guests and their often large quantities of luggage. Euston was the headquarters of the LMS Board of Directors, and an extra duty recalled was the 'lunch safari,' when groups of about five porters were to be seen carrying large trays on their heads en route from the kitchen to the Boardroom. For this duty, an extra shilling a month was paid. The war created many memories, especially the night of October 18 1940, when a near-miss by a bomb blew George Fordham, the hotel's fireman, across the front hall. Fortunately no one was seriously hurt. *(19)*

The sound of demolition hammer was heard in Scotland, too. The St. Enoch Hotel had been a vital part of the Glasgow scene for 96 years when the decision to close and demolish came in the mid-1970s. The Duke of Windsor had a soft spot for the hotel and could not leave Glasgow without calling at his 'dear old St. Enoch'. His brothers the Duke of Kent and the Duke of Gloucester also stayed at the hotel. Florrie Ford, a regular visitor, kept her pet parrot in the porter's lodge while she was on stage at the Empire Theatre. Enrico Caruso, Ivor Novello and Jack Buchanan were other famous guests. In more recent times the hotel was the meeting place of Glasgow Rangers Social Club. During the Second World War, a considerable part of the hotel was requisitioned by the Royal Navy and became HMS Spartiate. Mr Churchill came on board, but General de Gaulle decided not to venture beyond the station forecourt. *(20)*

It is sad when only memories remain of a famous building, but a more tangible reminder of the hotel can be seen in the Glasgow Museum of Transport. Here, carefully re-assembled, is to be seen the Coat of Arms of the owning Company, the Glasgow & South-Western Railway, carried out in mosaic, which was formerly laid in the hotel's entrance hall. It is a pleasant reminder of a once-great hotel.

APPENDIX 1:

This appendix contains a list of the principal railway hotels built or purchased by the railways in Great Britain and Ireland, arranged under the 'Big Four' grouping (LMS, LNER GWR and SR) in existence 1923-47. Following Nationalisation of the railways in 1947, the hotels were administered by the British Transport Commissions Hotels Executive until 1953 by the BTC's Hotel and Catering Services from then until 1962 and British Transport Hotels Ltd until 1983.

At the end of 1982, 21 of the remaining 23 BTH Hotels were offered for sale by tender. The 19 hotels marked * thus were sold; two more, the *Queens Hotel*, Leeds, and The *North British Hotel*, Glasgow, were sold in 1984 and the remaining two, The *Great Northern Hotel*, Kings Cross and The *Great Eastern Hotel*, Liverpool Street, have been let under management agreements pending decisions on the long term development at both the London stations.

The sale of the *Charing Cross Hotel* and the *Central Hotel* Glasgow were subject to 20 and 21-year leaseholds respectively. The *Grosvenor Hotel*, Victoria, and the *Great Western Royal Hotel*, Paddington, the *Queens Hotel*, Leeds the *Royal Station Hotel*, Newcastle Upon Tyne the *Royal Station Hotel Hull*, the *Station Hotel*, Inverness and the *North British Hotel*, Glasgow, were all sold subject to 125 year leaseholds and the *Adelphi Hotel*, Liverpool, were sold on 999 year lease (from March 1911). Hotels owned by the Irish Railways are listed on page 123/24. Many of the hotels listed were extended and some rebuilt. The dates of the original and subsequent work are shown, with the names of architects, where known.

CONSTITUENT COMPANIES OF THE LMS:

London & North Western Railway:

London: *Euston* and *Victoria Hotels*. Opened by the London & Birmingham Railway in December & September (respectively) 1839. Link block opened July 1881. Building renamed the *Euston Hotel*. Closed (prior to demolition) May 13 1963. (Philip Hardwick; Link by J.B. Stansby)

Birmingham: Curzon Street. *Victoria Hotel*. Opened by the London & Birmingham Railway in 1839 and renamed *The Queens Hotel* the following year. Later known as *Hardwick's Queens Hotel*. Converted to offices by 1900. (Philip Hardwick). Original building since restored.

Birmingham New Street: *The Queens Hotel*, Opened May 1 1854. Extended in 1911, 1917 and 1925. Closed (prior to demolition) December 31 1965. (William Livock).

Alderley Edge: *Queens Hotel*. Opened by the Manchester & Birmingham Railway in 1845. Sold 1965. Still open.

Holyhead: *Eagle & Child Hotel*. Built circa 1800 and later renamed *The Royal Hotel*. Acquired by the Chester & Holyhead railway in 1850. Taken over the by LNWR in 1857 and replaced by the *New Station Hotel* in 1880. Closed September 1951. Demolished 1978

Bletchley: *Station Hotel*. Opened circa 1860, rebuilt 1882. Closed circa 1934. Demolished 1963.

Lancaster: *County Hotel*. Opened 1864. Sold 1929. Since used as offices and inn.

Crewe: *Crewe Arms Hotel*. Built by Lord Crewe, 1836. Leased to LNWR 1864. Purchased 1877. Extended 1880. Sold June 1952. Still open.

Liverpool: *North Western Hotel*. Opened March 1 1871. Closed March 30 1933. (Alfred Waterhouse RA). Since used as offices/

Blaenau Ffestiniog: *North Western Hotel*. Opened April 1881. Sold 1906. Still open.

Preston: *Park Hotel*. Opened jointly with LYR 1882. Sold 1949. (Arnold Mitchell). Since used as offices.

Windermere: *Windermere Hotel*. Opened 1847. Two-thirds share owned with Mr Ullock until circa 1912. Still open.

MIDLAND RAILWAY:

Derby: *Midland Hotel*. Opened 1840. Purchased March 1 1862. Sold 1982. (Francis Thompson). Still open.

Normanton: *Station Hotel*. Opened 1840, Purchased 1861. Residential Business ceased 1902. (G. T. Andrews). Since demolished.

Leeds: *Queens Hotel*. Opened January 10 1863. Enlarged 1867 and 1898. Closed August 3 1935. (William B Perkin) Hotel completely rebuilt and reopened November 12 November 1937. Lease sold June 1984. (W Curtis Green and Wm Hamlyn).

London: *Midland Grand Hotel*. Opened May 5 1873. Closed April 19 1935. Used as railway offices until August 1985. (Sir Geo Gilbert Scott). To be reopened.

Morecambe: *North Western Hotel*. Opened September 11 1848 by the 'Little' North Western Railway. Taken over by Midland Railway 1871 and renamed *Midland Hotel*. Closed March 27 1933. Completely rebuilt on new site and opened July 12 1933. Sold 1952. (Oliver Hill). Still open.

Bradford: *Midland Hotel*. Opened July 1890. Closed 1975. (Chas Trubshaw). Since reopened.

Liverpool*: *Adelphi Hotel*. Opened 1826. Rebuilt 1876. Purchased by Midland Railway 1892. Completely rebuilt 1912/14. War damaged 20/21 December 1940. (R. Frank Atkinson).

Heysham: *Heysham Towers Hotel*. Opened circa 1830 as a private residence. Purchased 1896. Sold 1919.

Keighley:. *Queens Hotel*. Opened 1881. Purchased 1902, residential business ceased 1942. Sold 1958. Since used as offices.

Manchester:*. *Midland Hotel*. Opened September 1903. (Chas Trubshaw).

LANCASHIRE & YORKSHIRE RAILWAY:

Fleetwood. *North Euston Hotel*. Opened 1841 by Peter Fleetwood Hesketh in association with Preston & Wyre Railway. Closed 1859. (Decimus Burton). Since reopened.

Liverpool: *Exchange Station Hotel*. Opened August 13 1888. Closed July 3 1971. Since used as offices.

Preston. *Park Hotel*. Opened Jointly with LNWR 1882. Sold 1949. (Arnold Mitchell). Since used as offices.

NORTH STAFFORDSHIRE RAILWAY:

Stoke on Trent: North Stafford Hotel. Opened July 1849. Enlarged 1878. Sold January 1953. (H.A. Hunt). Still open.

Leek: Churnet Valley Hotel. Purchased C1900. Sold 1938. Still open.

Rudyard Lake: Hotel Rudyard. Purchased 1903 Sold 1955. Still open.

FURNESS RAILWAY

Barrow: *Furness Abbey Hotel*. Opened 1845. Leased by Furness

Railway from Earl of Burlington 1864. Closed March 1938. Partly demolished and open as inn.

COCKERMOUTH KESWICK & PENRITH RAILWAY:

Keswick Hotel: Opened 1869 and leased to Keswick Hotel Company, which had joint chairman with CKPR. Sold prior to 1923. Still open.

CALEDONIAN RAILWAY:

Glasgow*: *Central Station Hotel.* Opened 19 June 1885. (R. R. Anderson).

Edinburgh: *Caledonian Hotel.* Built 1899-December 1903 to design prepared in 1867. Sold 1981. (J. M. Dick Peddie). Since modernised.

Auchterarder. *Gleneagles Hotel.* Opened June 2 1924. (Alex Adam). Sold 1981. Since modernised.

Perth*: *Station Hotel* Opened June 1890. Ownership shared with North British and High Railway Companies. (Andrew Heiton).

GLASGOW & SOUTH WESTERN RAILWAY:

Glasgow: *St Enoch Hotel* Opened July 1879. Closed 1974. Demolished 1977. (Thos. Wilson).

Ayr: *Station Hotel.* Opened June 1866. Sold October 1951. (A. Galloway).Since modernised.

Dumfries: *Station Hotel.* Opened circa 1865. Rebuilt and re-opened June 1897. Sold April 1972. Since modernised.

Turnberry*. *Turnberry Hotel.* Opened 17 May 1906. (James Miller).

Greenock. Plans for a hotel at Albert Harbour in 1876 were abandoned.

HIGHLAND RAILWAY:

Inverness* *Station Hotel.* Opened 1856. Purchased 1878. (Jos Mitchell).

Achnasheen: *Station Hotel.* Purchased 1870 (Former House) Sold 1969. Still open.

Perth*: *Station Hotel.* See under Caledonian Railway section.

Kyle of Lochalsh*. *Lochalsh Hotel.* Purchased 1896 (formerly known as Kyle House). Extensively rebuilt 1932-35.

Dornoch Firth. *Dornoch Hotel.* Opened July 1904. Sold April 1965. (Cameron & Burnett). Still open.

Strathpeffer. *Highland Hotel.* Opened June 1911. Sold May 1958. (Cameron & Burnett). Still open.

LONDON MIDLAND & SCOTTISH RAILWAY:

Stratford Upon Avon*. *Welcombe Hotel.* Built as private House, 1869. (Henry Clutton). Purchased December 1930. Opened July 1 1931. New Wing opened April 1933.

Hotel Schemes at **Leicester** 1936/7 and **Coventry** 1945/46 were considered but abandoned.

In 1939 the LMS and Thos Cook opened the **Prestatyn Holiday camp** as a joint venture. The war intervened and the camp was sold in 1948.

CONSTITUENT COMPANIES OF THE LNER:

Great Northern Railway:

Lincoln: *Great Northern Hotel.* Former house, purchased and reopened following remodelling, 15 July 1848. Sold circa 1946. Demolished 1965. (Henry Goddard & Son).

London: *Great Northern Hotel* opened 1954. (Lewis Cubitt). Let under management agreement in 1984

St Neots: *Railway Inn.* Opened 1853 and later renamed *The Station Hotel.* Closed 1970. Demolished 1973.

Peterborough*: *Great Northern Hotel,* Opened 1851. (Henry Goddard & Son).

Leeds: *Great Northern Hotel.* Opened July 1 1869. Badly damaged by fire, July 26 1906. Sold January 1952. (M. E. Hadfield). Still open.

Bradford: *Victoria Hotel.* Opened 1867. Purchased by GNR 1892 and renamed *The Great Northern Victoria Hotel.* Sold April 1952. (Lockwood & Mawson). Still open.

Great Eastern Railway:

Harwich: *Great Eastern Hotel.* Opened June 1865. Closed temporarily. 1908-12. Finally closed 1922. Used as Town Hall from October 1951. Sold to private owner 1983. (Thos Allom).

Hunstanton: *Sandringham Hotel.* Opened 1876. Extended 1905.Sold to local Council for offices 1950. Demolished 1967.

Parkston Quay. *Great Eastern Hotel.* Opened March 1883. Closed 1963 prior to conversion into offices.

London: *Great Eastern Hotel,* Liverpool Street. Opened 1884. Extended 1901. Let under management agreement 1984. (C. E. Barry. Sir Robert W. Edis).

Felixstowe. *Felix Hotel.* Opened 1903. Purchased 1920 Sold 1952. (Hon Douglas Tollemache). Used as offices.

Colchester: *Victoria Station Hotel,* Opened 1843. Promoted by Samuel Peto and sold 1849 for use as a hospital. (Lewis Cubitt)

Great Central Railway:

New Holland: *Yarborough Hotel,* First known as *The Yarborough Arms Hotel,* Bought by Grimsby & Sheffield Junction Railway 1844. Rebuilt 1851. Sold 1946. Still open.

Sheffield : *Royal Victoria Hotel.* Opened by the Sheffield Hotel Co 1862. Taken over by Manchester Sheffield & Lincolnshire Railway. 1883. Extended 1901. Sold 1982.(M. E. Hadfield). Still open.

Grimsby: *Royal Dock Hotel.* Opened April 22 1865 by Grimsby Hotel Co. Taken over the MSLR May 1890. Sold Dec 1949. (M. E. Hadfield). Demolished 1966.

Grimsby: *Yarborough Hotel.* Built by 2nd Earl of Yarborough 1851. Taken over by MSLR August 1890. Sold April 1952. Still open.

North Eastern Railway:

Gateshead: *Station Hotel.* Built for the Newcastle & Darlington Junction Railway, June 1844. Closed 1852. (G. T. Andrews). Since used as offices.

Tynemouth: *Royal Hotel.* Opened March 1847. Closed Circa 1882. Since used as offices.

Tweedmouth: *Station Hotel.* Opened July 1847. Closed Circa 1920. Derelict, 1990.

Newcastle Upon Tyne*. Central Station Hotel, Opened 1854. Enlarged 1892. Renamed Royal Station Hotel. July 1930. John Dobson & W M Bell.

Hull*: *Royal Station Hotel.* Opened November 1851. Enlarged 1909 and 1935. (G. T. Andrews).

York: *Station Hotel.* Opened February 22 1853. Renamed *Royal Station Hotel.* (G. T. Andrews). * Replaced by the new *Royal Station Hotel* May 1878. Enlarged 1896 (W. Peachey).
Friars Garden Hotel (Annexe) Added 1981. (Former NER Catering Department. Opened 1912)

Saltburn by the Sea: *Zetland Hotel.* Opened 1863. Sold 1976. (W. M. Peachey). Due for conversion into flats,1990.

West Hartlepool: *Royal Hotel* Opened November 1853. Purchased Circa 1880. Sold 1913. Still open.

West Hartlepool*: *Grand Hotel.* Opened February 9 1901. Purchased January 1912. (Jas Garry).

Scarborough: *Station Hotel.* Opened 1883. (within station buildings) Closed 1898.

Withernsea: *Queens Hotel.* Opened 1854. Taken over 1862. Sold 1892. Since used as residential home.

North British Railway:

Edinburgh: *North British Hotel.* Opened October 1902. Sold 1981. (Scott & Beattie). Undergoing modernisation, 1990.

Glasgow: *North British Hotel .* Dates from 1780's. Taken over during remodelling of station in 1870s. Re-opened after modernisation May 1905. Sold 1984. (Scott & Beattie). Since renovated.

Perth*: *Station Hotel.* See under Caledonian Railway.

The Company also owned eight inns, including, *The Harrow Inn,* Dalkeith; *The Star and Garter,* Linlithgow; *The Lovat Arms,* Fort Augustus, *The Ivanhoe,* Glasgow, *The Crown,* Edinburgh; and *The Royal,* Burntisland.

Great North of Scotland Railway:

Aberdeen: *Aberdeen Palace Hotel.* Opened 1874. Purchased 1890. Re-opened following modernisation August 1891. Extended 1894. Destroyed by fire, October 30 1941. (Pratt & Keith, James Matthews).

Aberdeen*: *Station Hotel.* Opened 1870. Purchased 1910.

Port Erroll: *Cruden Bay Hotel.* Opened March 1899. Closed 1939. Sold September 1951. Demolished 1952. (J.J. Smith)

LNER:

London: *Great Central Hotel.* Opened 1899. Purchased for use as offices 1945. Used at British Rail Headquarters 1948-86. Sold 1986. (Sir R. W. Edis).

Great Western Railway:

In 1923 the Company absorbed the Taff Vale Railway, which owned three hotels, and the Cambrian Railway, which had an interest in one hotel.

Slough: *Royal Hotel.* Opened 1841. Closed c1852. Sold 1863 for use as a Orphanage. Now a school.

Swindon: *Queens Arms Inn.* Opened 1842. (This Hotel was sited in the twin buildings on the station platforms. The hotel was later referred to as the *Queens Hotel* and finally as the *Queens Royal Hotel.* Closed 1895. Partially demolished.

Swindon: *Queens Arms Hotel,* Station Road, Opened c1850. Sold 1931. Now known as *The Queens Hotel.*

London*: *Great Western Royal Hotel.* Opened June 1854. Leased 1854-96, To GW Royal Hotel Co. (P.C. Hardwick). Enlarged 1936-38.

Neyland (New Milford): *South Wales Hotel.* Opened 1858. Taken over with South Wales Railway 1863. Sold June 1922, demolished 1972. (Owen).

Bridgewater: *Railway Hotel.* Opened 1841. Taken over with Bristol and Exeter Railway 1875. Sold 1968. Still open.

Taunton: *Railway Hotel.* Opened 1842. Taken over with BER 1875. Closed 1854 and since used for offices.

Yatton: *Railway Hotel.* Opened c1850. Taken over with BER 1875. Sold 1966. Still open.

Bristol: *George Inn.* Opened c1800 and later referred to as the *George Inn* and *Railroad Tavern* and by 1852 as *The George Inn and Railway Tavern.* and now as the *George and Railway Hotel.* Taken over by BER 1875. Sold 1939. Still open.

Plymouth: *Pier Hotel.* Opened Circa 1850. Taken over with South Devon Railway 1878. Since sold.

St Ives*: *Tregenna Castle Hotel.* Built 1774. Taken on lease 1878. Freehold purchased 1895. Additions 1932.

Cardiff: *Central Hotel.* Opened 1881. Leased for five years 1962. Sold 1967. Still open.

Fishguard: *The Wyncliff Hotel.* Originally a private house. Purchased by Fishguard & Rosslare Railways and Harbour Company, 1894. Taken over by GWR in 1898. Extended and renamed *The Fishguard Bay Hotel* in 1906. British Transport Hotel operation ceased 1950. Freehold sold 1967. (A. H. Webbe,1906).Still open.

Moretonhampstead*: Built 1907 as *North Bovey Manor.* Purchased by GWR in 1929 and named *The Manor House Hotel.* Subsequently extended, 1935. (Detmar Blow).

Birmingham: (Snow Hill) *Great Western Hotel.* Built 1863. Purchased 1906, closed and converted for railway offices. Restaurant on ground floor remained open. Demolished 1970.

Bath: *Grand Pump Room Hotel.* Built 1869. Leased by GWR 1946, but not used for residential business owing to cost of refurbishment. Lease surrendered November 30 1956. Demolished 1959. (Wilson & Wilcox).

Newquay: *Great Western Hotel.* Opened 1878. The GWR was the principal shareholder in the owning Company until c1920. Still open.

PROJECTED HOTELS:
Looe: *Great Western Hotel.* Designed by Sir Edwin Lutyens 1936. Proposal abandoned 1938.

Birmingham: *Great Western Hotel.* Colmore Row. 1938. Plan abandoned at outbreak of war.

Swansea: *Great Western Hotel.* Scheme prepared 1939; abandoned

Taff Vale Railway:

Penarth: *Penarth Hotel.* Opened 1868, Sold 1917. Now a childrens home.

Penarth: *Marine Hotel.* Opened 1880. Sold 1958. Still open.

Penarth: *Railway Hotel.* Opened C 1885. Sold 1949. Still open.

Cambrian Railway:

Aberystwyth: *Queens Hotel* Acquired by Aberystwyth Queens Hotel Company in 1913. The CR had a controlling interest in the Hotel Co. Sold c1925.

CONSTITUENT COMPANIES OF THE SR:

London & South Western Railway:

SOUTHAMPTON: *Imperial Hotel.* Opened 1866. Purchased 1882. Renamed *The South Western Hotel.* Closed 1939, following war service, converted into offices and known as *South Western House.* (John Norton).

Eastleigh: *Junction Hotel.* Opened 1842. Purchased 1871. Closed 1966 prior to demolition 1970. (William Tite).

Lymington: *Freemasons Arms Public House.* Opened C1890. Since sold.

South Eastern Railway:

Folkstone. Royal Pavilion Hotel. Opened 1843. Sold 1896 and subsequently enlarged. Sir R W Edis (1896)

Dover: *Lord Warden Hotel.* Opened September 1853. Closed 1939. Following war service converted into offices. (S. Beazley).

London*: **Charing Cross Hotel.** Opened May 1865. (E.M. Barry). Reinstated following war damage, 1941.

London: *City Terminus Hotel.* Opened 1866. Renamed Cannon Street Hotel 1879. Closed following war damage 1941. (E.M. Barry).

London: *Holborn Viaduct Hotel.* Opened November 1877. Closed 1917 and used as offices. Ground floor refreshment rooms open until 1931 Demolished following war damage 1941. (L. H. Isaacs).

Hythe: *Seabrook Hotel.* Opened July 1880. renamed *The Imperial Hotel* 1901. Closed 1939. Sold 1946. Still open.

Port Victoria: *Victoria Hotel.* Opened 1883, closed 1949, demolished 1952.

Deal: *South Eastern Hotel.* Opened 1901. renamed *The Queens Hotel.* Sold June 1937. (J. A. S. Brooks). Still open.

London: *Craven Hotel.* Building dated from c1730 and known as the *Globe Tavern.* Later extended into adjacent Terrace. Renamed circa 1790. Purchased c1890. Lease surrendered 1963.

London Brighton & South Coast Railway:

Newhaven: *London & Paris Hotel.* Completed December 1847. Damaged by bombing March 23 1942. Demolished 1958. Requisitioned as HMS *Aggressive* 1939-42

London*: *Grosvenor Hotel,* Victoria Station. Opened 1861. Purchased 1893. Under British Transport Hotels control from 1977. (J.T. Knowles)

London: *London Bridge Terminus Hotel.* Opened 1862, bought 1893 for conversion to offices. Gutted by bombs December 29 1940. (H. Curry).

Brighton. *Terminus Hotel.* Built 1851 as *Terminus Tavern* . Purchased 1877. Demolished 1923.

Southern Railway:

Sidmouth: *Knowle Hotel.* House built to design of Sir John Soane circa 1805, subsequently enlarged. Purchased October 1947. Sold August 1951 and later used as Council Offices.

Dorking: *Deepdene Hotel.* Built c1652. Purchased C 1925 and used as a licensed premises until 1950s. Subsequently used as rail offices until 1966. Demolished 1969.

British Transport Hotels built one new hotel, the *Old Course Hotel,* St Andrews in 1968. Sold 1982. (Curtis & Davis). Still open and being extended, 1990.

IRELAND

The railway Hotels of Ireland passed through several changes of ownership and name before being nationalised or finally sold.

In Ulster, the Belfast & Northern Counties Railway was vested in the Midland Railway (of England) from July 1 1903 and took the title Northern Counties Committee. The smaller Belfast & County Down Railway kept its separate identity until October 1 1948, when it was absorbed by the Ulster Transport Authority. The NCC was likewise absorbed by the UTA in 1949.

In Southern Ireland the Great Southern & Western Railway and the Midland Great Western Railway were among the companies amalgamated to form Great Southern Railways in 1925. In January 1945, this company joined with the Dublin United Transport Company to form the Coras Iompair Eireann (CIE).

The Great Northern (Ireland) Railway kept its identity until 1953 when the Great Northern Railway Board was formed and administered by representatives of the Irish and Ulster Governments. From October, 1958, the assets of the GNRB were apportioned between the UTA and CIE.

The Dundalk & Greenore Railway (later referred to as the DN&GR Dundalk, Newry & Greenore Railway) owned by the London and North Western Railway (Of England) and its successor the LMS kept its title until closure of the railway and the Station Hotel, Greenore in 1951.

Belfast & Northern Counties Railway:

Portrush: *Antrim Arms Hotel.* Renamed *The Northern Counties Hotel* 1883. Leased 1891. Freehold purchased 1902. Sold 1966. Still open.

Belfast: *Midland Hotel.* Opened 1898. War damaged. May 1941. Reinstated 1942. Sold 1966.

Larne: *Laharna Hotel,* Purchased 1909, sold 1966, (D. Wise). Still open.

Londonderry: *City Hotel.* Purchased c1895. Sold 1966. (J.G. Ferguson).

Belfast & County Down Railway:

Newcastle: *Slieve Donard Hotel.* Opened June 1898. Sold 1966. Still open.

London & North Western Railway:

Dublin. *North Wall Hotel.* Opened 1885. Closed 1923. Used as offices.

Dundalk Newry & Greenore Railway (Owned by the (LNWR):

Greenore: *Station Hotel.* Opened 1873. Holiday Bungalows built c1903. Railway and hotel taken over by Great Northern Railway (Ireland) July 1 1933. Railway and Hotel closed December 31 1951.

Midland Great Western Railway:

Galway: *Railway Hotel* opened 1848. Renamed *The Great Southern Hotel.* (J. S. Mulvany). Still open.

Mulrany: *Hotel Mallaranny.* Opened March 1897. Renamed *The Great Southern Hotel.* Sold 1977. (Sir Thos Deane). Still open.

Connemara. *Recess Hotel.* House purchased in 1898 and converted for use as Hotel. Destroyed by fire during Civil War.

Dublin: *Broadstone Harbour Hotel.* Purchased from the Royal Canal Co and since closed.

Dublin: *Moy Valley Hotel.* Bought from Royal Canal Co; since closed.

Great Southern & Western Railway:

Killarney: *Railway Hotel.* Opened July 11 1854, jointly with the Killarney Jct Railway. Renamed *The Great Southern Hotel.* (F. Darley). Still open

Killarney: *New Hotel,* Opened 1908. since sold.

Caragh Lake. *Great Southern Hotel.* Purchased C 1890. and enlarged. Sold c1930.

Kenmare. *Great Southern Hotel.* Opened 1897. (J. F. Fuller). Sold 1977. Still open.

Waterville: *Great Southern Hotel.* Opened c1893. Sold c1930.

Parknasilla: *Great Southern Hotel* . Opened 1897. (J. F. Fuller). Still open.

Parknasilla: *Bishops House,* opened 1905. SInce sold.

Limerick: *Station Hotel.* opened 1856. Closed 1927.

Dublin: Kingsbridge, *Station Hotel* opened c 1875. Closed c 1914. Used as offices.

Cork: *Station Hotel:* Opened 1894. Closed C 1946. Used as offices.

Following the formation of Great Southern Railways in 1925, one new hotel, *The Great Southern Hotel*, Sligo, was opened in 1928. (J. F. Sides and C. Dewhurst) Sold 1977 and now known as *The Southern.*

New hotels added by Ostlanna Iompair Eireann (OIE), and now under the control of the state-sponsored Council for Education.

Torc: (Killarney): *Great Southern Inn,* opened 1969. Since renamed *The Torc Hotel.*

Rosslare: *The Great Southern Hotel* , opened 1970.

Belfast: *Russell Court Hotel,* purchased 1970. Rebuilt 1973. Sold 1983. Still open.

Corrib: *Great Southern Hotel,* opened 1972.

Great Northern Railway (Ireland):

Bundoran: *Great Northern Hotel.* Purchased c1895. Transferred to Great Southern Hotels 1953 and named *The Great Southern Hotel.* Sold 1977. Still open.

Warrenpoint: *Beach Hotel.* Purchased 1899. Sold 1922. Still open.

Rostrevor: *Great Northern Hotel.* Purchased 1899. Sold 1966. Still open.

Rostrevor: *Woodside Hotel.* Purchased 1899. Sold 1906. Still open.

Dublin & South Eastern Railway:

Rathdrum: *Station Hotel.* Opened C 1895. Closed 1911.

APPENDIX 2: ═══════════════════════════

LIST OF THE 19 HOTELS SOLD IN 1983, AND THEIR BUYERS:

LONDON:
The Grosvenor Hotel, Victoria Station.
The Great Western Royal Hotel, Paddington.
The Charing Cross Hotel.
M.F. North plc, 2 Hyde Park Place, London W2.

HARTLEPOOL:
The Grand Hotel.
Jifbarge Ltd, 4 Church Street, Hartlepool.

LIVERPOOL:
The Adelphi Hotel.
Oakleydene Ltd, (Shareholders Britannia Hotels Ltd), Piccadilly, Manchester.

KYLE OF LOCHALSH:
The Lochalsh Hotel.
Batchshire Ltd, Seacontainers House, 20 Upper Ground, London, SE1.

TURNBERRY:
The Turnberry Hotel.
Batchshire Ltd, Seacontainers House, 20 Upper Ground, London SE1.

YORK:
The Royal Station Hotel.
Batchshire Ltd, Seacontainers House, 20 Upper Ground, London SE1.

ST IVES:
The Tregenna Castle Hotel.
Batchshire Ltd, Seacontainers House, 20 Upper Ground, London SE1.

STRATFORD UPON AVON:
The Welcombe Hotel.
Batchshire Ltd, Seacontainers House, 20 Upper Ground, London SE1.

NEWCASTLE:
The Royal Station.
Virani Group UK, 82/83 Eccleston Square, London SW1.

HULL:
The Royal Station Hotel.
Virani Group Ltd, 82/83 Eccleston Square, London, SW1.

PETERBOROUGH:
The Great Northern Hotel,
Virani Group UK, 82/83 Eccleston Square, London, SW1.

MORETONHAMPSTEAD:
The Manor House Hotel,
Virani Group UK, 82/83 Eccleston Square, London, SW1.

GLASGOW:
The Central Hotel,
Virani Group UK, 82/83 Eccleston Square, London,SW1.

INVERNESS:
The Station Hotel.
Virani Group UK, 82/83 Eccleston Square, London, SW1.

PERTH:
The Station Hotel.
Virani Group UK, 82/83 Eccleston Square, London, SW1.

ABERDEEN:
The Station Hotel,
Virani Group UK, 82/83 Eccleston Square, London, SW1.

MANCHESTER:
The Midland Hotel,
Heathside Catering Ltd,
C/O Greater Manchester Economic Development Corporation Ltd,
Piccadilly, Manchester, M14 DD.

In 1984 two further sales followed:
LEEDS:
The Queens Hotel,
Trusthouse Forte Ltd.

GLASGOW:
The North British Hotel.
Archyield Ltd.

Management agreements for *The Great Eastern Hotel,* Liverpool Street, and *The Great Northern Hotel,* Kings Cross, were completed with Compass Hotels Ltd, C/O The Great Northern Hotel, Kings Cross, London N1

LEADING HOTEL OPERATORS IN BRITAIN AT THE END OF 1970

ORGANISATION	BEDS	HOTELS	LOCATIONS	NOTES
Trust Houses Forte	20,200	184	National; 13 in London	Also hotels and partnerships abroad.
Grand Metropolitan	10,900	30	National; 23 in London	Beds include 1,500 in Berni/Chef & Brewer Also, 15 hotels abroad
Strand Hotels	6,400	14	9 in London	Also hotels abroad
British Transport	6.100	32	National	British Rail
Centre Hotels	4,400	17	8 in London	
Bass Charrington	4,000	82	England and Wales	Crest Hotels. Includes 9 motels
Imperial London Hotels	3,600	7	London	Private Company
Scottish & Newcastle Breweries	3,000	80	National	Includes 24 Thistle Hotels
Ind Coope Hotels	2,800	48	England and Wales	Allied Breweries
De Vere Hotels and Restaurants	2,800	20	England	
Associated Hotels	2,600	10	9 in London	Includes Kensington Palace Hotel
Oddenino's	2,500	4	London	
Butlin	2,000	9	7 in Margate	Also Holiday Camps
Clydesdale Commonwealth Hotels	2,000	17	Scotland	Also hotel in Bermuda
Mount Charlotte Investments	2,000	17	England	Nuthall and Ocean Hotels
Rank Organisation	2,000	9	National	Also hotels abroad
North Hotels	1,800	11	7 in London	Unlicensed
Whitbread	1,800	80	England and Wales	Includes Sunshine Hotels and tenants
Allied Hotels Scotland	1,600	12	Scotland	Aberdeen Hotel Co.
Scottish Highland Hotels	1,500	16	Scotland	
Watney Mann	1,500	30	National	Includes 9 motels
Norfolk Capital Hotels	1,400	12	England	
Travco Hotels	1,400	9	England	Also 3 holiday centres
Courage	1,200	25	England	Anchor Hotels and Taverns
Queens Modern Hotels	1,200	16	England and Wales	
Vaux and Associated Breweries	1,200	30	Northern England & Scotland	Swallow Hotels. Beds Include some in Public Houses
Truman Hanbury Buxton	1,000	17	England	Haven Inns
Myddleton Hotels and Estate	1,000	7	5 South Coast	
North British Trust	1,000	14	Scotland	
Savoy Hotel	1,000	3	London	Also hotel in Paris.

SOURCE: S. MEDLIK.

LEADING HOTEL OPERATORS IN BRITAIN AT THE END OF 1976

ORGANISATION	BEDS	HOTELS	LOCATIONS	NOTES
Trust Houses Forte	16,600	199	National	Includes Ireland, also hotels abroad.
Grand Metropolitan	9,500	81	National	24 in London, 31 County Hotels 26 Steak House Division.
J Lyons	7,900	38	National	Strand Hotels and Falcon Inns also Hotels abroad.
Bass Charrington	7,000	104	England and Wales	Crest Hotels Including Europe and some smaller hotels.
Centre Hotels	5,300	24	National	Includes Holland
Scottish & Newcastle Breweries	3,600	66	National	41 Thistle Hotels 25 Ofer House Inns.
British Transport	3,500	28	National	British Rail
Rank Organisation	3,000	12	National	Also hotels abroad
Imperial London Hotels	2,400	6	London	Private Company
Allied Breweries	2,200	42	England & Wales	Ind Coope Hotels also some smaller hotels
Norfolk Capital Hotels	2,200	18	London & Provinces	
De Vere Hotels and Restaurants	1,800	16	England	
Whitbread	1,800	98	England and Wales	Includes Tenanted and leased hotels
Cunard	1,700	4	London and Cambridge	
Reo Stakis Organisation	1,700	26	National	
Vaux Breweries	1,700	48	N England & Scotland	Includes Lowlands of Scotland Hotels
Adda International	1,600	7	London	Also one in Amsterdam and one in Paris
EMI Hotels & Restaurants	1,600	17	London, Birmingham and Scotland	Royal London Hotels
Mount Charlotte Investments	1,500	22	England	Nuthall & Ocean Hotels
North Hotels	1,300	12	London and South	Unlicensed
Courage	1,200	38	England	Anchor Hotels and Taverns
Lex Hotels	1,200	3	London and airports	Also Hotels in US
Greenall Whitley	1,000	30	Midland, Wales, N England	Compass Hotels and Red Rose Grills and Inns.
Rowton Hotels	900	4	London and Suffolk	Townor Hotels also hostels
Queens Moat Houses	800	17	England and Wales	
Savoy Hotel	800	4	London	Also Hotel in Paris
Scottish Highland Hotels	800	15	Scotland and Yorks	
Travco Hotels	800	9	England	Also 3 holiday centres
Leisure and General Holdings	700	11	National	Mercury Motor Inns
North British Trust	700	14	Scotland and N England	

SOURCE: S. MEDLIK.

RECEIPTS AND EXPENDITURE INCURRED BY THE 23 HOTEL-OWNING RAILWAY COMPANIES IN THE UNITED KINGDOM & IRELAND FOR 1913 (COMPILED TO CONFORM WITH THE REQUIREMENTS OF THE RAILWAY ACCOUNTS ACT 1911)

COMPANY	NUMBER OF HOTELS	HOTEL CAPITAL EXPENDITURE	RECEIPTS	EXPENSES	NET RECEIPTS	RECEIPTS FROM RENTED HOTELS
MIDLAND RAILWAY	9*	£2,366,035	£691,659	£569,164	£122,495	-
LONDON & NORTH WESTERN RAILWAY	10**	£440,396	£467,840	£371,906	£95,934	£1,294
GREAT WESTERN RAILWAY	8	£110,331	£291,711	£225,381	£66,330	£404
GREAT EASTERN RAILWAY	4	£681,698	£278,518	£222,325	£56,193	
CALEDONIAN RAILWAY	3 (1 shared)	£469,490	£208,023	£172.024	£35,999	
LANCASHIRE & YORKSHIRE RAILWAY	2 (1 shared)	£92,553	£139,890	£110,325	£29.565	
NORTH BRITISH RAILWAY	10 (8 rented out)	£719,753	£138,532	£111,495	£27,037	£3,310
SOUTH EASTERN & CHATHAM RAILWAY	7	£869,581	£233,276	£208,383	£24,893	£5,459
GREAT NORTHERN RAILWAY	6 (2 not worked)	£209.465	£195,947	£173,624	£22,323	£365.
GLASGOW & SOUTH RAILWAY	4	£309,410	£102,110	£82,364	£19.746	
NORTH EASTERN RAILWAY	5	£352,877	£184,972	£165,287	£19,685	
GREAT CENTRAL RAILWAY	4	£132,149	£115,091	£102,735	£12,356	
GREAT NORTH OF SCOTLAND RAILWAY	3	£160,759	£41,397	£31,401	£9,996	
HIGHLAND RAILWAY	5	£151,471	£45,251	£36,182	£9,069	£201
MIDLAND GREAT WESTERN (IRELAND)	3	£69,366	£7,447	£6,211	£1,236	£1,523
BELFAST & COUNTY DOWN (IRELAND)	1	£98,728	£13,721	£13,163	£558.	
LONDON BRIGHTON & SOUTH RAILWAY	2	£406,246				£15,867
LONDON & SOUTH WESTERN RAILWAY	3	£97,006				£3,243
NORTH STAFFORDSHIRE RAILWAY	3	£25,274				£1,434
GREAT SOUTH & WESTERN (IRELAND)	8	£133,581				£868
GREAT NORTHERN RAILWAY (IRELAND)	3	63,904				£806
TAFF VALE RAILWAY	3	£10,758				£302
FURNESS RAILWAY	1	£5,013				£301
TOTAL	107	£7,975,844	£3,155,385	£2,601,970	£553,415	£35,377

* Excluding Belfast & Northern Counties Hotels at Belfast, Larne, Londonderry & Portrush.
** Including the *Station Hotel*, Greenore.

RECEIPTS & EXPENDITURE ON HOTEL, REFRESHMENT ROOM & DINING CAR SERVICES, INCURRED BY UK & IRISH RAILWAYS, 1933

COMPANY	NUMBER OF HOTELS CONTROLLED	RECEIPTS	EXPENSES	BALANCE
LMS	32	£2,636,945	£2,350,237	£286,708
LNER	30	£1,667,924	£1,582,244	£85,680
SR	9	£104,263	£104,851	£588 (Debit)
GWR	7	£637,826	£560,963	£76,863.
NCC (Northern Counties Committee)	3	£56,504	£57,773	£1,269 (Debit)
DN&GR (Dundalk Newry & Greenore Rly)	1	£1,200	£943	£257
TOTAL	82	£5,104,662	£4,657,011	£447,651.

OPERATING PROFITS OF THE HOTELS EXECUTIVE, 1948-1972 & BRITISH TRANSPORT HOTELS LTD, 1973-1982

DATE	NUMBER OF HOTELS	GROSS INCOME (£000'S)	EXPENDIUTURE (£000'S)	OPERATING PROFIT (£OOO'S)	NUMBER OF VISITORS
1948	44			104	
1952	38			42	
1957	38	7,236	7,051	185	1,110,633
1962	38	9,154	8,734	420	993,206
1967	32	9,728	8,915	813	943,924
1968	33	12,039	11,264	775	991,808
1969	33	13,309	12,446	863	1,038,417
1970	33	14,408	13,255	1,153	1,040,233
1971	32	15,325	14,111	1,214	1,024,874
1972	31	16,547	15,131	1,416	1,044,168
1973	31	17,577	16,374	1,203	1,075,214
1974	30	18,889	18,207	682	
1975	28	21,504	20,722	782	
1976	28	24,497	23,598	899	
1977	29	29,900	28,379	1,521	
1978	29	33,701	32,734	967	
1979	29	37,918	37,591	327	
1980	29	42,003	42,286	(283)	
1981	26	37,358	39,700	(2,342)	
1982	23	34,254	35,805	(1,551)	

OPERATING COSTS INCURRED BY BRITISH TRANSPORT HOTELS LTD, 1971-1972

1971 (£000's)	1972	
5,995	6,264	STAFF EXPENSES (2,106 SALARIED AND 9,244 WAGES STAFF IN 1972)
3,143	3,364	SUPPLIES
870	1,011	MAINTENANCE OF STRUCTURES, FITTINGS FURNITURE AND EQUIPMENT
547	619	DEPRECIATION OF FURNITURE AND EQUIPMENT AND AMORTIZATION OF PROPERTIES
380	410	RENTS AND RATES
774	956	GENERAL EXPENSES
2,402	2,507	MISCELLANEOUS
TOTAL 14,111	15,131	

GREAT SOUTHERN HOTELS, OPERATED BY OSTLANNA IOMPAIR EIREANN (OCIE)
THE WHOLLY-OWNED SUBSIDIARY OF CORAS IOMPAIR EIREANN (CIE)
TWENTY-YEAR STATEMENT

YEAR TO:	NUMBER OF HOTELS	GROSS RECIPTS	NET PROFIT/LOSS	TOTAL BEDNIGHTS
31/3/1963	7	£728,173	£68,962	£142,584
31/3/1964	7	820.113	117,158	154,368
31/3/1965	7	897,543	110,344	165,160
31/3/1966	7	924,461	114,892	160,682
31/3/1967	7	1,038,693	133,700	170,436
31/3/1968	7	1,137,328	160,417	185,303
31/3/1969	8	1,404,900	196,157	206,307
31/3/1970	10	1,714,477	162,416	237,759
31/3/1971	10	1,620,583	12,720	210,347
31/3/1972	11	1,913,863	53,428	227,488
31/3/1973	11	1,642,402	(35,275)	199,369
31/3/1974	11	1,856,308	(16,940)	218,734
31/12/1974	11	1,913,839	26,740	200,946
31/12/1975	11	2,585,857	(188,666)	233,651
31.12.1976	11	3,370,040	(322,041)	264,604
31/12/1977	7	3,649,488	91,110	217,640
31/12/1978	7	4,595,276	192,483	226,016
31/12/1979	7	5,220,770	327,918	216,953
31/12/1980	7	5,123,414	(76,380)	189,.248
31/12/1981	7	6,142,929	(245,632)	202,291
31/12/1982	7	6,565,776	(456,093)	188,345

LOCAL ACTS OF PARLIAMENT RELATING TO RAILWAY HOTELS

SESSION & CHAPTER	SHORT TITLE	EXTENT OF REPEAL
14&15 Vict c.xlviii	The Great Western Railway Act, 1851	Section 24.
24&25 Vict c.xvi	The Midland Railway. (Additional Powers) Act 1861	Section 21 - 25.
35&36 Vict. c.cxvi	The Lancashire and Yorkshire Railway (New Works and Additional Powers) Act 1872	Section 35
37 Vict c.xiii	The Lynn and Hunstanton and West Norfolk Junction Railway Act 1874	Section 29
40&41 Vict c.lii	The Midland Railway (New Works &c) Act 1877.	Section 39
40&41 Vict c.xci	The London and North Western Railway (Joint & Various Powers) Act 1877	Section 20
41&42 Vict c.cli	The Great Northern Railway (Further powers) Act 1878	Section 23
41&42 Vict c.ccxviii	The Rosebush and Fishguard Railway Act 1878	Section 48
43&44 Vict c.cxli	The Great Western Railway Act 1880	Section 41
44&45 Vict c.cxix	The Caledonian Railway (Additional Powers) Act 1881.	Section 10
44&45 Vict c.cxxxv	The Lancashire & Yorkshire Railway Act 1881	Section 30 - 32
45 Vict c.1	The North-eastern Railway Company's (Additional Powers) Act 1882	Section 25
45&46 Vict c.lxvi	The Great Eastern Railway Act 1882	Section 66
46&47 Vict c.liv	The Cambrian Railways Act 1833	Section 30
54&55 Vict c.cxiv	The Manchester Sheffield and Lincolnshire Railway (Various Powers Act 1891	Section 45 & 46
56 Vict c.lii	The Great Eastern Railway (General Powers)	Section 57
56&57 Vict c.xci	The Highland Railway Act 1893	Section 14
56&57 Vict c.xcviii	The Great Northern Railway Act 1893	Section 32
59&60 Vict c.lxx	The Cambrian Railways Act 1896	Section 13
60&61 Vict c.cxxxv	The Great North of Scotland Railway Act 1897	Section 4.
4 Edw.7.c xxxvi	The Cambrian Railways (Mid Wales Railways Amalgamation &c) Act 1904	Section 29.
4 Edw.7.c xliv	The North Staffordshire Railway Act 1904	Section 29
4 Edw.7.c cxlix	The Lancashire and Yorkshire Railway) Various Powers) Act 1904	Section 48
10 Edw 7 c.viii	The Stratford upon Avon & Midland Junction Railway (Various Powers) Act 1910.	Section 43
3 &4 Geo 5 c.xxix	The Caledonian Railway Order Confirmation Act 1913	In the Schedule, Section 29
10 &11 Geo 5 c.xv	The Great Eastern Railway Act 1920	In section 3 subsection (2)
13 &14 Geo 5 c.xxii	The Caledonian Railway Act 1923	Section 12
19&20 Geo c.xiii	The Great Western Railway Act 1929	Section 51
23 &24 Geo 5 c.xxxiii	The London Midland & Scottish Railway Act 1933	Section 29
10 &11 Geo 6 c.vii	The Southern Railway Act 1947	Section 7
10 &11 Geo 6 c.xlii`	The London & North Eastern Railway Act 1947	Section 76

1861....................................Midland Railway (Additional Powers) Act. Powers to build at Sheffield.
1876....................................Glasgow & South Western Railway Act. Powers to build at Albert Harbour, Greenock.
1881....................................London & North Western Railway (Additional Powers) Act. Powers to build at Manchester London Rd & Rugby
1881....................................Lancashire and Yorkshire Railway Act. Powers to build at Manchester, Bradford, Bolton, Blackburn and Fleetwood,
1882....................................Great Eastern Railway Act. Powers to build at Cromer.
1883....................................Cambrian Railway Act. Powers to build at Welshpool and Llanidloes.
1893....................................Highland Railway Act. Powers to build at Aviemore.
1896....................................Cambrian Railways Act. Power to build at Aberystwyth, Borth, Aberdovey, Barmouth, Towyn and Portmadoc.
1897....................................Great North of Scotland Railway Act. Powers to build at Ballater.
1904....................................Lancashire and Yorkshire Railway act. Powers to build at Drogheda.

Following the amalgamation of the railways, several hotel projects were considered but abandoned.

1930....................................Manchester. Site abandoned for extension to Midland Hotel. Scheme abandoned because of economic situation.
1935....................................Manchester. New Hotel considered on site of Old Swan Hotel.
1936....................................Leicester. Land purchased for hotel but scheme abandoned because of war uncertainty.
1936-38 ....Looe. Great Western Hotel project. Tenders received in July 1938 (lowest tender £223,479), but abandoned on account of
....high cost and war uncertainty.
1938....................................Birmingham. Great Western Hotel. Snow Hill. Drawings approved but scheme abandoned due to ware uncertainty.
1945....................................Coventry. Hotel project agreed in principle but subsequently abandoned.
1945....................................Birmingham. Rebuilding of Queens Hotel considered.

RAILWAY ownership also extended to about 180 non-residential hotels, inns and off-licences. These were acquired in property transactions and developments and have gradually been disposed of.

A list of the properties which passed to the LMS in 1923 is printed in this table. The terms of the lease made the usual provision that the tenant was responsible for the internal decoration, whilst repair of the building and the maintenance of the exterior was the responsibility of the railway company.

Rentals ranged from about £80 to £1,050pa. Comprehensive lists of the properties which passed to the LNER, GWR and SR at the Grouping have (at the time of going to press) not been located.

Ardrossan, Ayr..........................Ardrossan Hotel.
Barrow in Furness ....Roa Island Hotel.
Birkenhead ....Dock Hotel.
Birmingham..............................Bell Hotel; The Lion & Lamb Hotel;
                    Station Hotel, (Adderley Park) Samson
                    & Lion Inn
Blackburn, Lancs.....................Castle Hotel
Bolton, Lancs ....Rose Hill Hotel.
Bootle, Lancs ....Stanley Hotel.
Brighouse, Yorks ....Ring O Bells Inn
Brightside, Yorks ....Station Inn.
Burton on Trent.......................Mount Pleasant Inn.
Burton on Trent.......................North West Inn.
Couldon, Staffs ....Yew Tree Inn
Coupar Angus, Perth...............Strathmore Hotel.
Derby.......................................Brunswick Inn, Siddals Road.
Earlstown, Lancs ....Griffin Hotel.
Ellesmere Port, Cheshire ....Horse and Jockey Hotel.
Ellesmere Port, Cheshire ....Dock Hotel.
Gomersal, Yorks ....Shoulder of Mutton Inn.
Heckmondwike, Yorks ....Railway Hotel.
Huddersfield, Yorks ....Crown Hotel.
Killay, Glamorgan ....Greyhound Inn.
Kirkham Lancs ....Railway Hotel
Lazonby, Cumbria ....Midland Hotel.
Leicester ....Hind Hotel.
Liverpool..................................Bramley Moor Hotel, Regent Road.
                    Caledonian Hotel, Bankfield Street.
                    Royal Hotel, Lime Street.
                    St Paul's Hotel, Earle Street.
                    Savoy Hotel, Lime Street.
                    Tunnel Hotel, Tunnel Road.
                    Warwick Hotel, Sefton Street.
London.....................................Assembly Inn.
                    Bell & Anchor.
                    Cock Tavern, Highbury.
                    Constitution Tavern.
                    Euston Arms.
                    Globe, Seymour Street.
                    Kings Arms.
                    Marshall Keats.
                    Mitre Hotel

Old Bull, Kilburn.
Plasterers Arms, Seymour St, NW.
Queens Head Hotel.
Railway Tavern. Dalston Lane.
Royal Exchange Inn.
Royal George, Euston Square.
Russell Arms.
Seven Stars Inn.
Spread Eagle.
Sultan Inn.
Worlds End Inn
Longridge, Lancs ....Townley Arms Hotel.
Mansfield, Notts. ....Midland Hotel.
Manchester. ....Albert Inn, Didsbury.
                    Bay Horse, Long Millgate.
                    Boars Head Hotel.
                    Britons Protection.
                    Cleveland Hotel.
                    Crown & Anchor Inn.
                    Globe Inn.
                    Manchester Arms, Long Millgate.
                    Maypole Hotel, Pendleton.
                    Old House Inn.
                    Old Swan Hotel.
                    Roebuck Inn.
                    Queens Hotel, Denton.
Nottingham..............................Queens Hotel, (Sold before 1920)
Orrell, Lancs............................Station Hotel.
Pye Bridge, Derbyshire ....Old House at Home.
Sheffield...................................Reindeer Inn.
                    Durham Ox Hotel.
Salford ....Raven Hotel.
                    Albert Vaults.
                    Fox Tavern.
St Helens, Lancashire. ....British Lion Hotel.
                    Nags Head Hotel.
Swansea ....Oystermouth Inn.
Wincobank, Yorks ....Foundry Arms.
Windermere, Cumbria ....Greyhound Inn.

APPENDIX 3:

REFERENCES:

Abbreviations used:

BTH: British Transport Hotels, records kept at St Pancras Chambers, London, until December 1982.

GEN: General Records kept at British Transport Historical Records office at Porchester Road, London, before removal to new Public Record Office, Kew.

ILN: Illustrated London News.

PRO: Public Record Office.

SRO: Scottish Record Office

CHRONICLE: Staff newspaper published by British Transport Hotels.

INTRODUCTION:
1: Railway News, Jubilee edition, 1914

Chapter 1: Locations:
1: H.R. Stones, Britain's First Railway Owned Hotel, Railway World Annual, 1983
2: GEN, 3/55.
3: BTH
4: The City Terminus Hotel, Holborn Viaduct Hotel and Great Eastern Hotel, were the only large hotels in the City of London.
5: Bradshaw, February 1912.
6: 1879.
7: BTH
8: R.B. Dockray's Diary. Journal of Transport History, May 1965.
9: 4 December 1869.
10: Birmingham Mail and Post 28 January 1938.
11: J.B. Radford, Derby Works and Midland Locomotives
12: Mac Dermot. History of the Great Western Railway P152
13: J.G. Ruddock and R.E. Pearson. The Railway History of Lincoln.
14: The Midland Hotel, Manchester. A History 1903 - 1978.
15: The Times. 10 March 1982.
16: Uncommercial Traveller 17. All the Year Round 1860.
17: Out Of Town. Household Words 1855.
18: Dendy Marshall. History of The Southern Railway.
19: Southampton Times. 28 February 1920.
20: Bristol Mercury. 11 May 1839.
21: South Wales Ry Board., 25 April 1856 and 6 June 1856.
22: Liverpool City Library Records.
23: Liverpool Courier 2 March 1871.
24: Midland Railway, The History of a Great Enterprise. 1914.
25: Liverpool Mercury. 14 August 1888.
26: C.J.Allen. The Great Eastern Railway 1968.
27:LLN. 26 August 1865. P 183/4
28: Essex Telegraph 10 March 1883.
29: W.E. Lecky. A History of England in the 18th Century. Vol 2 P 199.
30: GEN. 4/263.
31: M Smith Withernsea. Child of the Railway.
32: July 1863
33: Hotels and Restaurants. 1830 to the Present Day. HMSO 1981.
34: LNWR Hotel Committee. Min 2325 15 July 1875 and GEN 4/730.
35: GEN 3/204
36: BTH
37: Great Northern Review. Vol 1, No 2, August 1964.
38: Thora M Aitken. A Palace in the Sandhills. Scots Magazine. September 1970.
39: 17 May 1906.
40: Inverness Courier 13 June 1911.

Chapter 2: Planning & Amenities.
1: PRO A2/Rail/236/491.
2: 28 March 1878.
3: Stones of Venice 1853. Vol 2 Ch 6 Sect 38.
4: Personal and Professional Recollections, 1879.
5: Hewitson. History of Preston.
6: Architect and Contract Reporter. 17 April 1903.
7: September 2 1903.
8: 27 March 1914.

9: 11 March 1932.
10: 19 November 1937.
11: H.R. Stones. Britains First Railway Owned Hotel.
12: See plan on page 61.
13: H. R. Hitchcock. Early Victorian Architecture in Britain. Illustration. XV23.
14: Ordnance Survey Map 1862.
15: 10 June 1854.
16: BTH.
17: 7 July 1860.
18: D Taylor & D Bush. The Golden of British hotels. Northwood. 1974.
19: ILN. 11 June 1864 and the Times. 16 May 1865.
20: ILN. 24 February 1866 and 13 April 1867.
21: J Simmons. St Pancras Station. Allen & Unwin 1968.
22: The Builder. 9/23 August, 1879. and 10/17 August 1880.
23: Glasgow Herald. 14/19 June 1883. ILN 14 July 1883.
Central Station Hotel Guide 1921.
24: The Builder. 8 November 1902.
25: Evening Dispatch. 1 October 1952.
26: The Scotsman. 13 October 1983.
27: 20 March 1914.
28: 1841-1917. 30 Years Architect to the Midland Railway.
29: Bradshaw. February 1912.
30: 8 April 1907.
31: L. E. Kent & Lt Col G. W. Kirkland. Construction of steel-framed buildings. The Structural Engineer July 1958.
32: 1871-1923. Other work included Waring and Gillow's building, Oxford Street, the interior decoration for the Cunard Liner Transylvania, and the Pullman Cars for the London Brighton and South Coast Railway. RIBA Journal 1923.P 566.
33. Buildings of England series.
34: S Jackson. The Savoy.
35: Aberdeen Journal. 9 July 1891.
36: British Architect, 2 January 1914. The Builder 10/31 May 30 June 1912.
37: The Builder. 10 May 1935. 19 Movember 1937. Architecture Illustrated June 1937. Architect and Building News 19 November 1937.
38: Darlington and Stockton Times. 17 January 1863.
39 Inverness Courier. 13 June 1911.
40: GSW/4/77 SRO
41: March 1925.
42: Builder, 11 March 1932. Architecture Illustrated September 1933.
42: BTH.
44: Press Journal. 31 October 1941.

Chapter 3: Management and Staff.
1: PRO Mid 1/9 51st Half Yearly Meeting 18 August 1869.
2: Railway World August 1892
3: 24 and 25 Vict.6.cvi.
4: PRO Rail 1022/10.
5: 19 and 20 GEO V cxliii.
6: 23 and 24 GEO.V. cxxxiii.
7: 10 and 11 GEO V. cvii and 10/11 GEO VI cxlii.
8: Chronicle. April 1963 and H.R. Stones. Britains first Railway Owned Hotel.
9: Mac Dermot. History of the GWR VOl 1. P331.
10: PRO SR 2048 Min of 22 March 1871.
11: BTH.
12: PRO GEN 4/3/132.
13: PRO GEN 4/263.
14: SRO Mins of Perth General Station Joint Committee.
15: 35 and 36 Vict. c.cxvi
16: PRO LNWR Hotel Committee. Min. 2325
17: PRO GEN 4/678.
18: PRO GW 9/251.
19: PRO GW 9/250.
20: Railway World August 1892.
21: PRO. LNW 3/46/
22: SRO.
23: PRO NER Hotel Committee. Mins 324/402/542.
24: PRO LMS Hotel Committee. Mins 1626/47 and 58.
25: SRO GNSR Hotel Commitee. 1890/96.
26: Derby Chronicle. September 1929.

27: Railway Gazette March 1914. P390.
28: As from 21 April, 1911, they were associated with their father as joint managers.
29: Railway Magazine April 1916.
30: PRO Midland Railway Hotel Committee. 14 June 1894. At this time Mr S W Johnson, The Midland Railway's Chief Mechanical Engineer received a salary ranging from £2500-£2750.
31: PRO North Eastern Railway Hotel Committee. Min 378.
32: PRO. Highland Railway Hotel COmmittee. April 1914.
33: PRO Mid. 1/275.
34: SRO NBR Hotel Committee. Mins 1890-95.
35: PRO LMS Hotel committee. Min 1January 1925
36: PRO LNER 1/108
37: Dendy Marshall. History of the Southern Railway.
38: Chronicle. Vol 2 No 1. March 1959.
39: R Christiansen and R W Miller. The Cambrian Railways.
40: D Taylor and D Bush. The Golden Age of British Hotels. 1974.
41: PRO Mid 1/9 51st Half Yearly Meeting. 18 August 1869.
42: Railway World. August 1892.
43: Sir M Barclay Harvey. History of the Great Northern Scotland Railway.
44: PRO NER Hotel Committee. Mins 575 and 598.
45: PRO GWR Hotel Committee. Min 19,4 april 1895
46: PRO Gen 3/204.
47: GEN 4/730.
48: BTH.
49: Liverpool Courier. 2 March 1871.
50: Chronicle March 1959.
51: Main Street. 1920.
52: Chronicle. Autumn 1961.
53: SRO GNSR Hotel Committee 24 January 1896.
54: ILN 8 July 1865.
55: Williams. The Midland Railway. P351.
56: Industries of Glasgow 1888.
57: S Jackson. The Savoy.
58: Thora M Aitken A palace in the Sandhills. Scots Magazine. September 1970.
59: SRO GNSR Hotel Committee 22 October 1901.
60: The Uncommercial Traveller V1. Refreshments for Travellers.
61: Chronicle, Summer 1964.
62: O R Goring. Fifty Years of Service 1960.
63: Railway Observor. 1964/5.
64: BBC Library./
65: PRO Rail 1022/3 X/K 1991.

Chapter 4: Publicity:
1: ILN 21 October 1854.
2: The Builder. 17 June 1876.
3: ILN 10 June 1854.
4: PRO GEN 4/678
5: PRO LNER Hotel Committee 10 July 1930.
6: SRO NBR Hotel Committee. 10 July 1901
7: Cecily Lambert. A Guider to Baedeker. Country Life 28 October 1971.
8: H R Stones. Britains first railway owned Hotel.
9: D Taylor and D Bush. The Golden Age of British Hotels.1974.
10: Cumberland Pacquet. 13 June 1854.
11: 1974 Guide.
12: 1801-72 A Founder member of the Royal Institute of British Architects and well known topographical Artist who frequently exhibited at the Royal Academy.
13: Essex Standard and Eastern Counties Advertiser. 2 June 1865.
14: Scotsman 24 June 1890.
15: ILN. 28 April 1855.
16: G Deghy and K Waterhouse. Cafe Royal Hutchinson 1955.
17: Birmingham Post. 3/8/29 and 31/12/65. Birmingham Mail 26 November 1965 and 1 January 1966.
18: D Taylor and D Bush. The Golden Age of British Hotels 1974.
19: Chronicle. Special Feature April 1963
20: Chronicle Summer 1964.

APPENDIX 4:

INDEX

ACCOMODATION:
American Bar 53/67
Arbitration & witness rooms 67
Bakery 70
Ballroom 30/76
Banking facilities 69
Bar 61
Bathrooms 62,67,70,79,108
Bathrooms,sea water baths 74
Bedrooms 61,62,65,67
Billiard room 30,61,67,70,73,74,75
Boardroom 62,65
Bowling green 42
Casino 69
Cellars 62,66
Club room 61
Coffee room 61,62,65,67,70,102
Commercial travellers 61,67,73,102
Committee room 62
Croquet 39,42
Dining room 67,69
Games facilities 30,39
Grill room 69
Hairdressing 66,67,70,89
Kitchen 53,61,62,66,68,70,73,74
Laundry 70,89
Masonic lodge 59,70
Musicians gallery & rooms 62,67
Public rooms 61,66
Restaurant 68,69
Rifle range 30,73
Schedule of accommodation .70,72,75
Shops 67
Smoking room 62,67,70,111
Solarium 76
Squash court 30,73,111
Staff accommodation 62,70
Sub Post Office 69
Suites 62,65,69
Swimming pool 30,76
Telescope room 74
Tennis courts 39,42,49,73
Theatre 69
Turkish baths 30,69,70,73
Verandahs, covered ways 69,74,75
Winter garden, palm court .67,69,70,73

ACTS OF PARLIAMENT:
Caledonian Railway Act, 1923 83
Caledonian Railway Order Confirmation Act, 1923 83
Gaming Act 74
Great Western Railway Act, 1929 81
Great Western Railway Act, 1851 81
Lancashire & Yorkshire Railway (New Works & Additional Powers Act) 1872 83
LMS Act, 1933 81
LNER Act, 1947 81
LNWR Additional Powers Act 26
LNWR Additional Powers Act, 1871 83
LNWR Joint & Various Powers Act, 1877 83
London Building Amendment Act, 1909 73
Midland Railway Act, 1892 81
Midland Railway Additional Powers Act, 1861 25,81
North British Railway Act, 1894 89
Southern Railway Act, 1947 81
Transport Act, 1947 81,90
Transport Act, 1962 81,91
Transport Act, 1968 81
Transport Act, 1981 5

Aston Villa FC 111
Architectural Association 55
Argyle, M 119
Army & Navy Canteen Board 86
Albert, Prince 102,104,118

ARCHITECTS, ENGINEERS, SCULPTORS & DECORATORS:
Adam, M 75
Allom, Thos 34,115
Andrews, G.T. 19,24,61
Armstrong, Sir W. 65
Atkinson, R.F. 73
Barry, C.E. 58
Barry, E.M. 56,62
Beattie, W.H. 67,89
Beazley, S. 28
Bell, W. 33
Brassay, Thos 115
Brooks, J. 75
Brunel, I. K. 29
Cameron & Burnett 47
Colcutt, T.E. 70
Cubitt, L. 10,63
Curtis & Davis 60
Dick-Peddie, J. 68
Dobson, J. 24,33,61
Dockray, R.B. 15
Donaldson, Prof. T. L. 55
Dorn, M. 77
Earp, T. 62
Edis, Sir R. W. 59
Fuller, J.F. 51,52
Gill, E. 77
Goddard, H & Son 18,23
Green, W.C. 20,60,73
Hadfield, M.E. 20,57,104
Hall, E. 70
Hamlyn, W.H. 60,73
Hamp, S. 70
Hardwick, P. 8,15,16
Hardwick, P.C. 9,29,55
Hawkshaw, J. 62
Heiton, A. 24
Hill, O. 35,59,60,76
Hunt, R.A. 23
Johnson, S.W. 65
Jones, O. 56,62
Livock, W. 16,17
Lutyens, Sir E. 41,60
Millar, J. 75
Mitchell, T. 59
Mulvany, J.S. 49
Owen, Mr. 29
Peachey, W. 74
Pevsner, Prof. N. 69,73
Pugin, A.W. 53
Reilly, Prof. C.H. 69
Revilious, E. 77
Royal Institute of British Architects 72
Ruskin, J. 58,73
Scott, Sir G.G. 10,57,62
Smith, J.J. 42
Stansby, J.B. 9
Stephenson, R. 17
Tegetmeier, D. 77
Thompson, F. 4,17,18,19,61
Tite, Sir W. 19
Trubshaw, C. 21,69
Waterhouse, A. 66
Wilson, T. 46

B:
Baer, Max 118
Banister, A. 36
BBC 101
Beeching 37
Belfast BBC 75
Bennett, Arnold 24
Betjeman, Sir J 4
Betws-y-Coed 40
Birmingham & District Hotels & Restaurant Association 118
Birmingham Football Club 111
Boot black 86, 114
Boulogne 28
Bourneville 75
Brazil, Emperor of 52
British Association for the Advancement of Science 15,74,78
British Railways Board 91,94
British Transport Commission 81,91
Brown, T 118
Buchanan, Jack 118,119
BUILDERS & FURNISHERS:
Chadwick & Son 83
Fryers Ltd 73
Hampton & Son 73
Hollands 62
Jackson, Thos 19
Liberty & Co 73
Lucas, C 115
Martyn, H.H. 73
Muggeridge & Co 75
Nicholson, D 19
Rigby, J&C 19
Waring & Gillow 10,73
Bulganin, Marshall 118
Burrell, Sir W 43

C:
Calais 28
Cardigan Bay 92
Carnera, Primo 118
Central Liquor Traffic Control Board.86
Channel Isle 29
Charles I. Statue 62
Chevallier, Capt 115
Chevalier, M 98
Churchill, Sir W.S. 119
Colman, Sir J. 43
Connacher, J 89
Connaught, Duke of 52
Conway Valley 40
Cook, Capt J. 37
Cook, Thos 113,114
Council for Education 5
Coward, Noel 118
Cromer 38

D:
De Gaulle, Gen Chas 118,119
Dickens, Chas 28,30,97
Dickens, Chas Jnr 113
Dieppe 29
Discipline 100,101
Dogs 85,114
Dow, G 4
Dunkirk 118

E:
East Coast Joint Stock 90
Edinburgh:
Cable tramway 67
Dean of Guild Court 89
Queen Street Hall 68

F:
Fields, Gracie 118
Filming 94
Fleetwood Hesketh, Peter 92
Fire Brigade, London 99
Fire Train 79
Ford, Florrie 119
Fyffe, Will 118

G:
Gaze, H. &Son 114
Geddie, J 108
Glasgow:
Empire Theatre 119
International Exhibition 75
Museum of Transport 119
Glasgow Rangers Football Club 119
Glouycester, Duke of 119
Goodson, J. 115
Great Exhibition 114
Grimsby, Royal Dock Co 33
Golf:
Courses:
Cruden Bay 42
Dornoch 47
Felixstowe 39
Gleneagles 45,111
Greenore 31
Holyhead 31
Hythe 39
Moretonhampstead 41,95
Mulrany 49
Strathpeffer 48
Tregenna Castle 39
Turnberry 43,45
Players, Designers Etc:
Abercrombie, Mr. 41,92
Aylmer,C 42
Bonallack, M 96
Braid, J 111
Cruikshank, Alex 43
Herd, A 48
McLean, Jock 111
Morris, Tom 74
Simpson, Archie 42
Sutherland, J. 48
Taylor, J. H. 48

H:
HOTELS IN TEXT -
(FOR COMPLETE LIST SEE APP. 1):
Aberdeen:
Douglas Hotel 86
Imperial Hotel 86
Palace Hotel 26,42,73,79,86,92,95
Station Hotel 26,42,92
Achnasheen: Station Hotel 47
Ayr: Station Hotel 4,48,94,114
Belfast:
Midland 52
Russell Court Hotel 54
Birmingham
Grand Hotel 17
Great Western Hotel, Snow Hill...17,19
Hen & Chickens Hotel 15,17
Midland Hotel 17
Queens Hotel 16,17,82,111,112,118
Victoria Hotel 15
Bradford:
Alexandra Hotel 26
Midland Hotel 21,26,69,86
G.N. Victoria Hotel 26,94
Brighton:
Grand Hotel 87
Hotel Metropole 89
Bristol:
George & Railway Hotel 102
Royal Western Hotel 29
Bundoran: Great Northern Hotel ..49,54
Buxton: Palace Hotel 40
Caragh Lake (Co. Kerry): Great Southern Hotel 52
Carlisle: County Hotel 82
Colchester: Victoria Station Hotel 92
Cork: Station Hotel 53
Corrib: Great Southern Hotel 54,79
Crewe: Crewe Arms Hotel 15,94,102
Cruden Bay: Cruden Bay Hotel 42,74,75,94,96
Deal: South Eastern Hotel 38,39,75,90,112
Derby: Midland Hotel 17,18,19,61,81,86,96,115
Dornoch: Station Hotel 46,47,48
Dover: Lord Warden Hotel 28,94,104,115
Dublin:
Broadstone Harbour Hotel 49
Kingsbridge Station Hotel 54
North Western Hotel 31,52
Dumfries: Station Hotel 4,48
Eastleigh: Junction Hotel (Bishopstoke) 19
Edinburgh:
Caledonian Hotel 7,26,68,89,104
Central Hotel 67
Clarendon Hotel 26,67
North British Hotel 7,25,26,67,69,70,89,90,103,104
Royal Hotel 67
Felixstowe: Felix Hotel 5,6,39,40,92,104
Ffestiniog: North Western Hotel 40
Fishguard: Wyncliff Hotel 30,94
Fleetwood: North Euston Hotel 77,92
Folkestone: Royal Pavilion Hotel28,104
Fort Augustus: Lovat Arms & Station Hotel 102
Furness Abbey: Furness Abbey Hotel 72,113
Galway: Great Southern Hotel 49,115
Gateshead: Station Hotel 24,61
Glasgow:
Central Station Hotel23,26,70,85,93,98
North British Hotel 26,103
St Enoch Station Hotel 4,26,46,48,65,119
Gleneagles: Gleneagles Hotel 44,45,75,76,92,93,94,101,112,114,115
Greenore: Station Hotel 31,52

Grimsby:
Royal Hotel 33,94,104
Yarborough Hotel 33,94
Harwich: Great Eastern Hotel ....
..............................31,33,34,74,106,115
Heysham: Heysham Towers Hotel 36,86
Holyhead: Station Hotel...........31,33,95
Hull: Royal Station Hotel ....
.....................................19,24,33,61,102
Hunstanton:
Sandringham Hotel ....
..............................38,39,75,94,104,106
Hythe:Seabrook Hotel...................39,94
Inverness: Station Hotel.22,26,77,84,93
Keighley: Queens Hotel.....................86
Kenmare: Great Southern Hotel 52
Killarney:
New Hotel......................................53,54
Railway Hotel....................................52
Great Southern Hotel 49,50,115
Kyle of Lochalsh: Station Hotel.........35
Larne:Laharna Hotel 52
Leamington: Regent Hotel...............115
Leeds:
Great Northern Hotel............................
...............20,25,79,94,101,104,108,113
Metropole Hotel 25
Queens Hotel 20,25,60,73,79,86,87,100
Lincoln: Great Northern Hotel...........23
Liverpool:
Adelphi Hotel 30,31,33,60,
70,73,81,86,88,93,94,96,98,101,104,105
Angel Hotel 30
Compton Hotel...................................30
Exchange Station Hotel 30,33,66,70
Lime Street Station Hotel.....................
....30,33,66,70,85
Queens Hotel 30
Stork Hotel 30
Victoria Hotel 30
Washington Hotel...............................30
Waterloo Hotel 30
London:
Berkeley Hotel 141
Café Royal..141
Cannon Street Station Hotel................
.........................12,13,62,81,83,107,114
Carlton Hotel..................................12,89
Hotel Cecil..................................12,70,118
Charing Cross Hotel ....
.................12,13,56,57.62,81,85,90,107
Craven Hotel 12,90
Dorchester Hotel 86
Euston Hotel ..5,8,9,13,61,81,84,85,86,
................104,107,112,113,114,117,118
First Avenue Hotel............................12
Grand Hotel...12
Great Central Hotel.........12,70,100,111
Great Eastern Hotel..............................
...............................12,58,66,106,113,114
Great Northern Hotel............................
......................9,10,12,62,63,102,113,114
Great Western Royal Hotel..................
..............................9,12,55,61,62,113,114
Grosvenor Hotel11,12,55,62,92,113,118
Holborn Viaduct Hotel.12,13,14,70,102
Langham Hotel 12,70,107,113
London Bridge Terminus Hotel...7,113
Metropole Hotel 12,86
Midland Grand Hotel 7,10,11,12,
................13,57,65,69,86,93,99,113,114
Mint Public House 9
Northumberland Avenue Hotel 12
Palace Hotel...12
Prince of Wales Hotel..........................9
Ritz Hotel..73
Hotel Russell 12
Savoy Hotel 70,119
Victoria Hotel 8,61
Waldorf Hotel 73
Westminster Palace Hotel..........12,113
Londonderry: City Hotel 52
Looe: Great Western Hotel...........41,60
Manchester:
Grand Hotel...26
Grosvenor Hotel 26
Midland Hotel...
4,7,21,59,60,67-70,73,86, 93,94,100,115
Queens Hotel 26
Victoria Hotel 26
Marseilles: Terminus Hotel.................80
Morecambe: Midland Hotel ....
....35,36,59,86,94
Moretonhampstead: (see next column)
Manor House Hotel......40,41,92,94,111
Moy Valley Hotel.................................49
Mulrany: Hotel Mallaranny 49
Newcastle: Central Station Hotel..........
....24,33,85
Newcastle, Co Down:
Slieve Donard Hotel..............51,52,111
Newhaven: London & Paris
Hotel 29,90,104
New Holland: Yarborough Hotel 94
Newquay: Atlantic Hotel 83
Neyland: South Wales Hotel..........29,30
Normanton: Station Hotel....................78
Nottingham: Victoria Hotel 111
Parkeston Quay: Great Eastern
Hotel 31,33,106
Parknasilla:
Great Southern Hotel 51,52
Bishops House Hotel 54
Peebles: Peebles Hydro 95
Penarth: Penarth Hotel 38,39
Perth: Station Hotel................24,26,103
Peterborough:
Great Northern Hotel.........................18
Preston: Park Hotel........................83,94
Rathdrum: Station Hotel.....................54
Recess: Recess Hotel.........................49
Rhyl: Claremont Hydro 97
Rosslare: Great Southern Hotel....54,79
Rostrevor:
Great Northern Hotel.........................52
Woodside Hotel 52
St Andrews: Old Course Hotel..............
.................................48,60,77,79,94,115
St Ives: Tregenna Castle Hotel..............
.....................................39,40,83,85,92
Saltburn by the Sea: Zetland Hotel........
....37,38,74,78,85
Scarborough: Station Hotel 38
Sheffield: Royal Victoria Hotel....55,104
Sidmouth: Knowle Hotel.....................94
Sligo: Great Southern Hotel 40
Slough: Royal Hotel 92
Southampton: South Western Hotel.......
....29,94
Stoke on Trent: North Stafford Hotel.....
....23,82,94
Stratford on Avon: Welcome Hotel41,79
Strathpeffer: Highland Hotel 47,114
Swindon:
Queens Arms Hotel...........................21
Queens Arms Inn 21
Queens Hotel 21
Queens Royal Hotel 21
Torc: Great Southern Inn..............54,79
Turnberry: Turnberry Hotel....................
...............................4,42,43,75,96,104
Tweedmouth: Station Hotel................24
Tynemouth: Royal Hotel 24
Venice: Victoria Hotel 95
Warrenpoint: Beach Hotel 52
Waterville: Great Southern Hotel.......52
West Hartlepool:
Grand Hotel...................................33,92
Royal Hotel 92
Windermere: Windermere Hotel.........83
Withernsea: Queens Hotel 36
York: Royal Station Hotel 24,61,85
HOTEL COMMITTEES:
Adelphi Hotel Extension Committee 85
Caledonian Railway Hotel
Committee.......................................84
Glasgow & South Western Railway
Hotel Commitee 84
Great Eastern Railway, Traffic, Conti...
nental Traffic & Hotel Commitee 84
Great Eastern Railway Hotel ....
Committee..84
Great Northern Railway, King's Cross
Hotel Committee...............................84
Great Northern Railway, Leeds & other
Hotels Commitee 84
Great North of Scotland Railway Hotel
Committee..84
Great Western Railway Hotel ....
Committee..............................81,85,86
Highland Railway Hotel Committee.....
....84,87
London Midland & Scottish Railway
Hotel Commitee 82,85
London & North Eastern Railway
Hotel Committee...............................85
London & North Western Railway
Hotel Committee..........................84,85
London & South Western Railway
Hotel Committee...................................84
Manchester Sheffield & Lincolnshire
Railway Hotel Committee 84
Midland Railway, Leeds Hotel ....
Committee.......................................85,87
Midland Railway, St Pancras Matters
Committee..85
Midland Railway Hotel Committee...89
North British Railway Hotel ....
Committee.....................................84,90
North Eastern Railway
Hotel Committee......................84,85,87
Perth Station Hotel Committee 83
Southern Railway Hotel Committee.85
Tregenna Castle Hotel Committee...85
HOTEL COMPANIES:
Adelphi Hotel Co 81
Bertram & Co 90
British Transport Hotels Ltd................
.....................................10,91,92,94
Buxton Palace Hotel Co Ltd...40,83,92
Cannon St Station & Railway Co 81
Carbis Bay Hotel Co.........................83
CERT 54
Charing Cross Hotel Co.........81,82,92
City Terminus Hotel Co....................82
Cornish Hotels Ltd 83
County Hotel & Wine Co (Carlisle)...83
Frederick Hotels Ltd 5,12,70,80,99,100
Gleneagles Hotel Co 83,92,93
Gordon Hotels 5,80,86,89,90,108
Great Western Royal Hotel Co ....
....81,92,113
Grosvenor & West End Railway ....
Terminus Hotel Co............................82,92
Hotels Executive 10
Keswick Hotel Co 24
LMS Hotels...10
London & Birmingham Railway Hotel
& Dormitories Co......................6,8,61,81
London Bridge Terminus Hotel Co......
....11,13
Ostlanna Iompair Eireann................54
Sheffield Hotel Co 83,102
Southern Hotels Co..........................52
Spiers & Pond............5,26,80,84,89,90
Strathpeffer Spa Co 47
Swindon Junction Hotel Co.............21
Trust Houses 5,82,99,101
Windermere Hotel Co......................83
HOTEL CONTROLLERS,
PROPRIETORS, BOARD MEMBERS,
MANAGERS & STAFF:
Anson, C.R...83
Armstrong, Mrs 97
Bacon R..81
Baker, T.H. 91
Balfour, J...12
Balzaretti, L.................................98,99
Bamford, Mr 97
Bannatyne, J.K.S........................82,93
Battersby, 'Flash' 118
Barry, H. A...82
Birmingham, Mr & Mrs......................28
Birrell, N.D...82
Bisserot, Mr & Mrs E. 94
Boase, Mr 89
Bonthron, A.S. 82
Bosworth, J.M.W. 91
Brunel, I.K. 92
Burcher, F.J. 89,90
Burland, W.H. 91
Burleigh, S.W. 90
Carlow, Mr 89
Collins, F.R. 82
Creighton, Mr......................................89
Cuany, A. H. L. 82
Currie, W.J. 82
Curtis, M. A. 82
Dethier & Vantini 81
Duffus, Miss..97
Duquenoy, R. D..................................82
Escoffier, M. 95
Etzensberger, R. 95
Farrimond, H. L. 9
Fordham, G. 119
Forshaw, Mr 86
Forster, J. 82
Forté, Chas...92
Frater, Miss 97
Gent, H. 87
Glen, Sir Alex......................................92
Gluckstein, Col, Sir Louis, QC 91
Gordon, F. 12,86
Graham-Bryce, Dame Isobel 91
Grierson, Mr 89
Hamilton, G. O'B.................................90
Harris, P. J. 82
Hatfield, A. 82
Head, G. 82
Heffer, Miss F......................................81
Hill, G. R. 91
Hole, F. G. 4,82,90,91,96
Horton, I 17
Howard, S. C. 87
Humphrey, S 99
Hutchinson, W. E................................92
Irwin, H. E. 82
Jack, I.M 82,91
Jones, R.F. 82
Jordan, Mr 89
Land, P. A. 91
Land, W. S. 82
Land, P...91
Lawrence, Sir Robert L. E.................91
Leigh & Rogers...................................29
Long, P. 4
Lord, Mr 90
McDermid, D. S. 82
McGuire, J. F. 82
McKilliam, Miss 86
McLeod, D. 82
Maple, Sir J.B. 12
Masser, H. 119
Moffatt, W. M 86
Moulin, F. H. 82
Nelson, J. W. 82
Pardini, A. J. C 82,119
Parker-Smith, Mr 89
Pearce, R. J. 82
Petre, J 82
Pine, Mr 89
Plock, F.H. 86
Portman-Dixon, E.K. 91
Pritchard, L. C. 82
Reavley, J. C. 82
Reid, J. G. 82
Ritz, C 93
Robertson, Mrs J. 96
Roberston, Mr 89
Salvin,T. 92
Schumann, C 95
Scott, Mr 82,86
Short, A. A. 82
Smith, G. M. 30,86
Smith, P. W. 99
Squires, R. 99,119
Stockton, Sir E. F. 90
Sutter, Mr 119
Tennant, Sir C 89
Theim, E & A 95
Thomas, J. H. 90,113
Thompson, M. W.................................66
Towle, Arthur ..68,73,76,82,85,86,87,90
Towle, Lt Col Sir F. W. 86,87
Towle, Sir William......5,10,68,69,80,81,
..............................83,86,87,89,95,101,109
Trenchard, Mr 97
Turnbull, R. L. 82
Turpie, J. W. 82
Tweedale, Marquis of 89
Vacher, E. J. 82,91
Vantini, Z 119
Wainwright, W.....................................82
Ward, H. H. 87
Watson, G. H. 82
Wemyss, Mr 89
Wieland, G. B. 86,89
Williams, E. O......................................82
Williams, J. 82
Wilson, A. E...82
Woodcock, V. P. R. 82
Haile, Selassie 118
Hambledon, Viscount 41
Headford, Marquis of 97
Heywood, Chas 26
Horniman, Miss 26
Hoy, Sir Jas 26
Hotel & Catering Institute 86
Hotel coupons & tickets 43,114
Hotels executive 90

I:
Insurance 79-90
International Hotel Alliance................85
Irving, Sir Henry 21,26

J:
Jervis, Capt, MP....115

K:
Kaye, Danny....118
Kent, Duke of....119
Kruschev, N....118
King Edward VII....97
King George V....118
King Wiliam IV....8

L:
Lancaster....35
Lascelles, Viscount....101
Laurel & Hardy....118
Leaseholds....81
Le Strange, H....38
Lewis, Sinclair....94
Licences....89,100
Llandudno Junction....40
Louis Philippe....115
Louvre....57,107
Luncheon baskets....86

M:
Mackintosh & Co....64
Mais, S. P. B....111
Matchboxes....104
Mayo, Chas....113
Mexico....6
Milford Haven....29
Ministry of Food....86
Minister of Transport....81,118
Moon, R....23
MUSIC:
BBC Dance Orchestra....101
Caruso, Enrico....119
Gleneagles Orchestra....101,111
Hall, Henry....101
Halle, Chas....26
Harwich GE Hotel....115
Midland Adelphi Orchestra....111
Midland Hotel, Leeds, Orchestra....111
Midland Grand Hotel, London, Orchestra....99,111
Midland Hotel, Manchester....100
Payne, Jack....101
Roman Orchestra....111
Savoy Hotel Band....101
NEWSPAPERS, PUBLISHERS & GUIDE BOOKS
ABC Guide....90,107
Aberdeen Daily Free Press....42
Allen & Unwin....107
Architect & Building News....60
Architect & Contract Reporter....90
Architectural Review....4
Ayr Advertiser....43
Baedeker, K....105,107,108,113,114,115
Black, Adam....105
Bradshaw, George....11,90,107,113
Burkart, A....113
Builder....60,75
Building News....57,62
Cairo & Egypt....90
Cornish, J....106
Cross Courtenay....105,111
Cumberland Pacquet....61
Gem of the Peak....61
Globe....26
Graphic....17
Guardian....59
Hull Packet....61
Illustrated London News....55,57,61,62,64,102
Industries of Glasgow....66
Leeds & Yorkshire Mercury....79
Liverpool Daily Post....60
LNWR Official Tourists & Picturesque Guide....8,17,107
McCorquodale....111,113
McMurray, J....105,106
Measom, George....106
Murray, J....106
Murray, Thomas & Son....107
Newcastle Guardian....37
Norton & Shaw....114
Railway Gazette....69
Railway News....92
Scotsman....45
Skinner, Thomas....107
Times....58,86
Tucks....113
Whittakers Almanac....10,65
Yorkshire Post....37

N:
Napoleon I....119
Napoleon III....115,118
National Council for Hotel & Catering Education....86
National SUnday League....100
New York....29,30
Nijinsky....118
Norfolk, Duke of....83
North Bovey Manor, Moretonhampstead....41,92
Novello, Ivor....118,119

O:
Orleans, Duke of....118
Ostend....28
Otis, E. A....62
Overend & Gurneys Bank....92

P:
Palmerston, Lord....58
Parkes, Mr....31
Parliament, Houses of....61
Peace Conference, Paris, 1919....86
Pease, Henry, MP....37
Peto, Sir M. MP....115
Phillips, M....41
Police....85,94
Postcards....112
Postmarks....69

Q:
Quebec....6
Queen Adelaide....8
Queen Victoria....8,18,96,102,104,115,118
Queen Eleanor Cross (Charing Cross)....13
Queen Mary....118
PLANNING, CONSTRUCTION, MATERIALS, FURNITURE & FITTINGS:
Air conditioning, heating & ventilation....67,68,72,73,75,76
Artificial stone,cladding....62,69,76
Brick arch construction....62,66,108
Carpets....74,75,76,85
Chamber pots....6
Clocks....67,89,111,115
Coal fires, chimneys....72,73
Costs....62,65,77,79
Curtains....75,77,90
Drainage....111
Electrophone....99
Faience & terracotta....59,62,69
Filler joist construction....67,69
Fire resistant construction and precautions....62,64,65,68,72,85,111,113
Furniture & furnishings....73,74,75,77,90
Lifts....62,64,65,68,73
Electricity, generators, lighting....67,70,75,85,107
Lightweight construction....73
Light well....67,69
Motor car, planning for....75,108
Noise insulation....62,64
Portland stone....73
Reinforced concrete....67,76
Windows, glazing....62,67,69,72,73
Sandstone....68
Steel frame construction....53,67,69,72,73
Suspended ceiling....73
Telephones....72,111,112
Vacuum cleaners....72,85,90
Van Kannel (revolving) doors....68,90,99
Wash stands....75
Water supplies and storage (including hot and cold services)....62,67,73,75,89,111

R:
RAILWAYS:
Belfast & County Down Rly....52
Belfast & Northern Counties Rly....52
Bristol & Exeter Rly....106
Caledonian Rly....26,45,54,68,83,104
Cambrian Rlys....92
Canadian National Rly....7
Canadian Pacific Rly....6
Cheshire Lines Committee....26
Cockermouth Keswick & Penrith Rly....83
Coras Iompair Eireann....54
Dublin & South Eastern Rly....54
Furness Rlys....113
Glasgow & South Western Rly....4,43,45,48,113
Grand Junction Rly....15,19,106
Great Central Rly....33
Great Eastern Rly....12,31,39,66,74,114,115
Great North of Scotland Rly....26,42,84,92
Great Northern Rly....10,21,25,26,57,83,107,113,114
Great Northern Rly (Ireland)....49,52
Great Southern & Western Rly....52,54,113
Great Southern Rly....54
Great Western Rly....9,17,21,29,30,39,40,41,60, 83,85,90,92,93,107,114
Highland Rly....23,26,45,47,83,84
Hull & Holderness Rly....36
Killarney Jct Rly....52
Inverness & Perth Jct Rly....83
Lancashire & Yorkshire Rly....30,59,83
Lancaster & Carlisle Rly....24,35,82
Liverpool & Manchester Rly....106
London & Birmingham Rly....8,15,19,81
London Brighton & South Coast Rly....11,12,28,82
London Chatham & Dover Rly....11,12,14,102
London & Greenwich Rly....11
London Midland & Scottish Rly....30,36,41,45,47,48,60,85,90,93
London & North Estern Rly....12,85,90,93,99,104
London & North Western Rly....8,9,15,17,26,31,40,52,59,81,83,107,108
London & Southampton Rly....19
London & South Western Rly....11,12,29,84
Lynn & Hunstanton Rly....38
Maidens & Dunure Rly....43
Manchester Sheffield & Lincolnshire Rly....26,33,83,84
Manchester South District Rly....26
Midland Rly....5,10,24,25,26,30,57,68,81,87,102,107,108,113
Midland Great Western Rly....49,113
Newcastle & Carlisle....106
North British Rly....26,67,83,84,85,108
North Eastern Rly....24,36,38,92,107,108
North Midland Rly....19
North Staffordshire Rly....23
North Western Rly....35,36
Paris, Lyons & Mediterranean Rly....80
Preston & Wyre Rly....92
Scottish Central Rly....83
Scottish North Eastern Rly....83
South Eastern Rly....11,12,28,38,39,82,85,107,112
Southern Rly....85,90,93
South Wales Rly....29,107
Stockton & Darlington Rly....37
Taff Vale Rly....30,38,90
Ulster Transport Authority....54
Western Railway (France)....29
York & North Midland Rly....61

R:
Railway Executive....90,91
Railway Guards Friendly Society....101
Reckitt, Sir James....37
Rogers, Roy....118
Rolls, Hon S....26
Ronay, Egon....97,115
Roosevelt, Presdident Teddy....41,111
Rotterdam....31,33
Royal Canal Co....49
Royal Navy....36
Royce, H....26

S:
Salaries....81,86,87,89,97
Sayer, J. P....111
Selfridges....73
Shakespeare, William....111
Stationery....90
Stock Exchange....99
SHIPS: (see next column)
HMS *Aggressive*....29
HMS *Spartiate*....119
Blenheim....31
Emmanuel....42
Great Britain....29
Great Eastern....30
Great Western....29,30
Liverpool....30
Nile....42
Royal William....30
Savannah....30
Togo....42
STEAMSHIP COMPANIES:
Allan....30
Anglo-Luso-Brazilian Royal Mail Steam Navigation Co....30
Brighton & Continental Steam Packet Co....28
City of Dublin Steam Packet Co....31
Cunard....30
Ford & Jackson....29
Great Western Steamship Co....29
Guion....30
Harwich Yacht Club....74
Inman....30
National....30
New Commercial Steam Packet Co....28
Newhaven & Dieppe Service....90
South Eastern & Continental Steam Packet Co....28
Transatlantic Steamship Co....30
White Star....30

T:
Tariffs....113
Teagarden, J....118
Telegraphic Addresses....108,113
Telephones....89,111,112
Thefts....85,90
Thurston, J....74
Toastmaster....100
Toronto....6
Trade Unions....6
Travellers Fare....94

U:
Uniforms....96,97,99,113

V:
Vancouver....6
Van Horne, Sir W....6

ACKNOWLEDGEMENTS

Since my research began, two people who provided a great deal of help have died; the late Frank Hole CBE, General Manager of British Transport Hotels Ltd gave unstintingly of his recollections of 35 years experience and the late John Thomas first drew my attention to the wealth of information available in the Scottish Record Office and helped with details gleaned from his own research.

Several other people have since retired: Paul Long, former Secretary of BTH was extremely helpful and E.H. Fowkes, former Archivist of British Transport Historical Records, made me welcome at Porchester Road on many occasions. I am indebted to Margaret Aitken, H.R. Stones, Professor Medlik for permission to use his work in my appendices and Peter Baughan for valuable help in listing Acts of Parliament and other data. Thanks also to the Royal Institute of British Architects Library, Guildhall Library, Manchester Central Library, Birmingham Library and the National Railway Museum. Valuable assistance also came from: Sir John Betjeman, Ken Hoole, Laurence Knighton, George Dow, Richard Casserley, Ted Higgs, Alan Meredith, David Froggatt, Dennis Lewis, Glyn Waite, John Alsop, Angela Meredith, Peter Billson, Claude Field, Harold Bowtell, David Tee, Margaret Brander, Andrew Biwandi, Brian Radford, Harry Barry, Bill Wainwright, John Edgington, Dorothy Crawford, John Marshall, Derek Taylor, Cliff Wrate, Gordon Biddle, J.R. Hollick and Michael Potter. Finally, thanks to Nan Maidment for typing my manuscript.